Carl Furillo,
Brooklyn Dodgers All-Star

Carl Furillo,
Brooklyn Dodgers All-Star

TED REED

McFarland & Company, Inc., Publishers
Jefferson, North Carolina, and London

LIBRARY OF CONGRESS CATALOGUING-IN-PUBLICATION DATA

Reed, Ted, 1948 April 2–
    Carl Furillo, Brooklyn Dodgers all-star / Ted Reed.
    p.   cm.
    Includes bibliographical references and index.

    ISBN 978-0-7864-4709-1

    1. Furillo, Carl, 1922–1989. 2. Baseball players—United States—Biography. 3. Brooklyn Dodgers (Baseball team)— History. I. Title.
    GV865.F83R44   2011
    796.357092—dc22   2010044514
    [B]

British Library cataloguing data are available

© 2011 Ted Reed. All rights reserved

No part of this book may be reproduced or transmitted in any form or by any means, electronic or mechanical, including photocopying or recording, or by any information storage and retrieval system, without permission in writing from the publisher.

On the cover: Carl Furillo (National Baseball Hall of Fame Library, Cooperstown, NY)

Manufactured in the United States of America

McFarland & Company, Inc., Publishers
  Box 611, Jefferson, North Carolina 28640
  www.mcfarlandpub.com

To Carl—
Sorry this took so long

Contents

Preface 1
Introduction 3

1. The Early Years 9
2. Home from the War 20
3. The Arrival of Jackie Robinson 28
4. The Reading Rifle 39
5. The Team Takes Shape 49
6. Forced to Grow Up 60
7. The First Bad Year 70
8. The Worst Bad Year 78
9. "I Couldn't Even See the Ball" 87
10. Batting Champ 93
11. Next Year Finally Arrives 101
12. "We're All Dagos in Here" 110
13. "I Should Never Have Moved Out There" 120
14. Number Six Passes On 127
15. The Game Turns Sour 136
16. Outside Looking In 149

17. Back Home for Good 162
18. The Right Way to Leave 171

Appendix: Furillo's Career Statistics 183
Chapter Notes. 185
Selected Bibliography 195
Index 197

Preface

I BEGAN TO WORK ON THIS BOOK 41 years ago after noticing that nearly every principal member of the famous Brooklyn Dodgers team of the 1950s had been the subject of a book—with the exception of Carl Furillo. I got in touch with Carl, conducted several lengthy interviews at his home in Flushing and once at the World Trade Center site, and wrote his "autobiography" as an honors thesis in American Studies at Wesleyan University. Wesleyan provided a $600 grant for my work. It was a lot of money at the time.

My periodic efforts to find a publisher were unsuccessful. In 2005, I submitted my work to McFarland, and was told that it might be publishable if rewritten as a third person narrative with appropriate historical context added.

In this pursuit, I have been assisted by many people. Most notable is Carl Erskine, who at this point is a national treasure, the greatest repository of information about the Brooklyn Dodgers because of his impeccable memory, his willingness to help and, in my case, his wisdom in being able to see every side of the conflicts that sometimes enveloped Carl Furillo. In his 80s, Carl Erskine became my e-mail correspondent, responding to dozens of questions.

Peter O'Malley and staff members Robert Schweppe and Brent Shyer, both former Dodgers executives, provided invaluable assistance. We discussed details of Carl's separation from the Dodgers, and of Peter's effort to ensure that Carl and the Dodgers reconciled.

Carl Furillo, Jr., and I have talked regularly since I began this work. This has enabled me to maintain an awareness of his father's perspective, which I hope has informed my work, and also of the need for his father's long-overlooked story to be told. Jon Furillo, Carl Furillo's other son, retrieved a scrapbook which an unidentified Furillo fan maintained from 1941 through 1956 before giving it to his father. I had also used the scrapbook while writing my thesis.

Most of the articles were from the Reading newspapers, and I quote often from them. It should be noted that reporters of the time—in Reading, at *The Sporting News*, and elsewhere—had a more liberal standard regarding their use of quotations and seemed to more readily substitute written English for spoken English.

During my research, I was provided an opportunity to review the transcript of the June 16, 1961, hearing in which Major League Baseball Commissioner Ford Frick considered Furillo's charge that he was unfairly dismissed by the Dodgers. I also reviewed Frick's findings, which were issued on July 13, 1961.

I had the good fortune to make contact with Judith Testa through an inquiry on the Society of American Baseball Research website. The author of *Sal Maglie: Baseball's Demon Barber*, she offered advice and encouragement and also volunteered to read a draft of my manuscript. My friend Dave Carpenter also read an early draft, while Jeff Siner helped me with photographs. Lyle Spatz, a baseball author and historian writing a book about Carl's predecessor Dixie Walker, provided encouragement and historic perspective. My membership in SABR has been exceedingly helpful and also enabled access to *The Sporting News* archives.

I also want to thank everybody else who agreed to be interviewed, including Bobby Bragan, Ralph Branca, Robert Erb, Jack Ferenchick, Ron Fairly, Gene Hermanski, Joan Hodges, Irv Noren, Jack Lang, Lester Rodney, Tom Villante, and Fay Vincent.

Finally, I wish to thank my wife Alexandra for her support during more than a year of continual weekend writing.

Introduction

OUR MEMORY OF CARL FURILLO does not shine as brightly as it should.

Furillo was a mainstay of one of baseball's most cherished teams, the 1946–1957 Brooklyn Dodgers. Like many players, he returned from combat in World War II to play the game at a time when it still reigned as America's pastime, and he excelled. A lifetime .299 hitter with 1,910 hits—one more would have given him a .300 average—he led the National League in hitting in 1953 and played in six World Series over 11 years. Well known for his strong, accurate throwing arm and his ability to play the caroms off the complicated right field wall at Brooklyn's hallowed Ebbets Field, he remains among the best right fielders who ever lived. And yet he's often reduced to a bit player—or worse, a villain—in Dodgers history.

In many ways, the Brooklyn Dodgers story in that decade after World War II was America's story. When the war ended, the country got back to business—and to baseball, which drew record crowds. Eighty years after the end of the Civil War, a slow march to equality for African Americans began to gain speed, with the Dodgers' Jackie Robinson at the forefront. The Dodgers story became a proxy for the story of the greatest domestic social movement of the twentieth century, the civil rights struggle.

Not only were the events dramatic—the timing was impeccable. The team flourished as post-war Baby Boomers were accumulating the childhood memories that, as they aged, would enshrine the team in legend. In a dramatic baseball story that played out in New York, the nation's media capital, the Dodgers finally defeated the Yankees in the 1955 World Series after five unsuccessful attempts. Then, shortly after the precise moment when they reached their greatest on-field ascendance, the Brooklyn Dodgers suddenly ceased to exist. They were lost to another major postwar societal movement, becoming part of a national migration shift to California, which by 1964 had replaced New York as the country's most populous state.

Furillo's teammates—Robinson, Roy Campanella, Don Drysdale, Sandy Koufax, Pee Wee Reese and Duke Snider—have been immortalized, even beyond their membership in the Hall of Fame. A fifth teammate, Gil Hodges, remains a perpetual Hall of Fame candidate, always on the edge of being inducted. But Furillo, somehow, ended up with less. In many ways, he became a footnote, his name tagged onto stories about the accomplishments of others. At worst, his memory has been darkened by two unfortunate incidents that have confounded his legacy.

First, Furillo came to be perceived in some quarters as racist, largely as the result of an early misstep during general manager Branch Rickey's move to add Robinson to the Dodgers roster in the spring of 1947. It seems clear today that the perception is inaccurate, but racial issues involve such intense sensitivity that—even 60 years later—it is hard to erase.

A major factor in the misrepresentation is that the events portrayed in a 1950 movie, *The Jackie Robinson Story*, have come to be viewed as fact. Specifically, the movie devotes a scene to a meeting between Rickey and four ballplayers who had organized a petition drive to oppose Robinson. Among them is an Italian ballplayer—called "Tony"—whom Rickey chastises for opposing Robinson, arguing that nobody took up a petition to prevent Tony's mother and father from working following their arrival in America. In this account and others, the extent of Furillo's limited opposition was expanded in an effort to embellish the Robinson story. The falsehood both wounded Furillo and diminished his reputation.

As Furillo recalled years later, "There was a funny thing that happened when they made the movie, *The Jackie Robinson Story*. They had a guy playing Mr. Rickey in there, and then there was this little Italian boy in there and he had all this discrimination and everything, he was against this and that, and I still say to this day that the little Italian boy was supposed to be me. And that's what gets me. It was the Southern boys who were the ones that fought against it and all. So to me, that movie to a certain point is sort of a joke."[1]

Secondly, the tangled circumstances of Furillo's departure from the Dodgers in 1960 left a bitter taste, as what could have been a graceful conclusion to his career turned hostile. The Dodgers intended for it to be otherwise, but anger—on both sides—poisoned a relationship that had flourished for two decades. In response to what he considered unfair treatment, Furillo sued the Dodgers. The team agreed to a settlement.

INTRODUCTION 5

Dissatisfied with some of the terms, Furillo demanded a hearing before the commissioner, who—not surprisingly—ruled in the team's favor. After he filed his suit—and this is not surprising either—Furillo could not find a job in baseball, despite writing letters to every team. He charged that he had been blacklisted.

For the decade following the end of his career, Furillo was an exile from baseball. His situation was particularly poignant because, in 1969, his onetime roommate Gil Hodges was lionized for managing the improbable New York Mets to a World Series victory one season after they finished ninth in the National League. At the time Furillo lived in Flushing, a few miles from Shea Stadium, and was employed as an elevator installer, helping to build the World Trade Center.

"A lot of the guys I played with are still in baseball right now," Furillo said. "But here I am, sitting on the outside looking in. And I often wonder, I say to myself: 'What is fair? What is wrong? What is right?' I'm out of baseball now because there was a little bit of ill feeling with somebody that I had a lot of faith in and I respected and then all of a sudden I got slapped in the face. It had a little sour note there. But then I say 'Well, that's part of life.' I don't really regret any of it. I think I've given baseball practically everything I had. I lived it, I loved the game, and it's been good to me as far as my family and I are concerned."[2]

Despite his misfortunes, Furillo possessed an innate ability to find contentment in his personal life. He liked to hunt; alone was fine. He preferred the company of his wife and family. He sometimes seemed to distance himself from his teammates, even before his separation from baseball. When he felt slighted, he would enter a sort of exile, at times self-imposed. When he left the Dodgers, and left baseball, both sides erected barriers. On the outside, looking in, Furillo seethed when he thought of baseball. He resented being deprived of something he felt he had earned.

The situation left a mark on Furillo's son. When Carl Jr. and his brother Jon were in their teens, their father seemed to ignore their burgeoning baseball careers. "My dad took a lot of interest in me and my brother," said Carl Jr. in 2009. "With hunting and fishing, he was right there. But he took no interest in my playing, even though I had scouts come to watch me play, and they came to watch Jon play too. They came to school to watch me, came to summer leagues to watch me.

"Dad was basically out of it. He would give me a tip if I asked him, and he would talk to the scouts when they came, but he would never say 'You did this wrong' or 'You should do it this way.' I think he thought he would try to keep us out of baseball because he didn't want us to get hurt, like he was. I was hurt and upset by that, because I felt that what they did to my dad ended up bleeding down to my brother and me."[3]

Furillo's family is not alone in believing that Furillo's departure from baseball ought to have turned out differently. Former Dodgers owner Peter O'Malley not only shared their belief, but also mounted a concerted effort to correct the wrongs of the past. He began in 1971, when he called Furillo and asked him to attend an old-timers game in Los Angeles. Later, he invited Furillo to be an instructor in the Dodgers' adult fantasy baseball camp in Vero Beach.

Teammate Carl Erskine also participated in the fantasy camps. "I managed the team; Furillo was my coach," Erskine said. "It was fantastic, we all were just thrilled that he would come back and identify himself with the team. He was very popular. He had this manliness about him: no nonsense, straight talk, and the campers really embraced him. I think that helped him to soften a little. My guess is he never quite came back 100%, he still had this feeling he had been jilted, yet he came back partially."[4]

In a final gesture, Peter O'Malley attended Furillo's funeral in Reading, Pennsylvania, in 1989, and gathered several of Furillo's teammates, including Erskine and Sandy Koufax, to join him. At the funeral, O'Malley declared, "When he left the Dodgers, it was the wrong way to leave. He was right and we were wrong. Being here today, I'm so very, very pleased that we were able to mend that fence."[5] (O'Malley said later he was referring specifically to the way Furillo's dismissal was handled.) To this day, says Furillo Jr., O'Malley still sends Christmas cards to his mother. "Peter was always respectful; my dad knew him and always liked him."[6]

Erskine delivered the eulogy at Furillo's funeral, saying in conclusion: "He had two sides, he was very strong-willed, almost on the stubborn side, but then he had a sensitive side, he was like steel and velvet. You saw the tough side mostly, but he did have a very tender side. But I think a lot of people missed the sensitive side."[7]

Indeed, Furillo was a complex man. Although he was movie-star handsome, widely recognized as a great ballplayer, physically strong and generally comfortable with himself, the barriers never seemed to disappear entirely. "I think his feelings were hurt unintentionally by some of us who lived in Bay Ridge, a section of Brooklyn, and used to ride together to the games," Erskine said. "Pee Wee Reese, Duke Snider, Rube Walker, Preacher Roe, and I—that was the nucleus of that group.

"Furillo lived away from us, on the east side of Brooklyn, and he had his following. He always had a bunch of Italian buddies around him. Somehow he got the notion he was kind of an outsider with this clique (from Bay Ridge), but that was never true. There was never one of us that didn't have great respect for Furillo. Like Jackie, he wasn't part of that either, he lived in Connecticut. When the game was over, we all went in different directions, but a handful of us lived in Bay Ridge. I think Carl misread that. He never made an issue of it, but I think he was sensitive enough that it bothered him. We always tried to convince him otherwise. I don't think we ever did."[8]

Furillo was also quick to anger, and prone to speak or act before he thought. "He stuck to his guns when he had a good point," Erskine said. "But sometimes his emotions got to him, more than his head."[9] In the two incidents that did the most to damage his image, the one involving Robinson's promotion to the Dodgers and the other involving his own departure from the team, Furillo subsequently acknowledged that he spoke without forethought. In another famous incident, in 1953, he charged into an opposing team's dugout to battle a nemesis, Giants manager Leo Durocher, who had instructed pitchers to throw at him. As usual, Furillo's hasty action may have been justified, but the result was unfortunate. In the scuffle that followed, his finger was broken and he missed the last month of the season, at a time when he was leading the National League in hitting. Nevertheless, he won the batting championship.

In the past decade, Carl Furillo, Jr., moved to correct some of the false impressions about his father. He worked closely with freelance writer Bill Ninfo, who self-published a book about Carl Furillo in 2002. The son provided details and family photographs and arranged interviews. The book sought to remove the blemish on Furillo's reputation, but its presentation was flawed and its distribution was limited. Still, the title *Carl Furillo: The Forgotten Dodger* was appropriate, said Furillo Jr. "Of all the ballplayers, a lot have been taken care of, but my dad was basically forgotten.

"There is a lot of stuff out there that isn't true," Furillo Jr. continued. "I would like to bring closure to this, especially for my mother, because for things to be said about my dad, when they are not true, hurts us all."[10]

1

The Early Years

THEY HAVE COME TO BE KNOWN as "The Greatest Generation." Most were born in small towns, grew up during the Depression, went off to fight World War II, and returned home to a country that prospered economically as no country had before. Their return triggered vast social movements, most notably the Civil Rights struggle and population shifts to California and the Sunbelt.

Baseball was a part of it, at every level. At the end of the war, baseball was still America's pastime, and Americans returned to it en masse. Baseball, movies and radio were the principal sources of mass entertainment. Television was an emerging technology and the National Football League was a secondary sports league, a distraction between the end of the World Series and the start of spring training.

In many ways, Carl Furillo's life was typical for his time. He was the last of six children, born on March 8, 1922, to immigrant parents from Naples who often spoke to one another in Italian. They resided in Stony Creek Mills, a small town just outside of Reading, Pennsylvania, which is about 50 miles northwest of Philadelphia. Like many kids, Furillo grew up playing baseball from dawn to dusk, unaware of how poor he was.

Often, he played in a playground a block from his home. His parents, unfamiliar with the sport, preferred that he work in the family garden plot or "truck patch." His father sold vegetables from what was then called a "huckster wagon," and his mother told him, "Baseball is for people who don't want to work."[1] In part, the lesson took. Furillo adopted a workman's approach to baseball. Years later, he would incessantly practice playing the caroms off the right field wall at Ebbets Field. After baseball, Furillo continued to take pride in his work, whatever it was, from running a delicatessen to working in construction to working in the fields with a tractor at his Stony Creek Mills home. "Dad always used to tell me to always be honest, do not steal and, if you give a day's work, you get a day's pay," said Carl Furillo, Jr. "He really believed in that."[2]

Recalled his father, "I never expected to be a major league baseball player. I always thought that the major leagues were in another world, and I didn't even have any idea of where Brooklyn or New York was. I never saw a major league baseball game in my life until the day I played in one. In fact, when I was in the seventh grade the principal asked me what I wanted to be, and at that time I wanted to be an undertaker. I wanted to take up embalming and all that, but when I came out of the war I was sick of it—to this day, I don't even like to go to a wake."[3]

While small-town American life had many advantages, freedom from discrimination was not always among them. Only four Italian families lived in Stony Creek Mills, which had a population of about 5,000. "When we lived there, it was all Pennsylvania Dutch," said Carl Furillo, Jr. "There was a lot of animosity towards Italians when Dad was a kid, even when I was a kid. That would have been my dad's first taste of being different."[4]

Even absent discrimination, Depression life was harsh. "Sometimes, we didn't even have a loaf of bread on the table for Christmas dinner," recalled Furillo, who dropped out of Pennside Junior High School in the eighth grade in order to earn money. "I worked at different jobs like picking apples in an orchard and picking weeds, and I was a bobbin boy in a mill, and then I was driving a truck for a while and I was hauling rocks, and some of these jobs were for money that you wouldn't believe. In fact, no matter what I did in those days I never made more than $15 a week, and for working in that orchard I remember I was getting $5."[5]

Michael Furillo, Carl Furillo's father, immigrated from Naples to Pennsylvania, where he sold vegetables from a "huckster wagon" (Furillo family photograph).

Furillo's Depression-era childhood was reflected in his lifelong concern about money. He wanted to be sure he got what was coming to him, with the result that he frequently held out for better terms during winter contract negotiations, and he rarely spent unwisely. Throughout his life, when he received a paycheck, he would write "for deposit only" on the back. "Dad came through the Depression, when times were tough and food was not plentiful on the table," his son said. "He always told me, the one thing he always vowed, was his children would never go hungry, there would always be food on the table.

"He was very conservative when it came to money. We always got the story about how hard he had to work for 50 cents a week, about how our grandfather used to resole his shoes with tire rubber. Dad always said, 'Money is a tool; if you don't break the tool, it will last you a lifetime,' and he would say, 'Why are you buying this?' or 'Why are you buying that? You are just making somebody else rich.' As a kid I used to like to play pinball machines, which cost a nickel a game, and Dad would always say, 'Every time you put a nickel in that machine, the guy that owns it goes to Florida and he watches me play baseball.'"[6]

Four-year-old Carl Furillo grew up poor in Stony Creek Mills, Pennsylvania, where he lived for most of his life (Furillo family photograph).

Baseball, it soon became clear, offered a way out of financial hardship. As a youth, Furillo played for a recreation league in Reading; when his second season ending, he was hitting over .300. The first person with baseball connections to notice his skills was Josh Haring, a former Reading city league player. Haring put Furillo, then 15, on the team he was managing in the Berks Recreation League. Furillo "immediately earned a regular outfield berth and proceeded to pelt the pellet at a neat .310 clip for the 1937 campaign," wrote Jerry Kobrin, employing the florid style of the time, in a 1941 article in *The Reading Eagle*.

Kobrin's article was one of the earliest to chart Furillo's career for Reading readers. At that time, mass communication involved radio and newspapers. Like many cities, even small cities, Reading had multiple newspapers—the *Times* in the morning and *The Eagle* in the afternoon. Kobrin had a unique relationship with Carl, because they had been classmates in school a decade earlier. In the 1941 article, Kobrin wrote that during the 1938 and 1939 seasons, Haring and another manager "groomed the Stony Creek DiMaggio" and that eventually they "began casting about for a springboard into organized baseball."[7]

Haring contacted Robert Eddington, a local entrepreneur who evidently understood the benefits of diversification, pre-war America style. Eddington owned a bowling alley, a Salisbury, Maryland, chicken farm and baseball teams in Reading and Pocomoke City, Maryland. He also understood business synergies; his Reading team was called the Chicks. Kobrin described the result of Haring's contact in the style of the day: "The general manager of the Reading Chicks allowed as how he might plant the Little Flower in the fertile farm of Pocomoke City, also owned by Eddington, and 'twas to this little Class D town in Maryland that Carl journeyed."[8] In 1940, around the time of his 18th birthday, Furillo was signed to a contract with Pocomoke City in the Eastern Shore League at a salary of $80 a month. Later, older brother Nick Furillo would also play, briefly, in the Eastern Shore League.

Two weeks before Furillo was due to report, his mother died. "My father said he figured I should go anyway because there wasn't anything I could do by staying home and losing baseball too," Furillo said. "So I went, and the manager there was Poke Whalen. And one day I remember Poke Whalen was watching me, it was just after I lost my mother, and he came over and he said, 'I'm going to make something of you, you little dago.' He was the first one that really pushed me."[9]

Although he was homesick, Furillo hit well at Pocomoke City, and he pitched as well. "His prodigious heaves from deep left field soon inspired Manager Poke Whalen, who was running woefully short of pitchers, to put our hero on the mound," Kobrin wrote. "Armed with only a sling-shot arm and a prayer, Furillo pitched five games, winning two of them."[10]

Gene Hermanski, later Furillo's teammate on the Dodgers, was also a teammate in Pocomoke City. He was 20, two years older than Furillo, and had two years of minor league experience. "He played center, I played left, but once a week he would pitch and get 10-plus strikeouts a game," Hermanski recalled. "The ball would be doing something. It wasn't a straight ball; it would move. But he did pretty well as an outfielder too.

"He was like me, a nice guy, but we didn't buddy around together," Hermanski said. "We lived with families. Management found people who would take in ballplayers for money. We paid $1 a day, and we walked to the ballpark. I was getting paid $125 a month, and when we would travel we would get meal money. The meal money was two quarters."[11]

Furillo got a break late in the 1940 season. One evening, the team was playing a game in Centerville, Maryland, when Whalen received a

1. The Early Years

Carl Furillo, right, with his brother Tony. Carl was the youngest of six children (Furillo family photograph).

telegram from Arthur Ehlers, president of both the Pocomoke City and Reading teams. Ehlers asked that another ballplayer be sent up to Reading, but for some reason the ballplayer declined. As Furillo recalls it, "The telegram said 'If he won't come, then send Furillo.' So Poke Whalen said to me, 'Carl, it looks like you're going up.' That night I was sitting the game out because I had hurt my ankle, but he had me pinch hit anyway because it was my farewell time at bat.

"The next morning, I was over at the park and I met the traveling secretary, and he says to me, 'What time will you be leaving?' I said, "What do you mean, leaving? I can't go anywhere because I don't have any money.' Whalen said, 'Well, I have none to give you.' 'I guess I can't go then.' 'Well, here's what I'll do. I'll give you your fare on the Greyhound to Philadelphia, and from there you can telegram Ehlers for more money.'"

Arriving in Philadelphia for the first time in his life, the young Furillo called the Reading ballpark and got the groundskeeper, who found Ehlers, who told him how to find the designated Western Union office. From there, after being awake all night, Furillo made it to Reading. "I went home first and slept and after that I went to the ballpark," he said. "I still had a sprained ankle when I got there, and in my first game I had a play covering first base and I sprained the other one. I wasn't worried except for one thing: I wanted an advance on my salary because I had to get something to eat. I was afraid they wouldn't give me any money because I was hurt."[12]

Reporting on Furillo's promotion, *The Reading Times* published a photograph of Furillo in the initial stage of a pitcher's motion, his front leg raised and the ball in his right hand, still at waist level, with the headline "Promoted to Peeps." The caption read: "Carl Furillo, Stony Creek boy, joined the Chicks for the first time last night after being called in from Pocomoke City. Talented both in the outfield and on the pitching mound, the young prospect will get into action as soon as a twisted ankle strengthens."[13] In fact, *The Times* writers had played a role in ensuring Furillo's promotion to Reading. "When the season opened, the sports department of *The Times* promised to hand (Ehlers) the best-looking prospect in Berks County," wrote sports editor Gordon Williams in a 1947 column. "Josh Haring, the real discoverer of Furillo, brought the big youngster to us and we delivered him to Ehlers. Furillo pitched and played the outfield with Pocomoke City (and) reported to Reading in the fall."[14]

Called up at the end of the 1940 season, Furillo played in just eight games for Reading, hitting .367 in 30 at-bats. More importantly to his future, Reading manager Tom Oliver determined that pitching was not going to be in his future. "Poke Whalen, down at Pocomoke City, was shifting Furillo from the outfield to the mound because of his powerful throwing arm," Oliver recalled in a 1946 interview. "That made me a bit curious. So when our ball club played the league's all-stars in a game at Wilmington, I gave Carl a one-inning shot at pitching. I saw enough to convince me he wasn't made for a pitcher and that he belonged in the outfield."[15]

The next season, 1941, Furillo became the property of the Brooklyn Dodgers in a transaction that became part of Dodgers lore. "The team was called the Reading Chicks but after that winter they became the Reading Brooks because the Dodgers bought out Eddington for $5,000," Furillo recalled. "When they bought him out, they got about 15 players, a set of old uniforms and a broken-down bus. At the time, Larry MacPhail was running the Dodgers and he was trying to build up the farm system. I was the only one out of the whole crowd that ever made it to the majors, but the Dodgers came out ahead on the deal because they sold one of the players to get the $5,000 back. Then, at the end of one season, they turned the franchise back to the league, but they kept some of the players, they made some money operating the team that year, and they kept the bus."[16] Buses at the time were in short supply, with most automotive production earmarked for the armed forces.

Another piece to the bargain was that Reading manager Fresco Thompson moved into the Dodgers organization, where he rose to become a top executive and remained until 1968. In a 1941 interview, Thompson raved about Furillo, saying he "is definitely a major league prospect. For a 19-year-old kid, who broke into organized baseball just last year, he's nothing less than a sensation. He has as much natural ability as any player in the league, and for my money, possesses the best throwing arm of any Class B outfielder you can name. At the plate, he's a diamond in the rough," Thompson continued. "A natural swinger and a powerful hitter, he has several rough edges that need polishing before he can step up to a higher league—and right now he is in the polishing process." Thompson was so sure of himself that he emphasized, "I repeat, Furillo is a great prospect. Some day your Chamber of Commerce will be proud of him."[17] *The Reading Eagle* suggested that Furillo could be the city's third contribution to the major leagues, following Dominic Dallessandro and Charley Wagner.

Like most Americans, Furillo did not realize that 1941 would be the last normal year until 1946. He spent the season ensconced as a hometown player and managed by Thompson, whom he called "one of the nicest guys I ever met in baseball." Playing at home had the advantage that "the Reading fans were always good to me," he said. "They would always root for a hometown boy to make good whether he was in a streak or a slump. Later on, when I went to play in Montreal and then in Brooklyn, those Reading fans were still behind me. And the sportswriters back home were terrific. They were always on my side and I always went to all kinds of functions and sports dinners and things like that for them. Some of the players would refuse to go but I never gave them any trouble."[18]

Furillo always spoke frankly, perhaps too frankly. An early example occurred in 1941, when the 19-year-old showed a clear lack of political correctness, telling *The Reading Eagle*'s Kobrin that he was thankful he was able to play in Reading, adding "I was afraid they would send me to some jerk town in the Middle West."[19] No doubt the statement reflected the sentiments of nearly everybody who read the article. Later, when Furillo was a major league ballplayer, talking to other players or to reporters for major dailies, his casual, truthful words would come back to haunt him.

There was one downside in Reading. Furillo's teammates included Al Campanis, who became a Dodgers scout after a brief major league playing career that included just seven games on the 1943 wartime team. He rose through the ranks, eventually becoming general manager from 1968 to 1987. During the 1941 season, Furillo and Campanis battled to have the Reading club's highest batting average and, by extension, to be selected by the fans as the team's most popular player. Furillo won both honors.

Several years later, Furillo ran into Campanis when both were with the Dodgers organization, and "he said to me then, because I won the contest, 'Well, I expected you to win it. A hometown boy would win it.' And to this day, I think he still holds a grudge against me. He's a vice president of the Dodgers now (in 1970) and at the time of the friction (over Furillo's release) he was director of scouting for them and someone said to me one day, 'Jeez, Carl, what was it you did to make Campanis so mad at you?' So there is a man who will hold a grudge."[20]

In any case, Reading fans celebrated "Carl Furillo Night" on August 19, 1941. "Stony Creek took a bigger place on the baseball map last night when Carl Furillo, from the little village down Oley Valley way, was honored with heaps of gifts from admirers at Lauer's Park," reported a Reading newspaper. "The leading hitter on the Reading club received a traveling bag, shotgun, portable radio, even a smoking stand from a fire company, plus other articles dedicated in his honor." (A smoking stand is an ashtray mounted on a pedestal so that it can be placed next to a chair or sofa.) A photograph shows a skinny, youthful Furillo being congratulated by manager Thompson and business manager Lee MacPhail, the son of Dodgers president Larry MacPhail. "Needless to say, there were plenty of Stony Creek fans in the crowd of more than 2,000 spectators," the newspaper reported.[21]

A week later, the Dodgers' top farm team in Montreal bought Furillo's contract. Furillo played out the season in Reading, his future defined by a path to a major league career, and in the spring of 1942 he climbed aboard a Pullman car bound for Florida. It was the first time he had ever traveled so far from home, and the first time he had ever been in a sleeping car. The war had begun a few months earlier, but its impact on baseball was not yet clear. When Furillo arrived in Daytona Beach, he reported to camp with the Montreal Royals, the Dodgers' top farm club.

The Royals' manager was former major league catcher Clyde Sukeforth, a Branch Rickey confidant who, a few years later, would be deeply involved in the signing of Jackie Robinson. Furillo met Sukeforth in the Osceola Hotel, an encounter described by *Montreal Herald* columnist Elmer Ferguson. "'My name's Furillo,' chirped the youngster with a smile, putting out his good right hand. Clyde Sukeforth winced a bit at the lad's handshake, so full of vigor. 'Oh yes, you were in Reading last year,' replied Sukey. 'We've got a room waiting for you.'"[22] Forty years later, Furillo's grip was still so strong that it continued to impress his friends. Initially, it seemed unlikely Furillo would play much, but he quickly proved himself. "After he watched me for a couple of weeks Clyde Sukeforth said he had to find a spot for me to play because, he said, 'I can't be sitting this kid on the bench, I got to play this kid someplace,'" Furillo recalled three decades later. "The thing he liked was that I never knew who was pitching out there, and I didn't care who we were playing against. I just loved to play. When it came to my batting average or my home runs I never looked in the paper. I always had the policy that every day when I went to play, I would say that I would get a few hits. If I went one for two or two for three or two for four, I always tried to get the third hit or whatever it was. But as far as knowing what my batting average was, I would never look at it except on that last day of the season because that's the one that counted on the paycheck."[23]

Montreal quickly took to Furillo. Though its image declined as the fate of the Expos dangled in the late 1990s and early 2000s, Montreal was once an enthusiastic baseball city, its interest in the sport stirred by robust competition between its newspapers, including three in English and others in French. The city's early moment in the baseball limelight would come a few years later, in 1946, when it enthusiastically embraced Robinson. But Furillo also received a warm reception.

In *The Herald*, Ferguson paid Furillo the highest possible compliment by comparing him to hockey star Howie Morenz, a revered former member of the Montreal Canadiens, then as now the pre-eminent Montreal team. "One glance at Furillo and you know he is aggressive, full of color," Ferguson wrote. "He reminded you, distantly, of Morenz breaking into hockey. Sliding head-first into a bag may or may not be the most effective way to get there, and it may not be the best way to elude a tag. Skating head-long into tough defense players wasn't the best way to get to the goals either. But that's the way Morenz did it when he first broke in.

"With Furillo it's natural, just as speed and velocity were natural with Morenz. He has to get to a bag, and he dives for it. Regardless of its merits, Furillo's head-first slides have attracted the fancy of the crowds. Montreal fans are taking this baby of the squad to their hearts. If he can continue to play the type of baseball he has shown up to this point, he's liable to be the most popular man on the 1942 team," he wrote.[24]

In another incident that boosted his fan appeal, Furillo, sliding into second base, was spiked on the head by the Toronto Maple Leafs second baseman in the first game of a doubleheader. He had stitches to close the wound, and returned for the second game so heavily bandaged that he appeared to be wearing a turban.

Ferguson paints a rare portrait of Furillo as a youngster, bathed in enthusiasm—some of which would soon be lost to a few years of combat in the South Pacific. The young ballplayer was "so full of excitement about everything—he is so happy to be alive and he gets a tremendous kick out of everything that happens," Ferguson wrote. "Everything is superlative with him." The story includes a list of Furillo's interests: hunting, riding horses, reading sports stories, taking pictures (a pursuit no subsequent writer ever mentioned), listening to the "Gang Busters" radio show and raising chickens.[25]

In May, *The Montreal Star* wrote about Furillo's appeal under the headline: "Furillo Quite a Fellow, Royals Fandom Finds." The story noted that "Furillo is a common subject amongst the fans nowadays, as he seems to improve day by day, almost every time out." Sukeforth described Furillo this way: "He's a wonderful type, got a great temperament. He doesn't know who's pitching out there, he doesn't care or possibly doesn't know who we're playing, but he's in the ballgame, every part of it.

"We show him off to the visiting clubs in fielding practice," Sukeforth continued. "We let him cut loose with a few throws to the plate. He throws strikes from the outfield. You can see their eyes popping out almost. That doesn't do them any good. That kid's got one of the great arms in baseball."[26]

As the team's baby, possessed of a cheery personality, Furillo was often kidded. Ferguson wrote that one clubhouse story had it that Furillo, asked to fill out a form that asked for his state of health, wrote "Pennsylvania." The youngster was called "Rocky" because he came from Stony Creek Mills, and "Little Flower" because his name sounded like New York Mayor Fiorello LaGuardia's. Another nickname was "the Reading Rifle," a reference to his strong throwing arm. "All in all, those were the years I really loved," Furillo said. "I was single at the time and I was making a fairly good dollar, three hundred dollars a month, and the money was secondary. The game was more important than the whole thing."[27]

It quickly became clear that Furillo was a major league prospect. In June, 1942, a story in *The Reading Eagle* speculated that he would be called up to the Dodgers before the end of the season. Not only did he seem ready, but also he would become available to other major league clubs if the Dodgers did not claim him. "So many scouts have followed the work of this youth that the front office of the Dodgers must be conscious of the fact that Carl could be claimed by a rival big league club in the baseball draft during the World's Series," *The Eagle* reported. "They can't afford to lose him that way."

The newspaper also sounded an ominous note. "If Furillo should get a chance in Brooklyn, his rise might come at a bad time, for it is evident that the major leagues can't be too sure of starting another campaign in 1943, despite statements to the contrary."[28]

Late in the season came a *Montreal Gazette* headline that proclaimed "Furillo Draws Praise as Sure Major League Prospect from Manager and

1. The Early Years

Several Scouts." It quoted Sukeforth as saying that Furillo "has been up with the first dozen hitters in the league all season. That's remarkable enough when you consider that it's his first year in the league. But it's more remarkable still when you think that it's practically only his second year in baseball, because he was a pitcher for the big half of the 1940 season when he broke in with Pocomoke City."[29]

At the end of the season, Furillo had a .281 average with three home runs and 51 RBIs, and appeared headed for the Dodgers the next season. He was living the dream—but of course it could not last. In October, a *Reading Eagle* headline declared: "Montreal Keeps Furillo on Reserve List," with this subhead: "Royals Count on Berks Lad for 1943."[30] But early in November, the story changed dramatically, as Furillo was inducted into the army. "Carl Anthony Furillo, (the) Stony Creek lad who was slated to go to spring training next spring with the Brooklyn Dodgers, had his baseball career cut short yesterday when he passed his final physical examination at Allentown and was inducted into the United States Army," *The Eagle* reported.[31] He was given 14 days to report to Fort George G. Meade, Maryland.

Within a month, he was in the army with the 77th Division, and he saw action in Guam, Leyte, Okinawa and Japan. His assignments included driving amphibian vehicles. He was cited for bravery in combat, and at one point he was hit in the head with shrapnel and offered a Purple Heart, but he turned it down. "He didn't like to be fussed over," said Carl Furillo, Jr. "There were guys out there who were much more severely injured, who deserved the Purple Heart, and my father felt he wasn't hurt as bad as they were and so he felt didn't deserve it."[32] Furillo himself recalled, "I saw quite a few bodies stacked up over there. By the end of the war I was the quartermaster of that division, and if there had been a third wave it would have been the doughboys, so thank the good Lord they didn't need it."[33]

2

Home from the War

THE BOYS OF AMERICA CAME HOME in 1946. By then, Furillo was 24 and had seen a lot of fighting and dying, although there is no indication that he ever subsequently discussed his experiences at length with anyone. Carl Furillo, Jr., recalls that when he and his brother sought to learn what happened during the war, their dad limited them to one question each and barely responded.

Many of the ballplayers who entered the service spent much of their time during the war years playing in games, some involving large numbers of professionals, in order to entertain the other troops. But during his 38 months in uniform, Furillo rarely picked up a baseball. "There were a lot of a lot of guys who were able to play ball in the service and some of them were saying that it was practically like the major leagues when they were in there," he said. "But I didn't get that kind of opportunity. The little ball that we got to play was only for a few get-togethers and it was only during about three weeks, which was practically nothing at all. So to make up for that, they let all the ballplayers who had come back from the war have an extra month or month and a half of spring training in Florida."[1]

Not surprisingly, baseball contributed to the feeling of joy that pervaded the victorious country. "When spring training started, it seemed like the war was really over and the country was getting started again," Furillo recalled. "Once the ballplayers came back, all you heard people talking was baseball, baseball, baseball."[2]

Montreal trained that spring in Sanford, Florida, while the Dodgers trained nearby in Daytona Beach. The team was run by general manager

Branch Rickey, who had taken over in 1942 from Larry MacPhail. Rickey was a colorful curmudgeon, characterized by bushy eyebrows, a propensity to quote biblical verse, and a superb ability to judge young baseball talent. He became a baseball icon, responsible for two of the most important developments in the sport's history: creation of the farm system, which he designed in St. Louis, and integration, which he masterminded from Brooklyn. Later, in Pittsburgh, Rickey would draft the first Hispanic superstar, Roberto Clemente. He built the pre-war St. Louis Cardinals dynasty, then built the Dodgers, and later went on to Pittsburgh to initiate the buildup of the young Pirates team that won the 1960 World Series.

In 1946, Rickey was focused on remaking the Dodgers, moving out many of the older war-time players and moving in youngsters, including Furillo. His top lieutenant was his son, Branch Jr., who was farm director. He also worked with the temperamental Leo Durocher, who had been the Dodgers manager since 1939. Over the ensuing decade, Furillo would have vastly different relationships with Rickey and Durocher. While the former was widely considered to be a cheapskate who underpaid players, he seemed to appreciate Furillo, a moral man who rarely drank and who was not afraid to speak up. Despite pointed annual contract negotiations, the two always got along, and Furillo's discussion of his early days in baseball is replete with incidents where he and Rickey amicably worked out minor misunderstandings. As for Durocher, he was in conflict with Furillo almost from their first meeting.

"The Rickeys had taken over the club, and I found out later that young Rickey told the scouts that he didn't want anybody to even give a comment on me until after 30 days," Furillo said. "That was until I got into shape and everything. So after 30 days they commented on me and I went to work out with the Dodgers. But I was still with Montreal because Branch Rickey had what he called 'the Montreal embargo': he didn't want any of the Montreal players to go up to Brooklyn right away. In fact, it was finally Durocher who told Rickey that he wanted to give me a trial with the Dodgers.

"I had first seen Durocher managing down in spring training when I was with Montreal before the war, and he was still the same afterwards. In fact he hasn't changed to this day (1970), because what he was doing when I first saw him was hollering and yelling his head off all day long. That's why they gave him the nickname 'The Lip.' Even back then he didn't get along with his players too well; he didn't know how to handle them." Not only did Durocher not get along with many players, he also had a conflict with Clay Hopper, who in 1946 was manager of Montreal. Somehow, Furillo ended up as a pawn in their battle, in an incident which shows that even as a rookie, he refused to back down when his integrity was questioned.

"When I got the word that I was supposed to go and work out with the Brooklyn ballclub, the waiters and some of the ballplayers that were down there threw a little party. We had altogether about a dozen beers, and I think I had one or half of one. When it was over, they cleaned up the room and they put everything in a wastepaper basket. Well, Hopper was bucking for Durocher's job, and he was sneaking around there, and he figured this would be a good chance to smack Durocher right in the mouth. So he went and turned me into to Mr. Rickey, saying that I was drinking and that he had caught me. Young Rickey saw me and I told him all about it and then, when I got to the ballpark, I told Durocher what happened. And Durocher told me, 'Don't worry about it, kid,' and it seemed like it was all over. But then on the following day he came up to me and said, 'Why didn't you tell me the truth?' I said 'I did tell you the truth.' And he said 'That's not the story I heard.' So I said 'I don't care what you heard, I'm telling you the truth.' So he was calling me a liar then, and I think from that day on I lost a little faith in Durocher."

"I stayed with the Brooklyn club and later on in the season we were on a train, and young Rickey came over and sat down beside me. And he said 'Carl, I'm sorry for what happened in Daytona Beach. We found out there was no truth to it, because we know you're not a drinker.' And it was true, I didn't start drinking beer or hard stuff until I'd say maybe the last six years of my career. Up until that time, if I took a beer or two beers a week I was lucky."

The young Furillo held his ground not only with Durocher, but also with the Montreal club, which initially offered him $300 a month. "It was the same salary they were paying me before the war," he said. "So I held out." The holdout established a pattern, because Furillo pursued a similar course throughout his career. The 1946 holdout was not widely publicized since Furillo was an unknown at the time, and it turned out to be meaningless, because Furillo ended up signing not with Montreal but with Brooklyn. "I went over to Daytona Beach to train with the big club, and they offered me $3,750, because I was still under a Montreal contract," Furillo said. "Then when I went to the Brooklyn team just as the season opened, they jumped my salary to $5,000. In those days right after the war, that wasn't bad for a single fellow, but you couldn't go out and do real fabulous things that you really wanted to. You had to pinch the dollar a little bit."[3]

Years later, *Reading Times* reporter Gordon Williams wrote that Furillo asked for more money after Rickey decided to move him to the Brooklyn roster. "'I'll stay with Montreal unless I get double what my contract calls for' was his ultimatum," Williams said, adding, "Seeking advice from your newsboy, Furillo was told to talk with Fresco Thompson, then a field scout for the Dodgers, who had managed Carl in Reading in 1941. Thompson straightened matters out and Furillo signed a Brooklyn paper."[4] Later in the 1946 season, after Furillo had signed, Major League Baseball raised its minimum salary to $5,000.

Initially, Furillo was just one among about 200 GIs whom Rickey had invited to the first post-war training camp at Sanford. "He was sort of a ragamuffin, represented no investment on the books and had no scout touting him," wrote *New York Journal-American* reporter Mike Gaven. "He was just a name on the Reading roster when Larry MacPhail purchased that franchise for $5,000 with about a dozen players and a bus thrown in for good measure. But not even in that confusing mob scene of six years ago with the spotlight on Jackie Robinson could Furillo's great class be overlooked."[5]

It was certainly not overlooked by Durocher. Although he lacked diplomacy, Durocher could spot talent and often got what he wanted. In 1946, he was willing to battle Rickey in order to start an outfield of three rookies, reasoning that the Cardinals would likely win the pennant that year but that he would be well-positioned the following year. The three rookies, sometimes referred to as "Leo's Kid Outfield," were Furillo, Gene Hermanski and Dick Whitman. Hermanski was the only one with big league experience, having played 78 games with the Dodgers in 1943. Furillo, meanwhile, was able to take advantage when the regular center fielder, the oft-injured Pete Reiser, suffered a shoulder separation in spring training.

In an early-season interview, Durocher declared, "I decided to use my kid outfield about the time we started north from Daytona. I figured maybe I could finish second behind the Cards with my old-timers in there, and then I got to thinking like this: 'What if I should finish second next year, I'd still have the same second-place outfield, with nobody to take their places. And the Cards still would have a first-place ballclub.' So I decided to cut bait, and to cut it short. I told Mr. Rickey to get me these boys, and now the only way they'll get out of there is if they eliminate themselves.

"Of course, my old-timers will be around if I need them, but these kids are going to get a real chance," Durocher continued. "That's the only way I could get Furillo and Whitman from Rickey. Either I promise to use them or he'd rather have them playing regularly at Montreal."[6] In fact, during the season, Durocher constantly shifted back and forth between the rookies and veterans like Dixie Walker, Augie Galan and Reiser, depending on who was hot as well as his own hunches. At one point in May, Durocher moved Reiser from third base, where he had been playing, back to center and put Furillo in left.

The arrival of Furillo, who was slated to play center field, represented an early step in the Rickey revolution in Brooklyn. Over the next few years, Rickey would put together the great Dodgers teams of the 1950s. Furillo was the second of the mainstays to join the Dodgers. In that first year, he teamed with shortstop Pee Wee Reese, a member of the team from 1940 until he went to war in 1942. The Dodgers, who had played in the 1941 World Series, had a strong lineup that included Eddie Stanky at second and Cookie Lavagetto at third. But the team also included a number of lesser wartime players. "In 1946 and 1947 some more of the boys came up, and it didn't take long to move out some of those wartime players," Furillo said. "Some of them were on borrowed time."[7]

The first time Furillo ever visited a major league ballpark was to play in a preseason April exhibition against the Yankees at Ebbets Field. "It was still freezing cold, but they had the largest crowd ever for a spring training exhibition game at Ebbets Field," he said. "They had just bought my contract from Montreal, and we won the game by one run when I stole home with two out in the 12th inning and I slid in on my stomach."[8] The steal came as Yankees southpaw Jake Wade was in his windup.

The belly slides quickly endeared Furillo to fans, and the excitement continued through the month. Furillo hit safely in his first three games with the Dodgers. In the seventh game of the season, on April 23, he made a spectacular running catch on a seventh-inning drive by Boston Braves hitter Tommy Holmes, saving a no-hitter for Brooklyn pitcher Ed Head. "I threw only one bad pitch in the entire game," Head told the Associated Press. "I meant to keep it on the outside to Tommy Holmes in the seventh inning, but it went right down the middle and he hit it a long way to centerfield. Luckily, Carl Furillo got under it for me. I was saying to myself 'Come on, Furillo.'"[9] The *New York Times* reported that Holmes hit the ball "soaring far and high down the right centerfield alley.... It was like a big balloon suddenly deflating to

Carl Furillo was considered a fleet center fielder when he joined the Dodgers in 1946, as Branch Rickey assembled the great Dodgers team of the 1950s. Furillo was the second mainstay to play for the Dodgers. He joined Pee Wee Reese, who arrived in 1940 (National Baseball Hall of Fame Library, Cooperstown, New York).

hear the collective sigh of relief that was expelled when Carl Furillo scuttled rapidly back and over to camp under the ball way out by the exit gate."[10]

Nonetheless, Furillo made his share of rookie mistakes. In fact, the day before the catch that saved the no-hitter, he misplayed two fly balls, turning one into a two-base advance for a Braves hitter when he collided with Dixie Walker in the outfield, and another into a two-base hit when he misplayed a fly ball by Phil Masi.

In the eighth game of the season, on April 24, the Dodgers made their first appearance against the Phillies in Philadelphia's Shibe Park. *The Reading Eagle* sent Furillo's former classmate, reporter Jerry Kobrin. Furillo hit his first major-league home run, inspiring a compelling lead sentence: "It's barely possible that the guy who coined the cliché 'local boy makes good' was endowed with a divine foresight that enabled him to see yesterday's ball game in Shibe Park." Furillo had four hits as the Dodgers won 11–3, and Kobrin mused on his transformation into a major-league hitter from a kid who, "until a few short weeks ago, was as unknown as a pound of butter."[11] In an interview, Furillo told Kobrin, "This is what I've been working and hoping for. I've reached the big time and I'm going to stick." When Kobrin asked how it felt, Furillo "feigned indifference and shrugged, 'Just like hitting it anywhere else.' But a happy grin belied his nonchalance."[12]

Despite Furillo's success, Kobrin wrote, "He's still the same quiet, determined, nerveless young man who earned the respect and praises of such seasoned baseball veterans as Tom Oliver and Fresco Thompson, his managers when he was getting his start with the Reading club."[13] Kobrin took the opportunity to interview everybody he could find on the subject of Reading's hometown hero. His subjects included Charlie Dressen, a coach who was managing the team while Durocher defended himself against a lawsuit regarding a fan who had fallen down some stairs in Brooklyn. Dressen, a friend throughout Furillo's career, said, "The kid's got everything it takes to develop into a star. He's cool and capable in the pinches and he has one of the best throwing arms in the majors."[14]

Veteran Dixie Walker said, "Carl's not like a lot of the rookies who think they know it all. He's eager to learn and asks a lot of questions. As a result, we're all glad to help him." Walker added, "Furillo has a magnificent arm, but he needs training and experience. For instance, he takes three strides before throwing, giving the runner an unnecessary advantage, but he makes up for it with his terrific speed. And he's plenty dangerous at bat."[15]

Meanwhile, reporter Harold Burr of the *Brooklyn Eagle* told Kobrin that Furillo was the best of the youngsters Rickey had brought up from the minors. In an indication of how much sports reporting changed over the ensuing six decades, Kobrin concluded his story by noting that he had given Furillo a ride home from Philadelphia to Stony Creek Mills. The young star wanted to visit his ailing father and to eat a spaghetti dinner prepared by his sister. "They don't make spaghetti right in New York," Furillo declared.[16]

Playing in New York posed other problems as well. "It was tough to play in Brooklyn because the fans were so serious about their baseball," Furillo recalled. "You were a hero or a bum with them from play to play in every game. In fact, they would call everybody a bum there, no matter what you did wrong or what you did right. If you struck out you were a bum and if you made an error you were a bum, and then they would always come out and say, 'Well, we still love our bums.' You had to get used to that kind of stuff. But right from the time that I started playing in Brooklyn, it seemed like I got to be adopted by the Italian fans there. They would want you out every night for a dinner or banquet or lodge meeting or whatever it was, and it seemed like I was being invited to a different affair every night of the week."[17] One indication of Furillo's strong fan support came on Sept. 25, when the Dodgers staged "Carl Furillo Day" at Ebbets Field, enabling both Italian-Americans and the 77th Division Association to honor him. His gifts included a watch and a radio.

During the season, Furillo continued to develop his contrasting relationships with Durocher and Rickey. "As we got into the season, we had a little slump and Durocher started platooning me," Furillo said. "Since I was a right-handed hitter he would only let me hit against left-handed pitchers. I wasn't too crazy about that because I had always played against all types of pitching, and I did okay. But Durocher was the type of guy that every time you came to the plate you had to get a base hit, which was especially hard on the rookies who were coming up. Durocher always kept the tension real high for his players. He put too much pressure on them and then he chewed them out and wouldn't play them if they didn't get a hit. And I know for a fact that he had the same problem with every club he ever managed."[18] Furillo included the Chicago Cubs, whom Durocher managed at the time of the 1970 interview.

For the full 1946 season, Furillo hit .284 and was a contender for *The Sporting News* Rookie of the Year award, but he was beaten out by Phillies outfielder Del Ennis. Denizens of the two cities argued over the selection, with the Philadelphia contingent citing Ennis' high average—he hit .313 with 17 home runs and 73 RBIs—while the New Yorkers focused on Furillo's clutch hitting during a pennant race as well as his strong arm. The battle for the National League pennant was also a close one. Although they were not expected to compete with the Cardinals, who had played in three of the previous four World Series, the Dodgers managed to tie them during the regular season and force a best-of-three playoff series. The Cardinals won and went to the Series once again, making their last appearance until 1964. The late forties and the fifties would belong to Brooklyn.

By the opening game of the National League playoffs, Furillo and Reese were the only players in the starting lineup who had also played on Opening Day for the Dodgers, and Durocher's management was being praised. "Leo Durocher's act in getting the Dodgers as far as this compares favorably with the greatest juggling act that ever opened a vaudeville show," reported the *International News Service*. For the playoffs, Durocher turned to veterans like Eddie Stanky, Cookie Lavagetto, Joe Medwick, and Dixie Walker. "Not a single soul—even Durocher or Branch Rickey—figured on this finale last spring," INS said. "Durocher looked into the Florida sun and mumbled 'maybe in 1947' ... but (he) lit the fuse and the firecracker never went out."[19]

Recalled Furillo: "We got into a real close pennant race with the Cardinals. We were in and out of first place all through the latter part of the season, and I was getting quite a few of my hits then. That's when I began to get that reputation for being a clutch hitter. The reason is that I wouldn't tense up or worry when I came up to bat in a tough situation. There is one thing I was taught that year by George Sisler, who was a Dodgers coach. He always said 'Carl, when you go up to the plate and you got men on base, that's just like dollar bill signs.' In other words, at contract time they would pay you based on the number of runs batted in that you had. So I didn't care so much about average or home runs or anything else, but I tried to get about 90 or 100 runs batted in every year." Throughout his career, Furillo would say that nothing was more important, when it came to signing a contract, than the number of RBI collected during the previous season.

"One other thing," Furillo continued. "At the end of the 1946 season, Rickey was so happy with the team that he bought each of us on the club a new Studebaker. He gave us each a check for $1,800 to buy it, if we wanted to. For Studebaker it was a big advertisement. So in return the boys all got together with Durocher and Charlie Dressen, and we all chipped in $150 apiece to buy him a boat. And then Charlie Dressen said 'That will be enough. Anything else to be added onto it, I'll add it on.' They bought the boat and had a day for Mr. Rickey. They brought the boat right onto the ball field and they made Mr. Rickey came down on the field to accept it. But he didn't want to come down. He had tears in his eyes. He was a sentimental man."[19] This no doubt was part of the basis for the bond between Rickey and Furillo.

3

The Arrival of Jackie Robinson

JACKIE ROBINSON JOINED the Dodgers in 1947.

More than six decades later, his story continues to be told, and his memory is regularly honored. Robinson led a societal change, and his story remains a gripping tale of right and wrong, filtered through the lens of baseball. The story of Furillo's involvement provides another dimension, one that is not so frequently explored; it is a story of misperception, of the occasional eagerness to find racism in a truth that is more complex and also of an effort to unnecessarily enhance an already compelling saga at Furillo's expense.

Branch Rickey micro-managed Robinson's ascension to the Dodgers, a move that was opposed by many, including the owners of the remaining major league clubs. Shamefully, they gathered at a secret meeting in New York in January 1947 to vote against Robinson's participation in baseball by a 15–1 margin. However, Rickey had the support of the baseball commissioner, A.B. "Happy" Chandler, who chose to allow the Dodgers' purchase of Robinson's contract from the Montreal Royals minor league team. Chandler wrote of his decision in his autobiography, noting that he told Rickey, "You know, Branch, I'm going to have to meet my Maker some day. And if He asks me why I didn't let this boy play, and I say it's because he's black, that might not be a satisfactory answer."[1] While Rickey is widely and justly regarded as a hero in the story of bringing Robinson into baseball, Chandler's contribution is sometimes overlooked. According to Chandler, that is because Rickey "and his whole outfit" worked hard to make sure that he got the credit for breaking baseball's color line. "I never could understand why he always cut me out of it," Chandler wrote.[2]

That spring, the Dodgers and Royals trained in Havana because Robinson was in camp for the first time and Rickey wanted to avoid racial incidents in the South, the more usual site for spring training. From Havana, the Dodgers made visits to play games in other Caribbean venues, including Venezuela and, in mid–March, Panama City. The latter venue was the site of the notorious petition incident, which shapes subsequent perceptions of Furillo's attitude and role regarding Robinson.

"From Havana we had gone into Panama to play some exhibitions there, and we were staying in the naval base in Panama," Furillo recalled. "That was where the big friction started among the Southern boys. Some of (them) were trying to get up a petition to keep Robinson from playing, and I'm sorry to say that at the time that it happened, I had to go and get myself involved in it.

"Robinson at the time was still with Montreal, and he and I, as far as I was concerned, were always friendly. I always spoke to him no matter where I saw him, and I talked to him on the side and everything. In fact, I remember running into him on the main street in Havana and I said to him, 'It looks like you may come up, huh?' So he says, 'Yeah, that's the way it sounds.'"

One afternoon, following the conclusion of a ball game, "we had

Like Carl Furillo, Jackie Robinson joined the Dodgers from the Montreal Royals, after enjoying enthusiastic support from the Montreal fans. Furillo played the 1941 season in Montreal, while Robinson played the 1946 season there (National Baseball Hall of Fame Library, Cooperstown, New York).

come into the barracks, which was an officers' barracks, and I was lying on one of the cots there," Furillo said. "They had a divider between the cots and it must have been about six feet high so you couldn't normally see over it. Right in the middle of this big room was where they had a lot of the Southern boys, and they were discussing this thing about Robinson. Some of the Southern boys that were there were Kirby Higbe, Hugh Casey, Dixie Walker and Bobby Bragan, and there were a few others, although offhand I can't remember them. And they wanted to sign a petition keeping Robinson from coming up into the major leagues, because they were against it."[3]

"Well, I just happened to be lying on the cot and I heard all this, I was hearing all these different remarks. So I got up—I was only a rookie at the time—and I went over to where they were talking, and one of them asked me what I would do if Robinson was after my job. So like a dumb jerk I came out and I made a remark like 'Well, I'd cut his legs off.' That was stupid for me to even say, but it came out, and from that day on I was pulled on the carpet because I was one that was supposed to be against Robinson. The whole thing was too bad because really, I didn't care who the hell came up. I was only a rookie at the time. I had a lot of friends who were colored in my hometown, I played against colored and I got along with everybody."[4]

The various accounts of what happened that spring agree that a group of Southern ballplayers opposed Robinson's ascension to the club, but vary wildly on the details. A principal question concerns whether a petition ever actually existed; while it is one thing to talk about drawing up a petition, it is another to actually do so. It is impossible to say who, if anyone, signed such a document; again, the accounts vary wildly. Another question involves Furillo's position on Robinson—specifically, at what point did Furillo's initial resistance to Robinson turn to full acceptance? In this matter, only the timing is disputed. The most credible interpretation is that, despite his slipup in Panama, Furillo never seriously opposed Robinson, although he made at least one and possibly more unfortunate remarks. However, in some accounts, the Robinson story was embellished by the creation of an Italian straw man. This embellishment came to be viewed as fact.

The Southern players' opposition, as well as the possibility of a petition, came to the club's attention one night when Kirby Higbe discussed it while drinking with Dodgers traveling secretary Harold Parrott in Panama. Parrot conveyed the news to Rickey, and Durocher subsequently called a late-night meeting of the club in the military barracks. Players had to be awakened, and Durocher conducted the meeting attired in a bathrobe. "Durocher had a clubhouse meeting and said he was the boss and he would be the one to say who played on the team," Bragan said.

Afterwards, according to Bragan, Rickey held individual meetings with the players who were involved.

Bragan, a Birmingham, Alabama, native and Walker's roommate, was a key member of the resistance to Robinson and, by 2009, was the last survivor from the group. Bragan recalls that Rickey met with him as well as with Walker, Stanky and Furillo to discuss their positions. Rickey "called us to his office there in Panama, and he had a writer, Arthur Mann, with him," Bragan said. "He called us in one at a time." Rickey asked Bragan, "Do you want to be traded?" and Bragan responded, "Yes, sir." Rickey asked, "But if you stay will you play the best you can?" and Bragan responded, "Yes, sir." The meeting was brief, with little additional discussion, Bragan said, noting "I'm sure he asked the same question of everybody." Walker, Bragan added, said he wanted to be traded.

At the conclusion of Bragan's meeting, "Arthur Mann said 'I guess that will be the end of Bragan on this team,' and Mr. Rickey said, 'No, we'll have to wait and see what he's made of.'" It should be noted that Bragan eventually became a Rickey disciple and regularly acknowledged he had been wrong about Robinson. In an interview, he proclaimed that "Mr. Rickey was the number one individual in sports" and that "Billy Graham and Mr. Rickey are the two greatest men I ever met."[5]

Rickey also met with Furillo. Neither man has provided a recollection. It is likely that Rickey drew a parallel between discrimination against Robinson and discrimination against Italians, and that he used this parallel to convince Furillo that he should play no role in the opposition—not a difficult task, given that Furillo both respected Rickey and also had no real interest in opposing Robinson. However, the story of Furillo's meeting with Rickey took on a life of its own because it provides an enduring fable. It was prominently portrayed in the movie *The Jackie Robinson Story*, although there the discussion takes place in a group meeting rather than a meeting between Furillo and Rickey. A slightly different version was conveyed in Parrott's 1973 reminiscence in *The Sporting News*. Parrott described Rickey's approaches to three players—Walker, Pee Wee Reese and Furillo—who initially expressed opposition to Robinson's joining the team. He said Rickey eventually traded Walker, "won Pee Wee over," and then talked with Furillo.

Parrott's account of Furillo's involvement is both unique and demeaning. He writes, "Some of the Southern gentlemen had framed a petition demanding that Rickey dismiss the controversial black 'for the good of the team.' Now the thing was all ready, complete with ball-point pen. But who would take it around to get it signed? They knew whoever did would be about as popular with Rickey as Judas Iscariot. The author of the document handed it to Furillo and suddenly fell ill, taking the day off so he wouldn't be suspected. Furillo, son of a simple Sicilian immigrant, was as out of place pushing an anti–Negro petition as he would have been unraveling calculus. Rickey had him on the carpet right now. 'Furillo,' the old man boomed, 'How long ago did your father come over on the boat?' The outfielder was bewildered. His lips moved and he counted on his fingers. Finally he announced, 'Thoity-five years, about.' 'Hmmm,' said Rickey. 'Now just suppose, and I want you to think seriously about this, Carl, before you answer. Just suppose that 35 years ago a few idiots got together and made up a petition to send him back to Sicily, and they got another idiot to take it around Reading, Pennsylvania, or wherever your father was living. Suppose all that had happened, and your father went back. Now I want you to think before you answer, Carl. My question is, where would you be today?' Furillo blinked. Finally he said, 'I never thought of that, Mr. Rickey.' End of petition. But not the end of Robinson's trials. Not by a long shot."[6]

The account contains at least three obvious factual misstatements. First, Furillo's parents were from Naples, not Sicily. Secondly, Furillo was not a semi-literate who counted on his fingers; in fact, he was financially savvy despite his eighth-grade education, enough so that in his post-baseball years co-workers regularly turned to him for financial advice. Thirdly, he did not speak with a Brooklyn accent, substituting "thoity" for "thirty'; in fact, he had never been to Brooklyn until a year earlier, when he was 25 years old. Why would Parrott, a one-time newspaper reporter, take such broad license to recast reality? Most likely he became caught up in the myth-making that was incorporated into the 1950 movie. This phenomenon was clear to Chandler, who wrote that Rickey and his associates were eager to define the Robinson story in a way that embellished Rickey's role. Among them, who would have cared about Chandler's actual role? Who would have cared about Furillo's? While the comparison between Robinson's struggle and the earlier struggle by Italians provides an emotionally appealing story, its frequent telling portrays Furillo in an untruthful and unflattering light, partially because of the manner in which Furillo is depicted and partially because it elevates the barracks remark into an indication of bigotry. Furillo was troubled and angered by the falsehood, which not only came to be viewed in some quarters as fact, but also contributed to his feelings of separation from the team and from his teammates.

It is particularly troubling that in response to Robinson's promotion to the team, Furillo behaved no worse than many other players—including Reese, who became a hero of the Robinson saga, and Bragan, who was known for his conversion to Rickey admirer—and yet he continued to be vilified for years afterwards. Erskine was not with the Dodgers in 1947, but he said he doubts that Parrott would have attended a meeting between Furillo and Rickey, if one occurred. In any case, "Harold was sort of a romantic" in his view of Robinson's ascension to the club, Erskine said, adding, "His writing shows that."[7] Carl Furillo, Jr., commenting on Parrott's account, declared, "There is no way my dad would have carried that petition. All along, he told me he had nothing to do with that. Dad told me they drummed up a lot of this stuff to use against him to keep him in line."

The son recalls watching *The Jackie Robinson Story* on television with his father. In one scene, Rickey meets with four ballplayers who are involved in a petition drive. He pointedly questions three of them; in the case of the Italian, he asks, "Your father was an immigrant laborer, did anybody get up a petition to keep him from working on the railroad?" Tony glumly responds, "Not that I know of."[8] After a similar exchange about Tony's mother, who worked in a shirt factory, Rickey proclaims, "Your parents came to this country from Italy and were allowed to work as free people. And yet you, a child and beneficiary of that freedom, want to deny the same opportunity to an American whose parents and grandparents and great-grandparents have been in this country for 200 years? Is that right?"[9] Tony was quiet and Rickey moved on to the next ballplayer, again deftly questioning his involvement. "The movie shows a meeting with Rickey, Southern boys on one side of the room and the Italian guy sitting on the far left on a couch, away from the other three ballplayers, and they called him 'Tony' in the movie," said Carl Furillo, Jr. "And my dad was very upset. He said, 'That's supposed to be me, but I was never at that meeting." He said, 'That's a lie' and he was furious about it. I made the remark, 'Can't you do anything about it?' and he said, 'No, that's the way they did the movie.'

"Then I said to Dad, 'Did you ever say, 'I'd break his legs?' And Dad said to me, 'All of us competed for the spots we had.' Dad said, 'It didn't matter if he was a white guy, a Chinese guy or whatever, I'd have said the same thing.' What he meant was, 'Nobody was going to take my spot.' It had nothing to do with ethnic groups."[10]

It is no wonder that Furillo was furious about the movie, because once an image as a Robinson opponent was assigned to him, it took on a life of its own and could not be excised. As another example, in his 1972 autobiography, Robinson discussed the effort to circulate a petition and named four "ringleaders" of the effort: Casey, Bragan, Walker and Furillo. Robinson wrote, "The ringleaders were called in individually, and Mr. Rickey told each one that petitions would make no difference (and) the petition protest collapsed before it got started."[11] In the 1997 book *Jackie Robinson: A Biography*, Arnold Rampersad writes that in Panama, a petition began to circulate, an effort supported by the southern ballplayers. Furillo "backed the revolt," he said, perhaps relying on Robinson's book.¹² In this account, the rebellion was largely quelled by Durocher in the midnight meeting. More recently, in the 2009 book *Perfect: Don Larsen's Miraculous World Series Game and the Men Who Made It Happen*, author Lew Paper says that Robinson described Furillo as a ringleader only because Furillo was not the type to have ever approached Robinson to explain what actually happened.

Various other Dodgers have also written or spoken about the petition. According to Carl Erskine, "When I came up in 1948, there was never a (negative) show of any kind about Jackie in the clubhouse or on the field. There was talk occasionally about a petition but Pee Wee never acknowledged that there was one."¹³ Tommy Brown, who had joined the Dodgers in 1944 as a 16-year-old, has also discussed the petition. Brown rarely gives interviews, but he did speak to Nashville writer Bill Traughber, a neighbor, who approached him in his yard and wrote about it in a 2005 article. "There was a little dissension when Jackie came into camp," Brown said. "I don't want to mention any names, but they got a petition against playing with Jackie. They came to me and said to sign it, but I never signed it. I don't know how many signed, but several did. Jackie was a great ball player. Of course, he was a little shy and timid in the beginning."¹⁴ In the 1984 book *Bums* by Peter Golenbock, Reese is quoted as saying that Walker, a good friend, asked him and Pete Reiser to sign a petition saying he would not play with Robinson. "I looked at it, and I just flatly refused," Reese said. Reiser also told Golenbock that Walker asked him to sign the petition, and he refused.¹⁵

In 2001, Buzzie Bavasi wrote an e-mail to Bill Ninfo, who was writing a book about Furillo. Said Bavasi, "The only thing I know about the petition is that Dixie (Walker) wanted players to sign a piece of paper stating their reluctance to play with Robby. I told Mr. Rickey about it and mentioned that the only signatures I saw were Dixie's and Higbe's. Higbe was gone the next week and later on Dixie followed him."¹⁶

Did Higbe sign? Who knows? Bavasi said he did. Higbe told Golenbock he did not. In his 1967 biography, Higbe said nothing at all about a petition. He wrote that the team was in Panama when Rickey announced that Robinson would play for the Dodgers, and five players confronted Rickey. "All of us were Southerners—Pee Wee Reese, Dixie Walker, Bobby Bragan and me—except Carl Furillo, who was from Pennsylvania," Higbe said. "We told Mr. Rickey that we did not want to play ball with a Negro." Rickey responded that Robinson would be playing for the Dodgers, so there was nothing more to discuss. Afterwards, the team went back to Havana. "Before we left Havana, Furillo and Bragan changed their minds and decided they would play with Jackie," Higbe wrote. "Just as we were leaving Havana, Pee Wee swung over to Jackie's side. That left me and Dixie."¹⁷ Higbe was traded quickly, but not as

3. The Arrival of Jackie Robinson 35

quickly as Bavasi recalled 54 years later; the deal with Pittsburgh was actually made on May 3.

Was there actually a petition? While much of the evidence supports the theory, Bragan consistently maintained in various interviews that none existed. "There was no petition," he said in 2009. "I don't know who started that rumor. I was Dixie's roommate (and) I never did see it. I'm sure I would have seen it." Bragan said that Walker wrote a letter to Rickey asking to be traded, and that later on, Walker sought the return of the letter. "Dixie felt so strongly he put it in writing, that he would prefer to be traded," Bragan said. "Then he tried to get the letter back and didn't get it."[18] Another player in camp in 1947 was Gene Hermanski. But Hermanski said Robinson's opponents paid no attention to him. "They ignored me," he said. "I was a rookie, trying to get a job, so what could I do? Besides, I was brought up in New Jersey, and we had Negroes in our classes. I thought Jackie was a wonderful person, the right man for the job."[19] Ralph Branca was not asked either. "I guess they figured I was a Northerner," he said.[20]

In no account does anyone remotely suggest that Furillo signed the petition. But it is clear that he initially enabled an impression that he was opposed to Robinson's joining the team. The impression was shared by Lester Rodney, then the sportswriter for *The Daily Worker*, a Communist newspaper. Rodney has become an iconic figure, a sportswriter with leftist leanings who was deeply involved in the effort to enable African American ballplayers to play in the majors. Despite antipathy towards Communism in some quarters, Rodney said, "I was accepted as a sportswriter. With the crew in the press box and on the field before the game, the abstraction of *The Daily Worker* falls away when you're in there working." The principal thing that differentiated his coverage, Rodney said, "being (with) a Communist newspaper, it influenced the proportion of space I gave to the racial problem."

Like Bragan, Rodney said no petition was drawn up, although the topic was discussed. "My own recollection is there was no actual piece of paper with signatures, but the players made their sentiments known," he said. Rodney did not travel to Havana or Panama with the team, but could easily have had knowledge of what happened, since he was intensely focused on the details of Robinson's acceptance on the team.

Rodney also said that in the early days of 1947, he heard Furillo declare, "I ain't gonna play with no niggers." Furillo "was basically just a guy from Pennsylvania," Rodney said. "He wasn't a bad guy. Originally he was hostile to integration, but he changed. He's the guy that changed before your eyes. Jackie changed a lot of people. He did that by his composure and what he did and how he did it ... (Furillo) became one of Jackie's best friends on the Dodgers, (although) that doesn't mean they went out together."[21] In several interviews, Rodney spoke of Furillo's transformation, a story that ends with Furillo's embrace of Jackie and Rachel Robinson at the 1955 World Series celebration. It is a heartfelt story, one that summarizes Robinson's ability to shape a country's attitude, told by a widely admired man of integrity who also fought against the harsh stereotypes of the day. However, it is also another story in which Furillo is used to make a point. Rodney's suggestion that Furillo used the word "nigger" and continued to voice opposition to Robinson following the barracks incident cannot be corroborated. Carl Furillo, Jr., said he never heard his father use the word, as did Furillo's co-workers from his post-baseball job as a security guard at a plant that made nylon resin pellets. Said Erskine, "I never heard Furillo use the N word or even make behind-the-back remarks about a black player."[22] Additionally, Carl Jr. said he once asked his mother if his dad had ever used the word, and she responded, "No, he always said 'colored' or 'colored people.'"[23]

It is clear that very quickly after Robinson joined the team, Furillo became an ally. "Carl played well with him; he got along with him fine, just like everybody else did," Bragan said. "Jackie sold himself to everybody. Carl was very outspoken. He wasn't the most intelligent person in the world. (But) it wouldn't make him exceptional. A lot of ballplayers were not too bright. Carl was likable. He got along with everybody on the team, including the black players."[24]

Reporter Jack Lang, who covered the Dodgers from 1946 through 1957 for *The Long Island Press*, said, "Carl had the natural biases many people had in those days, and he went along with those guys who didn't want Jackie playing with the club, (but) he later became a good teammate to Jackie Robinson." It is important to remember that Robinson, like Furillo, had a prickly personality. "Nobody loved Jackie," Lang said. "They put up with him. Jackie was not an easy guy to get along with. He didn't even get along with Campanella."[25] But through his play, Lang said, Robinson quickly convinced his teammates that he could help them win, and they were all friendly towards him.

While Robinson was high-strung, Campanella was easygoing, and he grew close to Furillo. On most days, they warmed up together before the games. They would talk constantly as they did so, recalls Carl Furillo, Jr., Erskine also spoke of the bond between the two men. "Campy and Furillo and I fished together, and when I didn't go, Campy and Furillo would go," he said. "I don't think there was any race thing with Furillo. I never heard one peep at any time that suggested that Furillo had any problem with any of the black players."[26]

In Furillo's 1989 obituary in the *Los Angeles Times*, Campanella was quoted as saying, "I'm really sorry to hear he's passed away. He was quite a good friend.... There were seven of us who played every day, and he was one of them."²⁷

As Roger Kahn wrote in a remembrance the day after Furillo died, "Early on he had a hard time accepting the integration of baseball. He grew up in all-white country and was never schooled beyond the eighth grade. But Furillo changed and grew, a quiet man learning from his times."²⁸

When Jim Gilliam joined the Dodgers in 1953, a few players complained and Kahn wrote a story that raised the issue of continued prejudice against black ballplayers. "By this point Furillo was warming up each night by playing catch with Campanella," Kahn wrote. "He had surpassed his boyhood and grown color-blind. Into the clubhouse I went and Furillo called me over. 'That stuff was years ago,' he said. 'I was wrong. I got nothing against the colored playing ball.'"²⁹

One particularly compelling piece of evidence supports the view that despite his early misstatement in the barracks at Panama, Furillo was receptive to Robinson very early in the process of the integration of the Dodgers. The 1947 Dodgers team picture was taken in early May and was the first official portrait of the team that year. Standing in the fourth row, Dixie Walker is looking away, perhaps a symbol of his opposition,

This early-season photograph of the 1947 Dodgers was taken in May. Dixie Walker, in the back row, is looking away from the camera. Carl Furillo, third from right, is seated next to Jackie Robinson in the first row (National Baseball Hall of Fame Library, Cooperstown, New York).

or perhaps an individualistic practice; baseball historian Lyle Spatz notes that Walker also looks away in an earlier-year team picture, and does not look away in a later 1947 team picture.[30] Still, "It's the first picture taken of Jackie and the guys," says Carl Furillo, Jr. "Dixie is looking away. But my dad is sitting next to Jackie."[31] In the end, it may well be that the picture provides the best indication of Furillo's attitude at the time, particularly by comparison with a series of conflicting memories clouded by the passage of time.

4

The Reading Rifle

As the Dodgers entered the 1947 season, much of America was focused on Robinson's arrival, the most important social change in major league baseball's history. But Carl Furillo was focused on a more pressing issue: his salary. As the season was about to begin, Furillo made it clear that—eighth-grade education or not—he was not about to let the Dodgers pay him whatever salary Branch Rickey chose to offer. "I want more dough to play with the Dodgers this year," Furillo proclaimed, in a Feb. 6 story in *The Reading Times*. The story, headlined "Carl Furillo Joins Holdout Ranks," reported that the 24-year-old outfielder was holding out after a rookie season in which he hit .284 with three home runs and 35 RBI in 117 games. He had mailed back his contract unsigned.

"I can't figure it out," Furillo told *Times* reporter Doc Silva, a former International League outfielder. "Here I play 117 games in my first season in the majors and they treat me as if I saw action in a few contests. I'm sure I helped keep the Dodgers in the thick of the scrap with the St. Louis Cardinals and what do I get? A minor league contract." The offer, Silva wrote, called for only slightly more than the major league minimum. "Now is the time to get the extra money," Furillo added. "I figure I had a great year despite my lack of experience and being away in the Army for three years. I know they have a lot of rookies coming up, but I have no worries as I proved my ability in 1946."[1]

This prelude to Furillo's sophomore year in the majors is revealing in several ways. First, it indicates that, even in his earliest days in baseball, he was not afraid to speak up. This never changed. "He was a tough man," said Ron Fairly, the young ballplayer Furillo would mentor two decades later. "And he had a lot of street smarts. He was nobody's dummy."[2] Furillo's ability to represent himself adequately was notable because, at that time, the idea of agents one day representing ballplayers was inconceivable. Later, as his career came to an end, Furillo may have been hurt by his tendency to reject offers he saw as unfair, and to fight back. But that is who he was.

Another trait that never changed, as the Reading coverage indicates, is that throughout his career, Furillo liked and trusted newspaper writers, and they in turn respected him. This was particularly true in Reading. The city's morning and evening newspapers, which were jointly owned, offered exhaustive coverage of the hometown athlete, and both treated Furillo favorably. In talking to reporters, Furillo "spoke with honesty rather than discretion and trusted you to keep him out of trouble," wrote Roger Kahn in the 1972 book *The Boys of Summer*. "Once in a while, when something he said fired controversy, he stood by his remark.... He was a man of uncomplicated virtues."[3] Importantly, Kahn noted, Furillo did not lie. He was proud of who he was, and comfortable with himself, and he saw no reason to say something untrue. "I knew Furillo for 37 years," Kahn wrote. "I do not believe he was capable of telling a lie."[4]

In the interview with Silva, Furillo detailed every intricacy of his contract discussions with the Dodgers. "I have been carrying on my contract negotiations with Branch Rickey, Jr., and he probably doesn't understand my case," Furillo said. "He told me in Brooklyn several weeks ago that I was getting a big raise on my record, but I fail to agree with him. I know that if his father handles things that he will give me a substantial raise. At least, I hope so, because I want to report for spring training early and get my eyes on the ball."[5]

In return for Furillo's willingness to confide in them, the Reading reporters offered their support. A few days after Furillo returned his contract, a *Reading Times* (2/12) reporter wrote, "Certainly Branch Rickey couldn't have been shocked when the Stony Creek giant returned his contract unsigned. If he was, we'll have to change our estimate of the boss of the Dodgers. Furillo doesn't want to be classed as a stubborn holdout. Right now he is in New York, probably conferring with Branch Rickey, Jr., before he has a final set-to with Papa Branch. Your correspondent happens to know what Carl is asking for and it is not too much. Matter of fact, he would be a foolish young man if he settles for a nickel less."[6]

The holdout ended after two weeks. Although terms were not disclosed, Furillo told *The Reading Times* that he agreed to sign after a 30-minute telephone conversation with Rickey. The amount, he later recalled, was $6,500. The negotiations were conducted under pressure, given the imminent departure of the train carrying the Dodgers to Miami, where they would catch a plane to Havana. Immediately after signing, Furillo drove to Philadelphia to catch the southbound train. Again, Furillo laid out the details to the newspaper. "Mr. Rickey told me that I was the last player to sign," he said. "He asked me what I wanted, told me what he thought the club could afford and what I was worth, and we had no trouble whatsoever reaching an agreement. It all ended with me receiving a fine boost in salary and no hard feelings on either side. Now I'm going to Cuba (to) clinch that center field job.

"I read in the papers where manager Durocher was counting on me to fill the centerfield spot this year, and it's going to take a derrick to get me out of that spot," Furillo added. "With my physical and financial worries now over, I'm looking forward to a great season."[7] Over the winter, he had an operation on his nose to clear up nasal congestion that he had contacted while serving in the South Pacific, had his tonsils removed and received treatment for a kidney ailment. Newspapers were reporting that Durocher planned to field an outfield of Dixie Walker in right, Furillo in center and Pete Reiser or Dick Whitman in left. On Feb. 27, Durocher confirmed his intentions, saying his starting lineup would be: catcher Bruce Edwards, first baseman Ed Stevens, second baseman Eddie Stanky, shortstop Pee Wee Reese, third baseman Arky Vaughan, and outfielders Walker, Furillo and Reiser.

Furillo played well in Havana, distinguishing himself not only by his hitting but also by his strong, accurate arm. Dodgers pitchers particularly appreciated his throwing skills, according to an article written for the Reading papers by *New York World Telegram* reporter Lester Bromberg. "As developed by conversation with many players, one's impression is that Furillo has the best throwing arm of the 12 outfielders in camp," wrote Bromberg, who described Furillo as "amiable but not garrulous" and said he "acts as if he never hears the compliments of teammates."[8] Interviewed on March 8, his 25th birthday, Furillo told Bromberg, "I guess I throw pretty fair but why shouldn't I? I guess some of the folks back home will remember when I pitched for St. Lawrence Dairy." Then, as he did throughout his career, Furillo made it clear that he was focused on the bottom line. "I've got to get some money together and sticking strictly to baseball is the one way I can do it," he said. "If we can get into the Series—well, that's what I mean."[9] On his birthday, Furillo scored the winning run as the Dodgers beat the Yankees 1–0 in a ten-inning exhibition game in Havana.

As the Dodgers prepared for what is arguably the most important season a major league team ever played, a second controversy arose. On April 9, six days before opening day, Commissioner Happy Chandler suspended Durocher for the season for "conduct detrimental to baseball." Durocher was replaced by Burt Shotton, a move that would benefit Furillo.

Chandler never fully detailed the unbecoming aspect of Durocher's conduct. However, Durocher was generally considered to be somewhat unsavory. His conversation was laced with obscenities. His relationships with ballplayers and others in baseball, including Chandler, were often tempestuous. His friends included gamblers, bookmakers and mob members. His habits included high-stakes card games in the clubhouse, and his personal life included an affair with actress Laraine Day, whom he married in 1947. He also encouraged his pitchers to throw at opposing hitters, and generally did a poor job of handling young ballplayers. Willie Mays was a later exception. Nevertheless, Durocher, who died in 1991, was posthumously elected to the Hall of Fame in 1994.

Opinions on Durocher varied widely. Bragan recalled him as a colorful character and a good manager. "Durocher was the best-dressed man in baseball, like a fashion plate," Bragan said. "He traveled in fast company. He knew all the actors; he would bring Abbott and Costello and Milton Berle into the clubhouse. And he was the only one I ever heard call Mr. Rickey 'Branch.' He was suspended for leaving tickets for Memphis Engelberg, a gambler. When the commissioner heard about it, he suspended (Durocher) for the year." Bragan also recalled Durocher as a talented manager who was fully cognizant of every play during a game. "Durocher was the best manager I ever played for," Bragan said. "After a game was over he could recall all 27 outs for the opposing team."[10]

Still, Chandler's decision to suspend Durocher can be easily understood, not only because of Durocher's background, but also in light of a series of events that occurred in the spring of 1947. For one, Durocher engaged in a feud with Larry MacPhail, who had left the Dodgers presidency to become a Yankees co-owner in 1945. Durocher crossed a line when he alleged, in a ghostwritten article in the *Brooklyn Eagle*, that MacPhail had invited gamblers into the Yankees clubhouse. Additionally, Laraine Day's husband sued Durocher for alienation of affection, and the Catholic Youth Organization of Brooklyn moved to end its affiliation with the team.

For the Dodgers, the distraction was unwelcome. Yet in some ways, it eased Robinson's monumental task. "The suspension of Durocher took the spotlight off me," Robinson recalled in a 1957 interview with Mike Gaven of the *New York Journal-American*. "Mr. Rickey had told me he wanted Leo to make the announcement of my coming up, stressing his need for me as a first baseman. So when he was suspended, they handed out a one-sentence announcement in the press box during the Montreal-Dodger game. It simply stated Brooklyn had purchased me from Montreal and I would join the Dodgers the following day."[11]

4. The Reading Rifle

On April 8, the day before his suspension, Durocher sought to denigrate Furillo. "Whatever gave you fellows the idea that Carl Furillo was sure of a regular job on this club?" he asked reporters. "He has to show me more than I've seen."[12] Analyzing the statement, Gaven wrote, "Obviously, the main idea is to take Furillo down a few pegs." Possibly, the effort represented a response to Furillo's brief holdout. "Rickey lives in fear of being put over the barrel and he would trade Furillo in a minute if he could obtain equal value in return," Gaven said.[13] Rickey also made similar comments, suggesting that Furillo had fallen out of favor. Not only had Furillo held out, but also the Dodgers had a number of outfielders in camp. As Furillo recalled it, "I was going to be in center with Pete Reiser in left and Dixie Walker in right. But then they had Gene Hermanski (and Dick Whitman) in camp too that year, and they began to watch him and talk him up, and it looked like Durocher and Rickey were trying to take me down a peg. Durocher was even saying that he was going to cut me from the squad or trade me or something, and most of the time he was platooning me and playing me only against lefties."[14]

On April 11, two days after Durocher's suspension, the Dodgers announced they had purchased Robinson's contract from Montreal. Furillo's status, however, had become less certain. That same day, Bill Reedy's column in *The Reading Eagle* referred to spring trade rumors involving Furillo, as the Dodgers dealt with the outfield glut and the possibility that Gene Hermanski might get an opportunity in left field. Hermanski was viewed as a potential long-ball hitter, but an erratic fielder, so playing him would require putting Reiser in center, where Furillo had been considered the leading candidate. "In recent exhibition games, Furillo has finished some games as a substitute for Reiser in center," Reedy wrote. Referring to Hermanski's strong hitting, he wrote, "If Hermanski has clinched the left-field post, that leaves no room for Furillo except as a substitute."[15] An

The first baseball card of Carl Furillo was issued by Bowman in 1949. Furillo played his entire career for the Dodgers (courtesy Topps Company).

April 16 story in *The Sporting News* was the first of dozens over the years in which Furillo's name was mentioned in a trade rumor. Rickey reportedly was offering five Dodgers—Furillo and four minor leaguers including catcher Dixie Howell—for Philadelphia outfielder Del Ennis. It is worth noting that the Phillies "snickered" at the offer,[16] and that Furillo concluded his career with the Dodgers in 1960.

On April 15, Opening Day, Robinson played his first major league game as the Dodgers' first baseman, the position he would occupy throughout the season. He was hitless. The next day, Robinson got his first hit, a bunt single, and Rickey named the 62-year-old Shotton to be the Dodgers manager. "As for Shotton, everybody loved him (and) his easygoing manner," Bragan said. "He was calm and cool, the opposite of Durocher."[17] Of course Furillo was pleased. Durocher's suspension "worked out well for me because it made Burt Shotton manager," he said. "I don't think that Burt Shotton was crazy with wanting to be manager, because he was well-fixed at the time and he was on the Brooklyn payroll as a scout. He took the job as a favor to Rickey because the two of them were good friends"[18] In July, he told Gordon Williams of *The Reading Times* that Shotton "never seems to get angry with anyone, whether we win or lose. (He) feels he can get more out of the boys by slapping them on the backs instead of clubhouse lectures."[19]

Shotton started off platooning Furillo, sitting him against right-handed pitchers, just as Durocher had done. Reiser generally started in center. In May, Shotton alternated Hermanski and Furillo in left, with Dixie Walker in right. The approach pleased neither Furillo nor Hermanski, who said, "I would face right-handers and he would face left-handers, and I was hitting pretty good against right-handers, but they still wouldn't let me hit against left-handers."[20] In June, Reiser ran head-on into a wall, and his subsequent performance deteriorated. Meanwhile, Furillo was hitting well; on June 30, his .348 average was the league's second-highest. In response, Shotton made Furillo the center fielder and moved Reiser to left.

In the July interview with Gordon Williams, Furillo said he was not thinking about winning the batting title, but he was—as usual—thinking about his salary. "All I want is for the Dodgers to win the pennant and get into the World Series," he said. "Maybe if I drive in 100 runs this season and hit in the select class, I will be in a position to ask for a decent salary."[21] Shotton wanted to convert Furillo into a long-ball hitter and constantly urged him to swing hard, Williams wrote, but Furillo "is satisfied with his doubles and singles and refuses to change his timing. In this, he is supported by Dixie Walker, veteran outfielder, who advised Carl not to cut from the heels, but to hit the way he has been doing. Walker has taken an interest in Furillo and coaches him with his batting."[22]

Furillo also spoke favorably about Robinson's play. "Robinson's fielding is improving every day," he said. "Next to Pete Reiser, he is the fastest man in the league. Jackie has a great eye and is a real good hitter. Minds his own business and hustles every minute."[23] In conclusion, Williams commented on Furillo as an interview subject, offering something of a contrarian view, since he and several other hometown reporters had grown close to Furillo. "If you think it is easy to interview Furillo, you have another guess coming," Williams wrote. "He doesn't say much, but when he speaks you know he is sincere in his remarks."[24]

Despite Robinson's improvement, the Dodgers did not excel in the first third of the season. On June 15, their record was 27–25. But as Robinson grew both in confidence and in the extent of his acceptance by the team, his play and the team's play improved. The Dodgers moved into first place in late June, led the Braves by a game at the All-Star Game break, and gradually increased their lead in the second half. For the season, Furillo batted 437 times, hitting .295 with eight home runs and 88 RBI. Robinson batted 590 times, batting .297 with 12 home runs and 48 RBI; he also led the league with 29 steals, scored 125 runs and was named *The Sporting News* Rookie of the Year. Surprisingly, a dozen home runs were enough to tie Robinson with Reese for the team home run lead. Meanwhile, Dixie Walker hit .306. Among the pitchers, Branca led the staff with a 21–12 record, while Joe Hatten went 17–8, Vic Lombardi was 12–11, Harry Taylor was 10–5 and relief ace Hugh Casey was 10–4.

Looking back on the season years later, Furillo said platooning was a barrier he had to overcome. "I had a tremendous year, against right-handers and left-handers, and I won quite a few games for them," he declared. "But it goes to show what I always said. You come up from the minor leagues, not now, but the minor leagues back then, you come up from Class D ball all the way to Double A and then into the major leagues. And you were hitting right-handers, left-handers, it made no difference how they were throwing it. Then all of a sudden you come into the major leagues and some guy says to you, 'You can't hit right-handed pitching.' Now, does that make him an authority? It does only because they put it in your mind that you can't do it. The only way that you can hit against right-handers is to play against right-handers, which Shotton let me do."[25] In his battle to avoid being platooned, Furillo of course had the support of the Reading reporters. "Furillo has been the most valuable man in Brooklyn's attack since he replaced Pete Reiser in center field," wrote Bill Reedy on July 27. "It's most significant that the Dodgers rose to first place and gained such a big lead over the Cardinals since the Berks boy got his chance for daily labor. Burt Shotton, who replaced Leo Durocher as manager of the Dodgers just as the campaign opened, cannot be criticized for the bad judgment in respect to Furillo's value earlier in the season."[26]

In April 1947, Burt Shotton replaced the suspended Leo Durocher as Dodgers manager. Durocher returned in April 1948, then departed for the Giants in July, enabling Shotton to manage through the 1950 season. This picture shows a convivial threesome: Shotton, Jackie Robinson and Carl Furillo (Furillo family photograph).

Furillo committed his share of rookie mistakes, but he made up for them. On August 16, he hit a single in the eighth inning, his 100th hit of the season, but failed to touch third as he ran home on an infield error. He was called out; the failure cost the Dodgers two runs. Nevertheless, the team defeated the Phillies, 5–4. Then on Sept. 10 in a key game against the Cubs, Furillo saved the win for the Dodgers with two sensational catches in deep center field. "Twice he climbed the old ivy at Wrigley Field to retire the Cubs runless in the seventh and eighth innings," reported *The Sporting News*. "There were two on in the seventh when he made a first leaping catch of a drive by Andy Pafko that otherwise would have been in there for extra bases, and in the eighth he repeated at the expense of Ray Mack with one on base."[27]

The Dodgers clinched the pennant on Sept. 22, finished the season five games ahead of second-place St. Louis, and headed into their first post-war World Series. To an extent, the Series provided a preview of what was to be, as it involved one of the greatest baseball games ever, a near no-hitter in the fourth game. During the next ten years, the Dodgers would play in four post-season games that would qualify for lists of all-time great baseball games. Others were the 1951 playoff game against the Giants where Bobby Thomson homered; the seventh game of the 1955 World Series, the only World Series victory in Brooklyn Dodgers history, and the fifth game of the 1956 World Series, the only perfect game in Series history. Some say the last game of the 1950 season, in which the Phillies beat the Dodgers in dramatic fashion to clinch the pennant, was also among the best games ever.

As they entered the fourth game of the 1947 Series, the Yankees were up two games to one. Going to the bottom of the ninth, the Yankees were winning 2–1, and pitcher Floyd Bevens was throwing a no-hitter, although he was en route to a World Series-record ten walks. The Dodgers had gotten a run in the fifth on two walks, a sacrifice bunt and an infield out. In the ninth, Furillo walked, and with two outs was taken out for a pinch runner, Al Gionfriddo, who stole second. Yankees manager Bucky Harris, in a controversial move, intentionally walked pinch-hitter Pete Reiser. Then Cookie Lavagetto came up with two men on base and hit a double, ending the no-hitter and scoring both runners to win the game.

The Yankees won the fifth game. The sixth was another classic, in which Gionfriddo again played a major role. Entering the game as a defensive replacement in the sixth inning with the Dodgers winning 8–5, he made a sensational catch off DiMaggio, racing to the left-field bullpen to pull down a 415-foot shot that appeared to be a three-run home run. In a well-known, rare display of emotion, DiMaggio reacted by kicking the dirt and turning disgustedly towards the dugout. But the Yankees won the seventh game 5–2, due largely to strong relief pitching by Joe Page, and thus the Series.

Furillo had a breakout Series, leading the Dodgers with a .353 average. Playing in six games, he recorded 17 at-bats and notched six hits, including two doubles and three RBIs. "Shotton put me into my first World Series, (although) he started off the first game of the Series with me on the bench," Furillo said. "But then the Yankees brought in Joe Page in relief, who was left-handed, and when Shotton sent me to the bullpen to warm up I knew I was in it. So my first time up I got a single and then I got a walk. And then I made a catch off DiMaggio deep in left-center that made their teeth fall out. It was a sure triple.

"But it didn't look to matter, any of that; I was out for the second game. Then Reiser twisted his ankle, and I had a fabulous Series for them. The Yankees were wondering why I hadn't been playing all year, which I was too, because in that Series I led the team in hitting and I made some throws from center that they didn't believe. The first-base coach they had was John Corriden, and he used to warn them not to run on me. He was the one who said to be careful because 'Furillo has a rifle hanging from his shoulder.' That was how I got the name 'Reading Rifle.' So the Yankees were wondering why I wasn't starting, and afterwards it looked like the Dodgers were having thoughts too, because they let Dixie Walker go."[28]

Rickey traded Walker in December, in a deal that some experts view as the best he ever made. For Walker and pitchers Hal Gregg and Vic Lombardi, the Dodgers got Billy Cox, considered the best fielding third baseman of his time, and southpaw Preacher Roe. Both became mainstays of the team. (Gene Mauch also joined the Dodgers in the deal.) Though he asked to be traded when Robinson came up, Walker had rescinded the request. Bragan recalls that "after the first road trip, Dixie came around just like all the rest of us; he became good friends with Jackie."[29] Walker by then was 37 and had played right field for the Dodgers for nine years. His departure paved the way for Furillo and Duke Snider to take over in right and center.

"I always liked Dixie Walker and I respected him," Furillo said. "He used to say that I wasn't a smart kid like some other kids that come up and are a little fresh and stuff like that. In other words, I knew my place and I respected the older ballplayers. After I moved to right, I used to always be compared to Dixie Walker because they would say 'Well, who was the best who ever played right field for the Dodgers? Was it Furillo or was it Dixie Walker?' Because it was a thing you had to learn, playing right field at Ebbets Field, and I guess that the two of us were there longer than anybody else. They always used to say that Dixie Walker had helped me a lot when I came up, but that wasn't the truth because he didn't really help me all that much. Because after all, let's face it: I was trying to take the man's job away from him."[30]

5

The Team Takes Shape

BY 1948 BRANCH RICKEY was in the final stages of assembling the great Brooklyn Dodgers teams of the 1950s. In the spring, Hodges, Furillo, Reese, and Robinson returned. During the season, Campanella, Erskine and Snider came up from the minors. And after Billy Cox and Preacher Roe came from the Pirates in the Walker trade, Rickey made another deal in March, 1948, moving second baseman Eddie Stanky to the Boston Braves. That cleared the path for Robinson to move from first base, where he had played in 1947.

By the time the season was over, Hodges was the first baseman, moved from catcher. Robinson was the second baseman, moved from first. Reese was the shortstop and Cox was the third baseman. The infield remained in place through the 1953 season. In the outfield, Furillo played 96 games in center and 12 in right—he would move to right permanently the following spring, clearing the way for Snider to take over in center. Both were regulars for the next nine years. And Campanella remained the first-string catcher until he was paralyzed in an automobile accident following the 1957 season.

"The 1948 season was the first time all those players who were with the Dodgers for all those years in the fifties played together on the same team, although we didn't really play a whole season together until the next year," Furillo recalled. "That Brooklyn club had pretty much the same lineup for eight years once they got started." Although the team failed to make the 1948 World Series, it played in five of the next eight Series and almost made it two other times before leaving Brooklyn after the 1957 season.[1]

Because the key players stayed together for so long, they became a close-knit group despite living in different parts of the city. "It wasn't just a team—they were brothers," said Joan Hodges, Gil's widow. Hodges said she was friendly with many of the wives, including Fern Furillo, while her husband was close to Carl, partially because both were avid fishermen. Furillo, she said, "was such a sincere, honest straightforward guy—he came to the ballpark and did his job."[2]

Furillo was also establishing an off-season routine. In the fall and winter, he would hunt and fish and wait to hear from Rickey about his contract. "The time that I used to get to be concerned would come around January, when they would mail out the contracts," he said. "I never used to accept a contract that I thought was unfair to me because I was playing baseball to make a living. I wasn't a sorehead, but when it came time to sign a contract I wanted to get enough to eat. I didn't usually work or get another job or do something to use my name over the winter. Instead, I would stay home with my family and maybe work around the house and go hunting. In fact, from October 15 I would duck hunt, and then I would go into pheasant hunting and rabbit hunting, and then at the end of November I would go into deer season. I kept myself in shape that way. I would sometimes be out with the dogs and maybe another guy or two, but mostly it was just the dogs and me.

"A lot of the years that I was with Rickey, before he sold the club, I would be a holdout or I would sign late. With Rickey, you were dealing with a man that I think was the shrewdest man there ever was in baseball. In fact, I was not educated in baseball until after I tried to get enough money out of Branch Rickey. The way it usually happened was that over the winter, I would go up to see him in New York. I would walk into the office and the first person you would see would be Branch Rickey, Jr. He would ask you about things at home and then he would talk about the new books that he got for Christmas. Then in would walk Arthur Mann, who was Mr. Rickey's assistant, and he would go through the same routine. And then eventually the big chief would stick his head out of a door and invite you into his office.

"We would sit down and he would talk about the weather, and the training camp in Florida, and about how much the Dodgers manager thought of me and my playing. I let him do all the talking because I knew that if I would so much as open my mouth, then all would be lost. Mr. Rickey had those bushy eyebrows and glasses and he would sit there and go over our chances of winning the National League pennant and all the other clubs and their chances of winning the pennant, and he would say how he thought we were going to lick the Yankees in the Series. And then all of a sudden Mann would knock on his door and say 'Time for your next appointment.' And we'd shake hands and I would go back to

5. THE TEAM TAKES SHAPE

Stony Creek Mills, and nobody would have said a single word about salary.

"When Rickey got ready to talk about salary, he would have Branch Jr. call me or come down to talk to me. That was always the way the Rickeys worked. Branch Jr. would talk to you about salary and he would sign you if he could, but if there was any trouble he would turn the negotiating over to his dad. According to baseball rules, the Dodgers had to have a contract in the mail to you by Feb. 1, but sometimes it would be the kind of contract that you would not even look at before you sent it back. In baseball at that time they paid off on what you did the year before, so you had to make sure that you got every penny you thought you were worth, because you knew that if you had a bad year the next time they would cut your salary. There were plenty of times that I saw player have a bad year and right away they would have their salary cut 25 percent, which was the limit according to baseball rules.

"I ended up talking to Mr. Rickey himself a lot of times. Sometimes I would go back to his office in New York, and I would sit down there, and it would be just like the last conversation I had with him was just a few minutes before. He would talk awhile, and then sometimes you would kind of argue with him about the salary, and then he would all of a sudden surprise you with the figure that you had in mind the whole time. I remember one time he was arguing with me, and he took off his glasses and wiped them off and put them back on, and then he made the offer I was thinking of and right away I signed. And then the photographers would come over and they would take a picture of me pretending to stick Mr. Rickey up. He would hold up his hands and look shocked and amazed. For him, it was all part of negotiating the contract.

"Some of the writers called him 'El Cheapo,' but it always seemed to me that old man Rickey was just a hard bargainer. The one thing I liked most about him was that if he gave you his word, his word was his contract. You would never have to go to Branch Rickey and say 'Well, Mr. Rickey, you remember the day you promised me....' In fact, he would come to you and he'd say 'son, remember the day we had....' And if he owed you money that was it. If he told you that you were going to get something, whatever it was, you got it. Every year I had with Branch Rickey, he gave me a raise, from $6,500 in 1947 to $12,500 in 1949 and $18,500 in 1950. If you held out or something, there was no ill feeling like you would get with Bavasi; Mr. Rickey didn't have any ill feelings. In fact later on I talked to young Branch Rickey and he said 'Carl, my father likes a person with a little spunk.'"[3]

Years later, Rickey declared: "The toughest player I ever had to sign was Carl Furillo when I was with the Dodgers. He was never out of line and our negotiations were never unpleasant, but Carl always delayed signing. Usually he met our train when it stopped in Philadelphia en route to training camp and came aboard with his signed contract."[4]

Thus, Furillo's third major league season began with his third holdout. "I think I proved my ability to play big league ball last year and I aim to get a good salary from Mr. Rickey," he told *The Reading Times*. "I just missed the .300 mark in hitting in my second year in the majors and I knocked across many a run to help the club in the pennant fight, and I believe I am entitled to big league pay. Mr. Rickey has a habit of sending out contracts with low figures to see if the boys will sign, and I am certain he will raise the ante when he reads the note accompanying my unsigned contract."[5] Rickey's initial offer was for $7,500, representing a $1,000 raise, while Furillo was seeking $12,500. In fact, the Dodgers sent Furillo a contract for $7,500 three times, and he returned it unsigned each time. On February 23, Furillo had an hour-long phone conversation with Branch Rickey, Jr., who then talked to his father, and called back with an acceptable offer, the newspaper reported. The amount was estimated at $8,500. "Now I feel better and I will hustle every minute for Brooklyn," Furillo said. "I will sign a contract which will give me the increase I figured I was worth to the Dodgers. There were no hard feelings between the front office and myself. It was a matter of business. Young Rickey has promised me I would get every opportunity to play in the outfield this season."[6]

This time, the team headed off to Ciudad Trujillo in the Dominican Republic for spring training. Furillo's stay was interrupted when he returned to Stony Creek Mills to visit his ailing father. "Trujillo is a fine place to train," he told *The Reading Times*. "Plenty of heat (with) nothing to do but play baseball, because the gambling casino is out-of-bounds."[7] On March 8, Furillo celebrated his 26th birthday; *The Sporting News* said he and outfielder Al Gionfriddo were "identical twins," both celebrating their 26th birthday on the same day.[8]

Unfortunately for Furillo, Rickey had rehired Durocher as manager in January. It seemed an odd move, since Rickey had as little affinity for Durocher as Furillo did. While Rickey was puritanical, Durocher was a profane, attention-seeking gambler who was drawn to the high life. Fans may have wanted Durocher back, and the obligation may have been there, but Rickey seemed to act with mixed feelings. Two months after hiring Durocher, he traded Stanky, a Durocher favorite, despite the manager's protests. Actually, the word "trade" is barely appropriate, Rickey dumped Stanky. The two players he received in return never played for the Dodgers, and the exchange helped the Braves to win the 1948 pennant. But Rickey was building for the future, and the trade opened up second base for Robinson.

Still another area of friction for Durocher was that he didn't get

5. THE TEAM TAKES SHAPE

along with Robinson. That spring, Robinson came into camp 20 pounds overweight, after spending the off-season on the banquet circuit. Durocher rode Robinson, even calling him "fatso," and at times starting Eddie Miksis at second. Campanella was also in camp, destined to be the Dodgers' catcher of the future. The spot was in flux because Bruce Edwards, the starting catcher in 1947, had a sore arm while backup Bobby Bragan was coming off a bad year. Campanella's path took a detour because Rickey wanted him to play for the Dodgers affiliate in St. Paul, Minnesota, in order to integrate the American Association. Campanella began the season with Brooklyn, was sent down in April, then recalled in July.

At that point, the third-string catcher was Gil Hodges. He had played in one game for the Dodgers in 1943 before joining the Marines, and in 28 games in 1947. "In 1947, Bruce Edwards was first-string, I was the extra catcher and extra infielder, and Hodges spent his time in the bullpen with me," recalled Bobby Bragan. "Then in July 1948, Mr. Rickey called me in and said, 'You've been on the bench so long they've started to call you Judge. Would you like to go to Fort Worth and be catcher-manager? We're going to make a change down there.' So I said yes, I would, and I was there for five years." As for Campanella, Bragan said, "He wasn't groomed to catch until July, when Rickey brought him back."[9]

As Furillo saw it, "They didn't have a first-string catcher at the time. Rickey knew that Campy would be coming back during the season and so Hodges didn't have much of a prayer there. So when Campy did come back Durocher—and this is one thing I have to give the man credit for—thought to put Hodges at first base. Actually, Pete Reiser was going to play first because he had run into so many fences in different parks around the country that his legs just gave out. They tried him at first and they tried some others too. But then they tried Hodges one day. He didn't even have a first-baseman's mitt the first time he practiced. He had to borrow Robinson's old one."[10]

In the outfield, Furillo was in center, Gene Hermanski in right and various players, including George Shuba and Marvin Rackley, played left. Snider was called up from Montreal in the middle of the season, and played part-time, becoming the full-time center fielder the following year. "Since they had gotten rid of Dixie Walker and they didn't use Reiser, they were using different guys," Furillo said. "For instance, Snider was up and down that year and they used Hermanski, and of course with the year I had just come off I figured that I was the center fielder unless I played myself out of it. But Durocher was platooning me there again so to tell the truth I was getting pretty fed up."[11] In April, on their way north, the Dodgers played an exhibition game in Asheville, North Carolina, against their Class B affiliate, the Asheville Tourists. Durocher started

Snider, who was a left-handed hitter, in center. In the third inning, the Tourists replaced the right-hander starter with a lefty. "Somebody on the Dodger bench then cracked, 'Look, Carl, they put in a lefty especially for you,'" wrote *Reading Eagle* columnist Bill Reedy. "Furillo didn't think the remark especially funny and retorted, 'Never mind that left-handed business. I've had enough of that.' It appears that the reinstated Dodger manager is still very much of a percentage man in baseball and hasn't overlooked the fact that Furillo batted only .250 against right-handers last season while clouting southpaws at a .340 pace."[12]

As the season opened, Durocher continued to platoon Furillo. Critics of this strategy included *Journal-American* reporter Mike Gaven, who wrote, "What has happened to Carl Furillo? The Yankees particularly want to know. The big Italian was the leading Brooklyn batter in the hectic Series with an average of .353. Of course you tell Bucky Harris' champs that Furillo is not supposed to be able to hit right-handers, but you cannot prove it by them. The Yankees had only one southpaw, Joe Page, and they recollect curly Carl did a rather fair job against all their hurlers." Additionally, Gaven noted, Furillo was by far the team's best defensive outfielder. "Another Durocher aim apparently is to avoid giving Furillo any idea that he is the best outfielder on the club," he wrote, "Naturally, Leo must have his own good reason for this sort of strategy, but if Furillo does not know he is the best outfielder wearing a Dodger uniform, he is not very observing."[13]

Recalled Furillo: "The pitchers would be saying, 'I like to have that Furillo behind me,' just for my fielding; they weren't even talking about hitting. One thing I had learned was that I should charge the ball more because then I could throw it sooner and cut off runners on the bases, and even though I might make a few more errors, it would be worth it. I could cut them off or they would just be afraid to run because they knew that I could throw them out. So there was a lot of fuss on account of that, and on some other things too, like for instance we were losing as many games as we were winning. Eventually Durocher just banned all the writers from the clubhouse, trying to stop all their speculation. And then I don't know what happened, he broke down or something during the first half of the season. He just said, 'Furillo is the center fielder,' and that was settled."[14]

Although the team fell into last place in early July, it is difficult to overstate how quickly Furillo's stock soared. He began to be viewed as one of the National League's best outfielders. Topping the list of his backers was legendary sportswriter Grantland Rice, whose list of the top ten National League stars included, in order, Stan Musial, Ralph Kiner, Hank Sauer, Enos Slaughter, Johnny Mize, Andy Pafko, Pee Wee Reese, Del Ennis, Tommy Holmes and Furillo.[15] Dick Young of *The Daily News*, another leading baseball writer, argued that Furillo ought not to be platooned. "(He) has a lot of supporters, respected baseball men who believe that, if played regularly, Furillo could develop into the Joe DiMaggio of the National League," Young wrote.[16] By this time, Furillo often batted fourth for the Dodgers. Other teams were noticing. In May, *The Sporting News* reported that the Pirates, trying to upgrade their outfield, "have made many passes for Carl Furillo of the Dodgers and always have been turned down."[17]

Meanwhile, Furillo had become friendlier with Robinson. In the ninth inning of the first game of a June 24 doubleheader with the Pirates, Robinson—the first baseman and number three hitter—homered with the bases loaded in the bottom of the ninth to give the Dodgers a 6–2 victory. After the game, Furillo told a Reading reporter, "You know what? When Mel Queen walked Preston Ward and loaded the bases, Robinson and I were standing together. Jackie said to me, 'The ballgame is over. I'll kill that fellow's fast ball.' And that's what he hit into the stands."[18]

At peace with a key teammate as his skills were coming to be recognized, Furillo was also enjoying the early days of the great romance of his life. On June 21 he obtained a license to marry Fern Reichart, also 26. Furillo was "thrown out at the plate yesterday by Dan Cupid," the Reading paper reported.[19] The wedding date, unfortunately, was problematic. Said Furillo, "She's a swell girl, believe me. The wedding? Well, you can't tell because right now Leo Durocher wants to keep us winning and it would be impossible to get a day off, even to get married."[20] Added Fern: "Maybe one of these days when the Dodgers aren't playing we'll find time to return to Reading for the wedding. That's the way it is with ballplayers, you know."[21]

Furillo met Fern shortly after returning home from the war. She made parachutes then and was working at Quality Hosiery Finishers in Reading when she got married. An oft-told family story involves an incident one evening during Christmas week of 1947, when Fern and Carl were sitting in his car outside her parents' house. When she stepped inside, she was confronted by one of ten brothers, intent on protecting her honor. He demanded to know the identity of her companion, saying he "had a mind to pull him out of that car." She responded, "Charlie, I don't think you want to do that." Told that Carl Furillo was the man in question, Charlie quickly lost his enthusiasm for taking action.[22]

The wedding took place on July 6. Once again, Durocher proved to be an irritant—perhaps reflecting the turmoil that was going on in his managerial life, as the team played poorly, or perhaps reflecting his predilection to make life difficult for those around him. "I asked Durocher for the three-day All-Star Game break off so that we could get married," Furillo said. "But he says, 'I don't know Carl—it looks like I might have to take you along to the All-Star Game.' So then he gave me the day off when we played in Philadelphia, and I missed the game there to get married. We had a small ceremony at St. Catherine's in Reading. There was only family and some close friends, including my father who was able to get there. I'm glad that he was able to make it, because he had gotten sick during spring training and there were times when I had to go back home to be with him.

"The following day I had to meet the ballclub in Philadelphia to go to Chicago," Furillo said. "And then the next week when the All-Star Game was held it turned out that Durocher didn't take me anyway. We could have had the three-day break to get married if he had let me. Later on in baseball I went to two All-Star games, one in Cincinnati and one in Philadelphia. Durocher and Dressen were the managers, and I didn't play in them either. In fact, I never played in an All-Star Game."[23]

The 1948 All-Star Game was played July 13 in St. Louis. Two days later, Durocher was out, replaced by his predecessor, Shotton. The Dodgers had slipped into last place July 2, before improving to fifth at the break, and Rickey was under pressure from owners Walter O'Malley and John Smith to fire Durocher. Not only was the team playing poorly, Durocher continued to be widely condemned for his lifestyle. A complex intrigue involving Rickey and Giants owner Horace Stoneham preceded the shift. With the Giants also playing poorly, Stoneham decided to replace his manager, Mel Ott, with Shotton, then employed in the Dodgers front office. When Stoneham sought permission from Rickey to approach Shotton, Rickey posed a surprising choice: Durocher or Shotton.

"I can't say I was unhappy when Rickey let Durocher go," Furillo said. "The team was in the second division and Rickey wanted to make a change, but I don't think he really wanted to fire Durocher outright. But it worked out that Durocher left and went right away to manage the Giants, and then Burt Shotton came back to manage us. Shotton was playing me pretty regularly and I was having a real good season in center field. People were talking about me and (Richie) Ashburn, and who was the better center fielder in the league."[24]

At the time, the pieces of the pitching staff were starting to fall into place. Roe had joined the team in the spring and Ralph Branca was coming off a 20-win season; Rex Barney and Joe Hatten were also mainstays and, in July, a young Carl Erskine arrived from Fort Worth. "When I came up, Carl and Pee Wee were already in place," Erskine recalled. "Carl was a solid member of the team and we became friends quickly. He went out of his way for me, a rookie kid, to invite me to go with him and some of his Italian friends. A couple of times we had big spaghetti feeds, and he had a friend who owned a pizza parlor. In Indiana in those

Carl Erskine (right) joined the Brooklyn Dodgers in 1948. He quickly became friends with Carl Furillo. The two men often fished together. This picture was taken in Miami in 1955 (courtesy Carl Erskine).

days, we had no idea what pizza was. I would watch those guys in the back sail those things in the air and make pizza out of them. Carl's nickname was Skoonj—I've heard it means snail in Italian—and I became known inside the team as Little Skoonj because of our first names both being Carl."[25]

One player who initially failed to win Furillo's friendship was utility player Tommy Brown, who joined the Dodgers in 1944 at 16 and stayed with the team through the 1951 season, although he rarely played. At some point during his tenure, Brown was Furillo's roommate, the two men had a fight and Brown got the worst of it. The most common explanation for the fight is that Brown refused to turn off the lights when Furillo asked him to. The story not only seems absurd, but also paints Furillo as an uncontrollable hothead. According to Carl Furillo, Jr., the true explanation is that Brown sought to bring women into the room, and the recently married Furillo objected strongly. "Tommy was pretty beat-up, with a swollen face," recalled Carl Erskine.[26] Later, Brown and Furillo became friends, said Carl Furillo, Jr. When he discussed the incident with his mother in 2010, she laughed at the suggestion that her husband would have cared whether the lights were on, because he could sleep through anything. "Your father could sleep on a bed of nails," Fern told her son.[27]

Within a month of Durocher's dismissal, the Dodgers were back in first place; they had managed to rise from the cellar in just 59 days. Robinson finally was back in shape and Erskine pitched well. Furillo was bothered by a broken nose, the result of being hit by a line drive from Coach Ray Blades while fielding another ball during batting practice in early August. On Sept. 9, 23-year-old fireballer Rex Barney threw a no-hitter against the Giants. He was assisted by Furillo, who made outstanding catches on three drives to center and also had three of the six Dodgers hits. The Dodgers won 2–0. Nevertheless, during a particularly poor September stretch, the Dodgers lost 11 of 14 games. That helped the Braves to capture the pennant, their first since 1914 and their last in Boston, as they beat out the second-place Cardinals by 6½ games. The Dodgers finished third, 7½ games out.

"We just had a run of bad luck," Furillo told Gordon Williams in the clubhouse after the last game of the season. "If Burt Shotton had been manager from the start of the schedule, we would have won the pennant in a breeze, (also) the loss of Stanky hurt us until Jackie Robinson got himself in shape. Stanky was a great team worker and we were much stronger with him on second and Robinson at first. Gil Hodges has improved at first and hits a long ball, but we were better defensively with the other setup."[28]

Meanwhile, speculation continued that Furillo would be traded or sold. Williams wrote that the Cubs were interested, that the Phillies "would not be averse to playing our Carl in the middle pasture," and that "when Furillo starts negotiating for his next year's contract, Rickey won't like the figures and that may bring about a deal."[29] In December, *The Sporting News* also reported that Furillo could be traded because, in Rickey's view, he lacked speed and did not run the bases well.[30] "That sounds like Rickey," laughed Whitey Kurowski, a veteran player who also resided in Reading. "Carl Furillo has become an outstanding National Leaguer and deserving of the kind of salary Rickey doesn't want to pay out when he has some younger players in line at lower salaries."[31] Later, during the 1949 season, reports surfaced that Rickey had offered to sell Furillo to the Pirates following the 1948 season, but had asked for so much money that a deal was unlikely. One report pegged the amount at $250,000, while Dick Young of the *Daily News* said the price was $125,000 and even that was too much for the Pirates.

Whatever the details of purported deals, and despite the constant fascination with reporting them, Furillo joined the Dodgers in 1946, left baseball in 1960 and never played a single game for any other major league team.

6

Forced to Grow Up

SUDDENLY, IN 1949, FURILLO was no longer carefree.

Not only did he become a father for the first time, but also his own father turned gravely ill, necessitating constant visits. Not surprisingly, Furillo slumped for the first half of the season. But he emerged in August so that statistically, he had his best year to date, hitting .322 with 106 RBI and 18 home runs as well as 10 triples.

For the Dodgers, 1949 was the first full year for the team Branch Rickey had put together, and the results were positive as the team reached the World Series after winning a thrilling pennant race by one game. The 1949 Series was the third Yankees–Dodgers matchup of the decade. Like the Dodgers, the Yankees had won the pennant by a single game—both teams finished with 97–57 records—so the excitement going into the Series was high. But the Dodgers again proved no match for their crosstown rivals.

Emotionally, the year was a complicated one for the 27-year-old Furillo. At one point, during his slump, he asked Shotton to bench him because he was playing so poorly. This was an early case where Furillo's fundamental integrity came to be misunderstood, even by the fatherly Shotton. In general, a young ballplayer should never ask to be benched, just as he should not have made remarks like "I'd cut his legs off" when talking about Jackie Robinson. Furillo was honest to a fault in a world where something different was expected, especially from a man who was so much in the public eye. He was politically incorrect long before the term gained currency.

It was as if there were "two different lives that I had that year,"

Furillo recalled. "One was in my family and one was in the newspapers and in baseball. I loved baseball, just like I always did, even when it wasn't easy keeping my mind on the game. I even had one of the best years I ever had. And in my family, it was one of the best years and it was one of the worst. I learned a lot from all of that. You can't have everything that you want exactly right, but you can still do a lot."

Furillo's father Michael fell victim to congestive heart failure. "He got very sick that year so that a lot of the time he could hardly recognize me," Furillo said. "During that season I kept going home to visit him whenever we were playing in Brooklyn or Philadelphia, and if I made that trip from Brooklyn to Reading once I must have made it 30 times during the year. That cut into my playing and I was in a slump for a long time, and the papers would be saying, 'What is wrong with Furillo?' and all that kind of stuff, but they didn't know about this. It was a (personal) matter and I didn't use it for an excuse."[1]

Furillo had signed his contract in early February, receiving an increase to about $12,500, and reported to spring training hopeful that he would play in every game that season. In March, Shotton moved him to right field, following up on an experiment tried during a dozen games in 1948. Despite Furillo's emergence as perhaps the best center fielder in the National League, Shotton wanted to open the spot for the young Duke Snider. One of Furillo's first appearances in right came in March, in a spring training game against the Philadelphia A's. His qualifications quickly became apparent when he threw out Elmer Valo at home as Valo rounded the bases after an errant pickoff throw by Dodgers pitcher Harry Taylor ended up in right field. "How about that Furillo in right?" asked Shotton afterwards. "Maybe he was the best centerfielder in the league but we need his class in right more than anywhere else. (He) made a play that no other outfielder on our team could have made. It saved the game. Can't you recall the same situation coming up several times last year? And what happened? We gave them the extra base or the run that cost us the game."[2]

The baseball world quickly came to recognize that Furillo's throwing skills were unique. Of course, in Reading, the story was old news. Furillo's spring training throws prompted this reminiscence by Williams: "Your newsboy never will forget the exhibition game in 1941 between the Dodgers and the Reading Brooks. Furillo was playing left. Joe Medwick, always a long-ball hitter, drilled a line drive into left center. Carl went over and took the ball off the fence and whanged a strike to second. Medwick was out by two feet. He got up, looked out toward left center, scratched his head and walked off the diamond talking to himself. On the bench, he asked his mates what happened. He could not figure how Furillo got his hands on the ball and had it to second in such a hurry."[3] Another headline that month proclaimed: "Furillo's Arm Rates with Any in Business." The story quoted Branch Rickey, Jr., as saying Furillo could throw harder than anyone on the team, pitchers included. At the time Rex Barney, thought to be the fastest pitcher in baseball, was on the Dodgers staff. Meanwhile, Shotton complimented Furillo's arm one rainy day as the Dodgers passed the time sitting in a hotel lobby in Greenville, South Carolina. Greenville was the home of renowned outfielder Joe Jackson, and the team had scheduled a pre-season exhibition game there. Jackson was "the sweetest hitter you'd want to see," Shotton said. "And throw? He had an arm like Furillo's."[4] Years later, Furillo recalled the transition to right. "I started playing right field that spring because Shotton had put me in right and Snider in center, because my arm was a little stronger than his, and they figured I could learn to play the rebounds off the right-field fence at Ebbets Field like Dixie Walker did."[5]

Over time, right field became the position where Furillo would be immortalized. One of Furillo's best-known nicknames, "the Reading Rifle," is a tribute both to his arm and his hometown. Today, he is often grouped with Roberto Clemente as having the strongest arm of any right fielder ever, and his arm is the first thing people will cite when asked about their memories of Furillo. For instance, former baseball commissioner Fay Vincent recalled, "He was a person I saw play many times. I admired him. I thought he had a great arm."[6] Carl Erskine, delivering the eulogy at Furillo's funeral, said, "I saw him, in Ebbets Field, throw runners out at all four bases: home, third base and second base, and twice I saw him throw runners out at first base."[7] In July, 1949, a *New York Herald-Tribune* writer penned a fanciful story about how Furillo was home for the winter when he spotted a flock of mallard ducks flying south for the winter. He stepped outside with a collection of baseballs and started throwing at the ducks. "His accuracy is such that he returns to the living room with the following report: 'I got three direct hits and three probables. I could have hit several more but I ran out of ammunition.'"[8]

It wasn't just Furillo's natural throwing ability that made him a great right fielder, however. It was also the hard work he put into learning to play Ebbets Field's unique right field wall, a task that took countless hours. Furillo often asked coaches and players to rap hits off the wall so that he could figure out how to play them. "Most people didn't understand that Brooklyn wall, it had so many angles," said Ralph Branca. "There was an angle off the scoreboard, which stuck out. The wall had a slant, then went straight up, and there was also a screen. If the ball hit the top off the wall, it went one way. If it hit the screen, it went another way. Carl played right field sensationally. He had the natural talent, and he had the experience that told him where the ball was going, and he had a gun for an arm."[9]

In 1989, Clem Labine recalled that "Carl used to get me to hit him fly balls, and he just didn't want lazy fly balls, he wanted me to hit them off the fence so he could do his thing. People used to come just to see Carl play the fence. I used to hit him sinking line drives, which are not nice to catch, very heavy balls to catch," Labine said. "Carl would come in, and you know, he had those big hands. He'd take his glove off and show me his hand swelling up from catching those balls."[10]

A 1953 article in *Collier's* magazine used a series of photographs to illustrate how Furillo covered 14 different angles off the right field wall. The story noted that Furillo led the league in outfield assists in 1950 and 1951, reaching 24 in 1951, but after that the totals declined to 12 in 1952 and 11 in 1953 because opposing players were reluctant to challenge him.

Still, the switch to right field also had a negative consequence: it removed Furillo from the continuing discussion of New York center fielders in the 1950s. Today it is Mays, Mantle and Snider who are immortalized in a 1981 song by Terry Cashman commonly referred to as "Talkin' Baseball" but best known for its refrain "Willie, Mickey and the Duke." Excluded from the centerfield comparisons, Furillo came to be known more as an underrated ballplayer, one who despite his achievements was outshone not just by his outfield companion but also by the three other future Hall of Famers in the Dodgers lineup, Campanella, Reese and Robinson, as well as by Hodges, who stayed in baseball as a manager and has come close to Hall of Fame election. It is not unreasonable to suggest that Furillo also merits Hall of Fame consideration, given the combination of hitting performance, consistency and excellence as a right fielder, both in terms of fielding balls off the wall and throwing. Unfortunately, even in the most statistics-oriented sport at a time when statistics are being more widely developed and used, Furillo's unique fielding skills remain impossible to quantify. Yet 50 years after his career ended, Furillo is still regularly mentioned as one of the very best rightfielders in the history of the sport. Is something more required to be in the Hall of Fame?

"Of course (the switch from center) took a little of the publicity off (me)," Furillo recalled. "A few years later in New York they had Mantle and Mays and Snider all playing center field and hitting home runs, and they were always comparing them and saying that one or the other was the best and everything else. And then they would come out and say that I was underrated. But I was always taught to keep my mouth shut and play my ballgame and publicity would follow in its pattern. And of course I didn't care so much about the home runs; I didn't go for them so much. I don't think that I lost out on anything or missed out on anything that I would have wanted anyway."[11]

All of this is not to say that Furillo's career in right field got off to a brilliant start. In fact, the opposite was true. In the early days of the 1949 season, Furillo was in a deep slump. While it seems clear that family issues created diversions that diminished the level of concentration required to hit a baseball, the solution was not so obvious.

Carl Jr. was born April 16, three days before the Dodgers' opening game. In those days, ballplayers did not skip games to be with wives who were giving birth, even if the games were just exhibitions. "We were playing the Yankees in a preseason exhibition in New York then, and I got a couple of RBI and handed out the Perfectos when I found out," Furillo remembered fondly.[12] On a trip to Reading the next day, Furillo joked that his son would not grow up to be a pitcher or an outfielder. "The way he's been hollering, he'll be a manager or an infielder," Furillo said. He also discussed again the benefit of playing for Shotton rather than Durocher. "Last year when we came up from spring training Durocher was the boss," Furillo said. "Nobody was sure of a job. He kept changing things until none of the players were certain whether he was an outfielder, an infielder or a pitcher. But with Barney Shotton in charge, we have some semblance of order and routine." As far as moving to right field, Furillo declared, "It doesn't make any difference to me where I am stationed as long as I get the chance to play.... It won't take me long to get used to the boards in right, like Dixie Walker. I haven't had any trouble judging line drives, although they come at you a bit differently in right."[13]

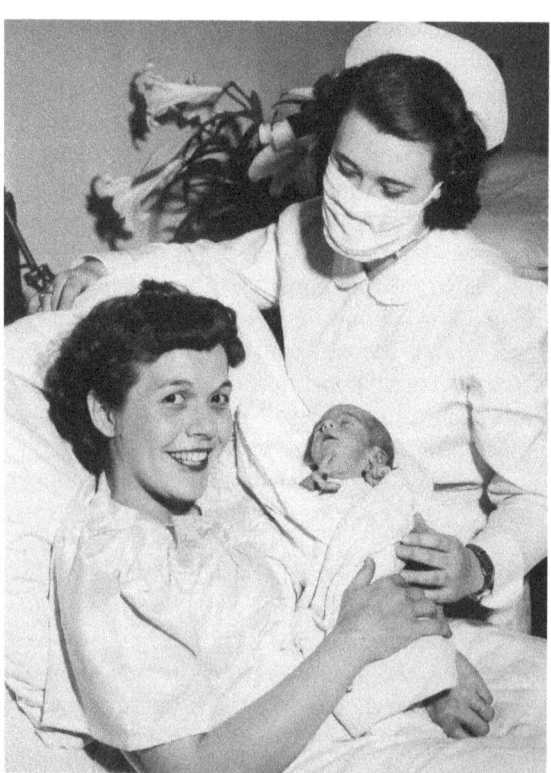

Carl Furillo, Jr., was born in April 1949. "The way he's been hollering, he'll be a manager or an infielder," his dad said (Reading Eagle Company).

Furillo slumped early, even as the team blossomed. The slump was so deep, Furillo recalled years later, that "if it wasn't for my arm and my fielding, they probably wouldn't even have had me in the lineup. I guess I must have been thinking about my dad's health then, but baseball is a game that you have to eat, sleep and play it and not have anything bothering your mind or interfering with your game at the time."[14]

However, in 1949, Robinson was at his peak, his .342 average and 37 stolen bases led the National League, and he won his only MVP trophy. Additionally, Snider and Hodges each hit 23 home runs, while Campanella hit 22. Six regulars hit .285 or over, led by Furillo and Robinson. Among the pitchers, Don Newcombe, the third black player signed by Rickey from the Negro Leagues, was called up from Montreal in May. His first start on May 22 was a 3–0 shutout against Cincinnati. By the end of the year, he was 17–8, was named Rookie of the Year, and was the staff leader. Meanwhile, Roe was 15–6, Joe Hatten was 12–8, Ralph Branca was 13–5, Jack Banta was 10–6 and Erskine was 8–1.

In late June, Furillo's hitting started to pick up. "Fortunately, Carl rallied greatly with the stick in the last six weeks," wrote Bill Reedy in *The Reading Eagle.* "He is now hitting consistently." Even when Furillo was not hitting, Shotton kept him in the lineup because he could throw. "That arm has proved to be Carl's greatest asset as a major leaguer," Reedy wrote. "Only once was he taken out of the lineup, and then for a single day's rest during a long batting slump. The Dodgers, especially their pitchers, want 'The Arm' in every game."[15] In a subsequent interview, Shotton said that part of Furillo's problem had been that he came to believe he could not hit right-handed pitchers. "Carl had been taken out of the ball game so often when right-handers were on the mound that he actually began to believe he had a batting weakness," Shotton said. "I gave him the chance to play regularly against all kinds of pitching, and Carl proved to himself something I believed all along."[16]

Still, in July, Furillo found himself in Shotton's doghouse. "The Brooklyn skipper expressed visible annoyance with Furillo when the outfielder, who had played in every game until July 27, asked for a rest. Shotton declared that Furillo would not see action again "until the player requests it."[17] Furillo recalled later that he asked to be benched because he thought it would help the team. "But when I asked Shotton, he got mad and I just kind of let it go. Then a couple of days later he decided to bench me anyway and he made a big deal about it and he told the press. If I had known that he was going to make such a big fuss about it, I would never have asked him in the first place. Burt Shotton was usually a great guy to play for, but he was a guy who thought that if you could walk and you cared about the team you would play no matter what you felt like."[18] Additionally, Furillo noted, "I couldn't figure why Shotton didn't sit me down when I was going real bad, when he had somebody who could help the team more. Maybe I shouldn't have said that, because when it got back to Shotton he was given the idea I wanted to rest. I never asked for a rest in my life."[19] Those words rang true until the day Furillo died.

It is possible that Shotton was unaware of the extent of the demands on his young outfielder. Michael Furillo was ill with congestive heart failure, and during the last month of the season he lingered between life and death. His condition required frequent visits to Reading by his son. Yet, until late in the season, Furillo "could not, nor would not, disclose to the manager why he had become so tired with little more than half a season gone," wrote Milton Gross, in a profile of Furillo that appeared the following year in *Sport Magazine*.[20] While it seems difficult to imagine that Shotton did not know, Furillo's work ethic was extreme, his private struggles were always private, and he consistently avoided making excuses. Furillo visited his father weekly. Sometimes he left New York early in the morning, returning for batting practice before a night game; other times, he flew to Reading. Gross wrote that eventually, Furillo disclosed details of his father's health to Shotton and received permission to miss some games. It was not until late in the season that reporters wrote anything about the state of Michael Furillo's health and the strain that put on his son.

As August began, the Dodgers found themselves in a pennant race with the Cardinals—and Shotton declared that Furillo and Snider would play every day. The move had a positive impact on Furillo. "I just started hitting like I hadn't been able to do all season, and the thing of it was that my father was getting worse around then," he said. "Around late August, they even called me home because they thought it was all over. He didn't recognize me, but he was still breathing, so I stayed home and missed a few games, but then he looked like he might hang on for awhile. So I started playing and driving home to see him every chance I got—that's how it got to about 30 times during the year."

On the field, "I was getting my hits and everyone else was coming through for us, like Robinson was leading the league in hitting and Campy and Snider were really fighting in that stretch. Then there was a night in late September when we beat the Cards 19–6. I got seven RBI in that game, and Robinson got the (hitting) lead back, and so after that we were just half a game back. That night we flew home and we were getting off the plane at LaGuardia, and they had the crowds and the red carpet and everything else. Everyone was all smiles but me, so the reporters were saying 'How come Furillo ain't smiling?'"[21] Even then, Furillo's concern about his father was not publicly known.

During the last 46 games of the season, Furillo hit .431, boosting his season average from .269 to .322. During one stretch, he collected 22

RBI in 15 games, and he emerged as the Dodgers' top player during a torrid National League pennant race. With four games left to play, the Cardinals led the Dodgers by one game. But while the Dodgers were taking a doubleheader from the defending champion Braves, the Cardinals were losing to the Pirates. "It was Furillo's bat that carried the Dodgers through their late surge to beat the Cardinals, and he hit viciously to all fields," according to *The Sporting News*.[22] On Oct. 2, the last day of the season, Furillo had four hits as the Dodgers beat the Phillies 9–7 in ten innings to clinch the pennant. Once again, It ought to have been a joyous occasion for Furillo, but continuing the pattern of the entire year, it was marred because he suffered a groin injury while sliding into a base.

After the game, Furillo recalled, "the team went back to New York and they got a big greeting from thousands of fans. It was even bigger than for that game when we beat the Cardinals. But I couldn't even be there that time. I had driven to Reading to see my father. And I think that was when the story (finally) came out about his being sick. On top of that it began to look like I was injured pretty bad, and they were all wondering whether I could play in the Series."[23] On the train ride back from Philadelphia to New York, Dodgers captain Pee Wee Reese was asked to name the player who did the most for the club in the stretch. "Furillo," Reese responded. "Furillo and about 24 other guys, but put Furillo first."[24] As a result of his spectacular finish, Furillo ended the season fourth in the league in hitting with a .322 average. Robinson led the league at .342, and two Cardinals—Stan Musial and Enos Slaughter—finished second and third. Likewise in winning percentage, the top five pitchers included two Dodgers, Roe and Newcombe, and two Cardinals, Howie Pollet and Red Munger. The individual statistics provide one more indication of how close the teams were.

As the Dodgers and Yankees prepared for the World Series, Furillo was the talk of the town. "Carl Furillo spent all day yesterday in Reading, Pa., worried about his father, who continues critically ill, while all Brooklyn spent the day yesterday worrying about Carl Furillo," wrote Dick Young in *The Daily News* on Oct. 4, the day before the first game. "Upon the healing progress made by the pulled muscle in Carl's right groin during the two days between the season's close and the Series' opening tomorrow depends much of Brooklyn's long-shot chance against the Yankees." Young added that while it was commendable for Furillo to insist he would play, the sad truth was that "it will be considered nothing short of a miracle if Furillo can carry through the Series without aggravating the soreness. He plays hard and slides gas-house style."[25]

Meanwhile, a story in *The Reading Eagle*, written by a correspondent in New York, began, "The line forms on the right in this baseball-mad city for the members of the Carl Furillo Admiration Society."[26] The story quoted various baseball insiders on Furillo's importance to the team. They included Jackie Robinson, who declared, "Furillo brought us through these last five weeks."[27] Shotton, meanwhile, called Furillo "the greatest rightfielder ever to wear a Brooklyn uniform." Shotton said he expected Furillo to play the first game of the Series, despite his injury. "Certainly he'll play," the manager said. "He'd play if he had a broken leg. He could hardly run in that game Sunday with Philadelphia, but he got four hits, didn't he? And with these couple of days of rest, Furillo will be okay."[28]

But it was clear in the first game that Furillo's determination did not serve him well. Playing with his right leg heavily taped, he was hitless in three times at bat. He reached first twice, on a walk and then on an error, when he "staggered to the bag, dragging his right foot behind him," *The Reading Eagle* reported. Additionally, he limped back and forth to right field, but "luckily for Furillo and for the Dodgers too, he was called on to handle only one ball during the entire game and he did that poorly."[29] His slowness in retrieving a Jerry Coleman double into the right field corner did not affect the outcome, however, as the Yankees won 1–0 on a Tommy Henrich home run. Afterwards, Furillo said, "I couldn't charge the ball the way I should have. It came off the wall and I just had to wait for it because my right leg wouldn't respond when I wanted to dash in after the ball." The injury also affected his hitting. "I couldn't get a level swing," he said. "To get power I have to push off with my right leg. Well, the darn thing hurts so much that I just can't put all that pressure on it."[30]

Asked if Furillo would play the second game, Shotton responded, "Furillo didn't hurt us out there today, and he might help us tomorrow. He won't come out till I have to take him out—and that won't be till he says he has to come out."[31] In response, Furillo declared, "Shotton wants to win at any expense. And he thinks by keeping me in there I'll be of some good. But the club would be better off if someone else were playing right field. If anything happens out there, I'm going to be the goat."[32] Injury was not Furillo's only worry. Before the first game, as he walked to the clubhouse, a reporter inquired about his father's condition, and he responded, "Not so good. It sure is tough to see a fellow as jolly as Pop being so sick. He doesn't even know me any more when I go to see him."[33]

Eventually, Shotton decided to bench Furillo for the second game, using him only as a pinch-hitter in the ninth inning, when he popped out weakly in a 1–0 Dodgers victory. He played the third game, going one for four, as the Dodgers lost 4–3, and then sat out the rest of the Series, which the Dodgers lost in five games. Years later, Furillo recalled, "At first I was saying 'I'll play if I have to carry a goddamned crutch' and stuff like that, but after awhile I saw there wasn't any use in it. I couldn't hit and I couldn't run. I had my entire career ahead of me and I wasn't going to throw it away for the sake of a few games, even World Series games, where I might injure myself worse and I couldn't help the team anyway. But Shotton, as I said, wasn't the type of guy to take a 'no.' I remember how Burt felt because of an incident that took place when I was supposed to pose with him for a newspaper picture. They told both of us to stand on the dugout steps and he was supposed to point at my injured leg; that was what they asked him to do. But he wouldn't do it. He stood there and he said, 'What injured leg?' He said, 'There's nothing wrong with this guy, he's going to be great in the Series.' And because of that incident in July, I was in no position to ask Burt to take me out."[34] After the Series was completed, *The Sporting News* columnist Franklin Lewis wrote that the "biggest blow" of the affair came when "Carl Furillo, the crack all-round outfielder, had to give up after the first game because of a leg injury. His absence demoralized the eventual losers."[35]

Furillo wasn't the only Dodger hitter to fail in the Series; the team had a collective batting average of .210. The Yankees weren't much better, hitting .226 as a team, but they did manage to win four of the five games. The Dodgers' only victory was Roe's 1–0 second-game shutout. "The whole team was lousy," Furillo said. "We had a horrible Series and it only went five games. To tell the truth, I thought that sitting on the bench while we were losing those Series games was as bad as anything that ever happened to me in baseball, even worse than a slump that you figure 'I'm going to play my way out of it sooner or later.' But sitting on that bench I just couldn't do anything, and I was thinking about my dad then too. When I went home I just forgot about that whole World Series except for the money; we got about $4,000 each. I rested for awhile, I built a new home for the family in Stony Creek Mills, and I went hunting. My father held on all that year and the next, and he passed away in March, 1951."[36]

7

The First Bad Year

Despite the promise that preceded them and the excitement that accompanied them, both 1950 and 1951 concluded as failed seasons for the Brooklyn Dodgers. In retrospect, the two seasons fit exactly into the tapestry of a story that captivated baseball for a decade, in which a slow, tortured lesson in perseverance led to the team's single world championship after six World Series losses to the Yankees. In practice, they were excruciating.

"One thing I found out early in baseball is that luck has an awful lot to do with it," Furillo said. "If you are a hitter, there is no difference between a .320 average and a .290 average except for luck. And if you are a team, it is the same. I guess we had some luck in winning that '49 pennant by one game. That was our first whole season together and by the time it was over people were already beginning to say that we looked like the best Dodgers team they ever saw. Those Brooklyn fans were always making those signs that said 'Wait 'Til Next Year' and it looked like maybe next year had come in 1950. We expected to do pretty well (but) we lost the pennant at the last minute, on the last day of the season. On the field, Furillo had a solid year in 1950. He played in 153 games and went to bat 620 times, both new highs that were indicative of his status as a mainstay on the team. He hit .305, with 18 home runs and 106 runs batted in.

"When the 1950 season started the writers said I was in Shotton's doghouse because of the year before, but it wasn't true," Furillo said. "There was some talk about trading me. They said the Cards wanted me and the Dodgers wanted Ted Wilks, but it never worked out. And Shotton had nothing to do with it anyway. There wasn't any friction between us. Burt was usually all for me, always saying how he had been the one who first saw that I should be playing every day."[1]

As usual, one of the earliest signs of the impending baseball season was detailed coverage of Furillo's contract negotiations in the Reading papers. That January, Furillo, who had finished sixth in the balloting for National League Most Valuable Player, told reporter Gordon Williams that he would ask for $27,500. When Williams asked, "Why the extra $500?" Furillo responded, "That's what Rickey will wonder too."[2]

This time, the negotiations went fairly smoothly. Branch Rickey, Jr., visited Stony Creek twice to chat. When no deal was reached, the Dodgers mailed Furillo a contract with his 1949 salary filled in, a formality to comply with the requirement for an initial contract offer by Feb. 1. Furillo sent it back. In late February, he went to Brooklyn to speak with Branch Rickey. Wrote Williams, "Rickey mentioned a figure, but Furillo, who says little in the presence of the shrewd Rickey, shook his head no. Papa Branch raised an eyebrow, took off his glasses and proceeded to wipe them off. He took another look at the .322 batting average which Furillo compiled in 1949. Then he made another offer. Furillo said yes and out came the contract."

How much was it for? Williams wrote that Rickey never allowed a player to mention his exact salary and that Furillo "had to be content with figures quoted by Harold Parrott, public relations chief, to newsmen. Needless to say, Furillo was tickled with his new $20,000 salary."[3] Subsequent reports placed the number at $18,500, representing a $6,000 raise. A few days after Furillo signed, a *Reading Times* photo showed him packing to go to Philadelphia to catch the Dodgers' train to Florida. His young son was preparing to put Furillo's glove in the suitcase.

Given Furillo's strong finish in 1949, the Dodgers had high expectations for him. During spring training, Dodgers executives repeatedly praised him. In an interview with *The Associated Press*, Shotton "talked willingly about every Dodger on the roster, but Furillo was the apple of his eye," wrote Frank Eck. "He would talk about Carl, go off on a tangent about another Dodger, but always came back to his right fielder, who has the best arm in the major leagues."[4] Meanwhile, Parrott told Reedy, "Furillo had as much to do with our pennant victory by hitting right-handers as did Duke Snider in hitting the lefties. Without him, well, let's not talk about that."[5] During the exhibition season, Furillo repeatedly hit home runs, further enhancing his standing as a principal member of a star-studded team, and boosting expectations that the Dodgers would again play in the World Series.

In May, Furillo was the subject of a lengthy, incisive article in *Sport Magazine*, then the country's leading sports magazine. This was the arti-

Spring training trips to Florida became a Furillo family ritual. Here Carl Jr., called "Butch," helps his dad and mom pack his dad's glove in a suitcase (Reading Eagle Company).

cle that revealed the difficulties Furillo had in dealing with his father's illness. Writer Milton Gross described Furillo as a man of few words, "not a quick thinker," distrustful of the world, distant from his teammates and difficult to interview until he opens up, and attributed his makeup to the difficulty of his early years, when he dropped out of school in the eighth grade and began working a variety of manual labor jobs. "You dig back into Furillo's beginnings and little by little you discover why Carl is tight-lipped and distant," Gross wrote. "The personality of the child living the life of an adult never developed along with his strength."[6]

At the same time, Gross noted that Furillo found happiness in his home life and his family. Despite being Pennsylvania Dutch, Fern Furillo learned to cook Italian food, Gross wrote. Furillo, he said, liked to hunt, listen to Italian records and play card games like horse-and-pepper or poker, until two or three in the morning. The study concluded by emphasizing Furillo's consistency, his value to the Dodgers and his standing as one of the top ten National League hitters in seven categories—triples, RBI, total bases, slugging, runs scored, hits, and batting average.

Although Gross presented a fully drawn, well-written profile, it is possible to quibble with some of the points he made. Furillo did eventually become close to several players, including Erskine, Campanella and Koufax. He may have been a man of few words at times, but he consistently opened up to the reporters whom he trusted, including this writer, a college student who was, by appearance, on the other side of the nation's cultural divide during a series of lengthy interviews in 1970. And while Furillo was "not a quick thinker," he possessed a high degree of self-awareness; he fully described the intricacies of his life to Gross; he very quickly realized the mistakes in his initial response to Robinson; he not only managed his finances well but also advised others in his later years, and he was obviously capable of finding happiness in his marriage and his home life. Moreover, despite a healthy, working-class skepticism about management, he developed positive, lasting relationships with Rickey and with two managers, Shotton and Dressen, who would replace Shotton at the end of the 1950 season and manage the team through 1953. As Gross made clear, while Furillo's life in baseball was not a Pollyannaish story, full of constant sunshine, neither was it a bitter, unhappy, unrewarding story, either before or after the 1950 season.

Certainly, one of the least pleasant aspects of Furillo's career was his relationship with Leo Durocher. While he managed the Dodgers, Durocher was the primary proponent of the theory that Furillo could not hit right-handers, a theory that Shotton was proud to disprove. When he left the Dodgers, Durocher regularly instructed his pitchers to throw at Furillo. An early incident occurred on June 28, 1950, when Giants pitcher Sheldon Jones hit him just below the left ear with an eighth-inning pitch, after Furillo had hit a two-run homer and a single. Although he did not lose consciousness, Furillo was hauled away on a stretcher and sent to a Brooklyn hospital for X-rays. He was not seriously hurt, but he spent the night in the hospital and returned to the lineup three days later. The beaning followed a 12-day stretch in which Furillo had hit .558, bringing his average to .325.

"I had a hell of a lot of trouble with Durocher," Furillo recalled, years later. "Some of us didn't care for the man even when he was with the Dodgers. When he went to the Giants in the middle of 1948 we figured that he was a traitor. And he couldn't have liked it that we started doing better as soon as he left." The day before Jones threw at him, Furillo said, "I was in the clubhouse and their clubhouse was right next to ours and there was a door dividing the two clubhouses. So Durocher comes through the door, and I'm sitting in the corner there, and Durocher looks over at me and he says to me 'Hey, dago, we're going to stick one in your ear tonight.' "So I say, 'Oh, I don't think you're that type of guy, Leo.' "And he says, 'Well, we'll see tonight.' "About ten minutes later who comes in but Herman Franks, the coach then, and he looks at me and he says, 'Well, dago, we're going to stick one in your ear tonight.'

"I didn't pay any attention to it, I acted like you would normally, and then all of a sudden I go out to play a ballgame and Larry Jansen's pitching and he's trying to hit me all night. But I got through that game all right anyway. Then the following day we went out to play and they had a big right-hander, Jones, pitching, and I got a homer and a single off him the first two times up. Then in the eighth inning he hit me right in the head, behind the ear, with a fastball. I just couldn't get out of the way. I wasn't unconscious but it was quite a wallop. That was the first time that I was ever hit by a pitcher, but it certainly wasn't the last. In fact, less than a week later Koslo was pitching and he hit me on the foot. So I looked over at Durocher, who was coaching third, and he was yelling at me. I called to him to come over and fight me himself if that's what he wanted, because I was ready for him. He said something else to me so I went for him, but the umpire broke it up. And from that day on I hated Durocher's guts. I knew that if I could have gotten my hands on him I would have torn him in half." This second hit by pitch incident came on July 4, in the second game of a doubleheader.

"Altogether, I got hit six times in the head. They even gave me the nickname 'Skoonj' which is from the Italian 'scungilli' for a fish with a hard shell. When those beanings happened they used to give me a real burning feeling in my head, and sometimes they would last for quite a few weeks. Even now I still get headaches, not like I used to, but if I wear something tight around my head, like a cap, I get the headaches. I couldn't

7. The First Bad Year

tell you why it always would seem that pitchers, besides the ones on the Giants, would be throwing at me. I think it might have been because I used to hit the fastball a lot and I would get a lot of hits in the clutch. Also, I wasn't like some of these other ballplayers who would pull away from a ball. I would always lunge into it. I think they said, 'Well, if I loosen him up a little then he won't dig in like he would normally' and so I think a lot of them were trying to get a fear in me more than anything else. But with Durocher and the Giants, I figure Durocher held a grudge against me because he had said that I couldn't hit right-handed pitching, and then there I was after he left, hitting all different kinds and playing regularly. In fact, in 1950 there was one day when I was three for four or something like that off Blackwell and I got a home run too. And that was after Durocher had been saying stuff like 'Furillo couldn't hit Ewell Blackwell with a paddle.' You look at my record and you can see that every time I played against the Giants, right-handers or left-handers, I used to have my fun with them. I'd get my base hits and all because the madder he got me, the better I played."[7]

Following the Aug. 6 game against Blackwell and the Cincinnati Reds, Bill Reedy wrote, "Carl Furillo continues to make Leo Durocher, his original boss in Brooklyn, look very bad. Leo the Lip made so many disparaging statements to the press about Furillo's hitting ability before and after leaving the Dodgers, they now boomerang to haunt him. The baseball writers in New York are not allowing him to forget what he said about Furillo in trying to justify his own stand for never using him against right-handed pitchers."[8]

Meanwhile, the Phillies were dominating the National League. The team was led by future Hall of Fame pitcher Robin Roberts, 33-year-old reliever Jim Konstanty, who would become the first reliever to be named the league's Most Valuable Player, and a nucleus of players known as the "Whiz Kids" because they were so young. At an average age of 26, the Phillies were the youngest team in baseball. Curt Simmons was 21, Richie Ashburn was 22, Roberts was 23, Del Ennis was 24 and Willie "Puddin Head" Jones was 24. Excitement in Philadelphia was high because the Phillies had last won the pennant in 1915, and had never won a Series, while the once-great Athletics had last won the pennant in 1931. The Phillies got off to a strong start, winning 17 of their first 26 games, then played even with the Dodgers into the summer, when they got hot. They won 34 of 50 games and by Sept. 15 were 7½ games ahead of the Dodgers.

Then came the fall. The Phillies lost nine of 13 games, while the Dodgers won nine of 12, so that the Phillies led the league by two games going into the final weekend of the season, when they were scheduled to play the Dodgers in a two-game set at Ebbets Field. The Dodgers needed to win both to tie and force a playoff. On Saturday they won 7–3, push-

Cal Abrams (left) was one of the many left fielders who sought to complement outfield mainstays Duke Snider (center) and Carl Furillo. Abrams joined the Dodgers in 1949 and lasted into the 1952 season (National Baseball Hall of Fame Library, Cooperstown, New York).

ing the season's resolution to the final game, in which Roberts faced Don Newcombe, with both going for their 20th win. Both lived up to their reputations, and the game was tied 1–1 after eight and a half innings. In the bottom of the ninth, left fielder Cal Abrams walked, Reese singled and Duke Snider hit a single to center field. As Abrams rounded third base and, for some reason, headed for home, Phillies center fielder Richie Ashburn fielded Snider's hit and threw a strike to catcher Stan Lopata, who tagged Abrams out 15 feet from home plate. Then Roberts walked Robinson and got both Furillo and Hodges to fly out. In the top of the tenth, Philadelphia's Dick Sisler hit a three-run home run off Don Newcombe. That enabled the exhausted Phillies to move on to the World Series, which they lost to the Yankees in four games.

"In the last week of the season we got hot and it looked like we could catch the Phillies," Furillo said. "We beat them in the second to the last game, and so if we won, there would be a playoff. Everyone was real

7. THE FIRST BAD YEAR

excited, and where I lived in Pennsylvania people would say to me afterwards that they didn't know who they were for, me or the Phillies. In fact, I was in court that winter, over a little thing with the guy who built my house, and the judge talked to me about it before the trial. He said, 'Carl, I was on the fence. I was for the Phillies and for you.' Well, he had a tough choice when I came up in the ninth inning with the score one-all and Robin Roberts had loaded the bases by walking Robinson to pitch to me. But I just popped out. Then when the Phillies came up in the tenth Dick Sisler got a home run with two on and they won the game 4–1. I remember walking off the field after that game. I've seen pictures of it, and to this day I have never seen anybody in baseball look as sad as me and Robinson and the others were in that picture, all just walking off the field kind of dazed and looking down at the ground. We had gotten almost all the way but we blew it on one hit."[9]

It seemed to the Dodgers that things could get no worse. But of course, they could.

8

The Worst Bad Year

To state the obvious, 1951 was not a good year for the Brooklyn Dodgers. They blew a 13½-game lead. They lost the last game of the season, a playoff game they were winning 4–1 in the ninth. The heartbreaking loss replicated a similar loss a year earlier. Even worse, it was a loss to a bitter rival and to a manager who three years earlier had left the Dodgers, some of whom despised him. Their failure was at least partially traceable to the Dodgers manager's misguided policy of not using a young pitcher whom he thought had crossed him.

At the same time, the continuing awareness of "the shot heard round the world," in a baseball game played more than half a century ago, points up the transcendent importance of a sports team that for a decade was at the very center of the intersection of sports and society. In 1946, when World War II ended, baseball became a symbol of America's homecoming. In 1947, baseball was integrated, with the Dodgers on center stage. In 1951, the country stopped to watch a game remembered as one of the most significant sports events ever.

As the 1951 season began, the Dodgers organization was in transition. Walter O'Malley had replaced Rickey as the team's president in October, 1950. The move was triggered by the mid–July death of team co-owner John L. Smith. Four parties—O'Malley, Rickey, Smith and James and Dearie Mulvey—each owned 25 percent of the franchise. When Smith died, O'Malley took control of his share. O'Malley's 50 percent ownership stake assured that when Rickey's contract expired in October, it would either not be renewed or it would be rewritten to give Rickey far less power. Rickey decided to leave and, after intense, hostile negotiations over the price, he sold out to O'Malley. He then took over as general manager of the Pittsburgh Pirates, where he laid the groundwork for a third championship team, following the Cardinals and Dodgers, before retiring in 1955. Among the players who most regretted the change were Robinson, whose appreciation for Rickey could never be matched, and Furillo. Furillo always felt that he was treated fairly by Rickey, and maintained a fundamental respect, even though both men were known for the high value they placed on money. Furillo's relationship with O'Malley was not as close.

O'Malley moved quickly to put his stamp on the team. In November, he named Charlie Dressen to replace Shotton, who was Rickey's man, as manager. "O'Malley wanted to get rid of the Rickey crowd," Furillo said. "He brought up Fresco Thompson and Buzzie Bavasi from the farm system as his vice presidents, and Bavasi was like his right hand from then on. Dressen had been like the assistant manager when Durocher was manager, and he had a lot to say then about the plays and players. In fact, sometimes it seemed like he supplied a lot of the brains when Durocher was manager. Shotton had been a good manager and I figured he would come back that year, but Dressen was a good manager too. One thing about him, if you had an argument with an umpire or something, he would battle for you right or wrong. He might chew you out about it in the clubhouse, but on the field when the chips were down he was for you.

"Bavasi always handled the contracts for O'Malley, and I had my first signing with him (at the start of the 1951 season). It wasn't like signing with Rickey, I'll tell you that. Bavasi was saying that the ballclub couldn't afford to give me much of a raise because the settlement with Rickey had cost so much. Of course I told him that it wasn't any of my business what they gave Rickey because I still had to eat. And I was going in there with about ninety RBI and that new record for games played so I figured that I should be eating pretty well. I must have turned down two or three offers until he says, 'Okay, Carl, we'll give you a cost-of-living increase,'" which was partly because we had another kid on the way. He only raised me from $18,500 to about $20,000. Then he gave me a raise the next year and a big one to $30,000 after my big year in '53.

"One thing about Bavasi I'll never forget: One day he said to me, 'Furillo, do you ever cash any of your checks?' And I said, 'I don't understand you, what are you talking about? I gotta live.' And he said, 'Every check I've seen come back it says 'deposit, deposit, deposit.' He said, 'I don't see where you ever cash a check.' So I told him, 'I deposit it in my savings account or my checking account or whatever it is, and then I write a check later.' I used to take my salary check or my World Series check and every check I got from baseball, and I used to put on the back of my check, 'for deposit only.' That way in case the check was lost or whatever it was, it would go straight to the bank. I made sure that nobody would steal it or anything like that.

"Bavasi was always trying to be a cutie pie. He would always say 'Well, Jesus, Furillo, you're making so much money now, you don't need this kind of money,' and stuff like that, joking around. Except for that one time, the raises I got from him were small. But I always took some part of my money on the side. For instance, they would pay my expenses for the wife and kids to come to spring training. They would pay for our houses down in Florida."[1]

Whatever the early dynamics with Bavasi were, the process by which Furillo signed his 1951 contract was familiar. He sent back two early contracts, and refused to sign during a trip to Ebbets Field in the first week of February. But he agreed to terms on Feb. 8 after a telephone conversation with Bavasi. "So 'The Arm,' as he is called in Brooklyn, gets another assist for himself, this time a financial one, for continuing his annual policy of holding out on contract talks until he is completely satisfied," wrote Bill Reedy. "He has never forgotten the tough days of his baseball career and is capitalizing on his good years."[2] Meanwhile, Gordon Williams quoted Fresco Thompson as saying, "We need Furillo and he needs us. Carl is the type of athlete who needs encouragement. When he is happy, he is a great ballplayer. I managed him in 1941 and know all about it." Williams wrote that if Furillo were with the Phillies or the Boston Braves, he would be earning at least $7,500 more than the Dodgers were paying him. Robinson, the highest-paid Dodger at the time, was earning $35,000 annually. Williams also said that Furillo was the National League's second-best right-handed hitter, after Del Ennis, in addition to having the best arm in the game. In 1950, Furillo led NL outfielders with 18 assists, and he had thrown out 62 runners since entering the majors. "He is the best center fielder in the National (League), yet he is playing right for the Dodgers because of his value to the club in that position—keeping the runners from advancing," Williams said.[3]

In another off-season story, Reedy addressed Furillo's positive relationship with Robinson, noting that "Jackie Robinson gives Carl credit for helping him over some tough spots" and that "the great Negro second baseman and leading hitter for the Dodgers said the most gratifying thing to him now is the realization he has been accepted 'as one of the gang' on the Brooklyn team and he is able to participate in their banter."[4] He quoted Robinson as saying, "I'll never forget how Reese and Furillo kept kidding me when I was in a batting slump last summer after I had been hurt. Reese would say to me, 'My, what power number 42 has' when I would pop a foul straight up in batting practice, and then

Furillo would chime in, 'Yeah, a home run if we're playing the game in an elevator shaft.' When they talked to you like that, they're with you, boy.'"⁵ The story provides additional evidence, in Robinson's own words, that the two players managed to forge a bond during their careers. Meanwhile, for the Furillos, the generational transitions continued. Furillo celebrated his 29th birthday on March 8. His father died at 74 on March 9. His second son, Jon, was born on March 28.

As a sixth-year player and star on a prominent team, Furillo was being noticed by advertisers. During the 1951 season, he became a spokesman for Camel cigarettes. In one advertisement, he reported that "I made the mildness tests you read about. My own 30-day Camel test sold me. Camels taste swell—and they're mild."⁶ A photo showed Furillo, in a jacket and tie, holding a cigarette between his fingers. "They paid us each a price for that, and I always had to carry a pack of Camels," Furillo said. "But I was smoking Luckies, so what I did was I always carried a pack of cigarettes with me in my left-hand pocket and in my right-hand pocket I carried my other cigarettes. And sometimes someone would walk up to you and say, 'How come you're smoking a different brand?' And I'd say, 'Oh, no, I got a Camel, and here they are,' and I'd show them the Camels."

Such endorsements provided a side benefit for well-known players in the 1950s, as did personal appearances, particularly in Brooklyn. "The people there would know us and we would get meals at restaurants we walked into and gifts from fans and stuff," Furillo said. "We did a lot of personal appearances where you would make like $50 or $100 or $150, or you could go on television shows and you would get paid."⁷ Additionally, in the weeks following the 1950 season, Furillo went on a barnstorming trip in the mid–Atlantic states with a team known as Danny Litwhiler's All-Stars, apparently earning several thousand dollars. Some of his money went to the off-season purchase of 60 acres near Bernville, Pennsylvania, where he kept about 20 head of cattle and more than a dozen pigs. During the season, his brother-in-law oversaw farm operations.

Furillo did not accept every opportunity presented to him, however. That summer, he rejected a chance to appear on the Giants' pregame show, which was hosted by Durocher's wife, Laraine Day. "Durocher has his pitchers throw at me and no one else in the league does it," Furillo explained. "One day last year he told me he was going to throw at me. The same day I got hit in the head. If it happens again, I'll get him. For every day I spend in a hospital, he'll spend two."⁸ Furillo later recalled, "I put my foot down; I said I wasn't going to appear with her."⁹ In October, after the Giants won the first playoff game against the Dodgers, Fern Furillo told *The Reading Eagle*, "the one thing that irks me is that Mrs.

Durocher, the way she crows when the Giants win." Asked if she was seated near Ms. Day, Fern Furillo responded, "Gosh, no. She was on the third-base side. If we sat any closer, I think there'd be some hair-pulling."[10]

On the field, the Dodgers got off to a good start. By Aug. 11, they had a 13½-game lead. But the Giants won their next 16 games. "For a while in 1951, it looked like the Dodgers' year," Furillo recalled. "Bavasi made a good trade (in June) when he got Andy Pafko from the Cubs to play left field. The Cubs got Hermanski and Joe Hatten and some others; we got Pafko and Rube Walker and a couple more. They said afterwards that it looked like the Dodgers had just traded into the pennant, and we opened up a big lead over all the rest of them."[11] Soon afterwards, Rickey proclaimed the outfield of Furillo, Pafko and Snider to be among the greatest in baseball history. While the proclamation is debatable, it is clear that the time when Pafko played for the Dodgers (84 games in 1951 and 150 games in 1952) marked the only time when it can truly be said that the team had a suitable complement to Furillo and Snider in right and center. (Pafko was traded to the Braves in 1953: the official justification was that the Dodgers needed to make way for younger players.) In a July interview, Furillo declared it was a "real pleasure" to play for Dressen. "He has everybody hustling and he's a great hustler himself," Furillo said. "Give Dressen credit for Ralph Branca's great comeback. All Branca needed was confidence in himself, and now he's got it." As for Hodges, Furillo offered this insight: "This guy Gil Hodges is no flash in the pan." At the time, Hodges had 28 home runs, but Furillo said he "doesn't even think about Babe Ruth's record. He's in there to win games for the Dodgers and you've got to admit that he's doing a pretty good job."[12]

In August, the Giants started a winning streak. "We began to look over our shoulders, which you should never do," Furillo recalled. "And things began happening. Like one day we played the Giants when it was getting near the end, and they (not) only beat us but they pulled a triple play against us. You know a triple play doesn't happen every day. I guess it was like when that black cat walked in front of the Cubs dugout last year (as the Mets pursued the Cubs in 1969). You don't want to think about those things. I especially used to just try and play my ballgame. But you could see that the whole team was upset."[13]

Furillo played what had become a typical year for him, hitting .295 with 16 home runs and 91 RBIs. From 1949 through 1955, he hit over .290 with at least 16 home runs and 91 RBI in every year except for 1952. Additionally, in 1951, because of the three playoff games with the Giants, Furillo led the league in durability, playing in 158 games with 667 at-bats and 724 plate appearances. His reputation continued to grow. In a

8. THE WORST BAD YEAR

Andy Pafko (left) joined the Dodgers to play left field in June 1951. Soon afterwards, Branch Rickey said the outfield of Pafko, Snider (center) and Furillo was among the best in baseball history. But Pafko left after the 1952 season (National Baseball Hall of Fame Library, Cooperstown, New York).

July interview, Dressen declared that Furillo was the best right fielder in Dodger history, better even than predecessor Dixie Walker. "Dixie Walker was a good hitter, but Furillo is also a .300 batsman and miles ahead of Dixie in the outfield."[14] In June, Dressen took the unusual step of making Furillo the Dodgers' leadoff hitter, defying the conventional wisdom that a leadoff hitter should be able to get on base and then use his speed to advance. Furillo was not particularly fast. He rarely walked, preferring to swing at bad balls and hit first pitches. Nevertheless, the gambit worked because Furillo often came to bat with men on base, and was able to drive them in. "The Dodgers are riding high wide and handsome these days and no little part of their success is due to Carl Furillo, who may develop into the greatest leadoff man the game ever knew," wrote INS reporter Pat Robinson in August. He wrote that Furillo had three leadoff, first-pitch home runs by early August, complementing "the strongest throwing arm in the National League."[15]

The following month, UPI reporter Fred Down tagged Furillo and the Giants' Monte Irvin as baseball's most underrated stars. "Chances are Furillo's arm is as strong as any the game has ever known," Down wrote. He added that Furillo was better than either of his outfield mates, Pafko and Snider, because "he has outplayed Pafko in every department this year, of course, and he is less prone to the occasional periods of brooding that afflict Snider." Down added, "Irvin, a hard-hitting Negro, is even less-known than Furillo because he does not have a comparable arm."[16] Again, it is worth questioning whether Furillo ought to be in the Hall of Fame. Both Irvin and Snider are members.

In a curious, somewhat inexplicable interview that September, Furillo asserted he should not be so widely characterized as a "tough guy." Talking to UPI reporter Milton Richman, he said, "I don't know where I ever got the reputation for being tough. Of course, I don't let anyone step on me, but believe me, I don't go around with a chip on my shoulder. I never look for trouble."[17] Discussing the interview, Reading's Reedy commented, "Anyone knowing Furillo intimately, as many of his friends and neighbors in Berks County do, will agree Carl was speaking truthfully and sincerely when he made that statement. He's certainly easy enough to get along with." But Reedy acknowledged that he did not fully accept Furillo's premise. Furillo "has suddenly come to be regarded as one of the toughest customers in the National League playing ranks," he wrote. "That's chiefly because Carl has steadfastly refused to be intimidated at the plate. It's no longer considered healthy to brush him back. The fact that he is quiet and conservative by nature misled some rival players to believe he could be intimidated. They were quickly disillusioned. He probably has carried modesty too far, however. Known as a rather difficult player to interview, he has not received nearly enough publicity in major league cities considering the fact that he is one of the best in baseball today."[18]

The last week of the 1951 season provided a gripping New York narrative, at a time when baseball was the country's predominant sport, as the Dodgers and Giants battled. On Monday, Sept. 24, the Dodgers, who were off, saw their lead fell to 2½ games as the Giants beat the Boston Braves. On Sept. 25, the Giants won at Philadelphia. The Dodgers lost a doubleheader to the Braves; they dropped the second game 14–2 after committing three errors, and their lead fell to one game. On Sept. 26, both teams won.

On Sept. 27, the National League arranged a coin toss to determine which team would have home-field advantage if there were to be a playoff. Jack Collins, the Dodgers' business manager, stood in for Walter O'Malley; he won the toss and chose Ebbets Field for the first playoff game, which meant that one and possibly two games would take place at the Polo Grounds. Meanwhile, the Giants beat the Phillies while the Dodgers lost to the Braves 4–3, cutting their lead to a half-game. "This game was decided on a disputed play," Furillo said. "Somebody (Bob Addis) slid into home and Frank Dascoli was the umpire and he called him safe, and Roy Campanella must have jumped four feet into the air. Before he came down Dascoli had thumbed him out, and that was just about the only time I ever saw Campanella so mad. But there was nothing that he or any one of us could do."[19]

On Friday, Sept. 28, the Giants were off, while the Dodgers lost again to the Phillies, falling into a tie. For the final two games of the regular season, the Dodgers faced the Phillies at Shibe Park, while the Giants were in Boston. On Sept. 29 both teams won, preserving the tie. On Sept. 30, the last day of the season, the Giants clinched a 3–2 victory while the Dodgers were still playing. "They were home free," said Furillo. "Either they would win it all or there would be a playoff. I don't know how we did it, since it was just like the year before in Philadelphia, and it even went into extra innings, but Robinson hit one that won the game in the 14th (by a 9–8 score). It seemed like that was the only break we got all year. But we were ready for the playoffs. We hadn't forgotten about first-place money."[20]

The playoffs were a best-of-three affair. The Giants won the first game 3–1 at Ebbets Field as Bobby Thomson hit a two-run homer off Ralph Branca. Furillo, the Dodgers' leadoff hitter, could not get a hit in four at-bats against Jim Hearn, who pitched a complete game for the Giants. After the game, "Carl Furillo stepped from the steaming showers in the Dodger locker room, reached for a Turkish towel and groaned 'Geeze, I'm weary,'" *The Reading Eagle* reported. "Furillo rubbed himself hard with the towel, and then sank down on a stool. He reached for a cigarette, took a long puff, and continued, 'I don't have very much left, I guess. I haven't missed a game this season and I'm just plain tired.' The Berks County product, however, didn't want his weariness to be interpreted as defeatism. 'Look at it this way. We played good ball today. It wasn't a sloppy game. And it's about time the percentages start falling our way, instead of that way.' And he pointed in the direction of the Giants' dressing room."[21]

The Dodgers won the second game 10–0, a complete game shutout by rookie Clem Labine, played at the Polo Grounds. In the third game, the Giants started Sal Maglie and the Dodgers started Don Newcombe. In the first inning, Jackie Robinson singled home Pee Wee Reese. The Giants scored a run in the seventh, but in the eighth the Dodgers scored three times. They headed into the bottom of the ninth with a 4–1 lead with Newcombe still pitching, even though he had pitched a complete game the previous Saturday and $5\frac{2}{3}$ innings in relief on Sunday. After he put two men on base and gave up a run, Dressen brought in Ralph Branca. The first pitch was a strike. Thomson homered on his second pitch, scoring three runs for a 5–4 victory. For most fans, perhaps the clearest memory is of broadcaster Russ Hodges repeating the phrase "The Giants win the pennant, the Giants win the pennant, the Giants win the pennant."

In a 2009 interview, Branca recalled that after the game, "Jackie came over and said 'if it wasn't for you, we wouldn't have been there.'" Branca also recalled that he led the league in ERA in August, but "in the last seven weeks, the team went flat." He put much of the blame on Dressen's management of the pitching staff. Dressen "was a vindictive guy," Branca said. "He used Newcombe and me too much." He also overused two other starters, Carl Erskine and Preacher Roe, to the point that both had sore arms, as did bullpen pitcher Clyde King, Branca said. One reason was that Dressen refused to use Clem Labine after an incident on Sept. 21 when, in a game against Philadelphia, Labine disobeyed an order from Dressen to take a full windup when pitching to Phillies third baseman Puddin' Head Jones. Instead, Labine, using his own best judgment, pitched from the stretch, and Jones hit a grand slam home run. "Dressen wanted Clem to take a windup, and Clem said no," Branca recalled. "Then Clem hung a curve, the guy hit a grand slam, and Dressen didn't pitch him anymore." Even though Labine had won four straight games before the loss, Dressen used him just one more time during the season. "Non-pitchers don't have a clue," Branca said. "Once a pitcher loses his confidence, he gets tenuous out on the mound and he doesn't make good pitches."[22]

Furillo had played every game that year, setting Dodgers records for most games and also, because he was the leadoff hitter, for most at-bats. Recalling the game years later, Furillo said: "They won the first game but we won the second, and in the ninth inning of the third we were winning 4–1 and people had started leaving because it looked to be all over. After it ended, we sat around the clubhouse and wondered about whether the Dodgers were just unlucky, whether we were cursed. We thought we were unhappy the day we lost out to the Phillies in 1950, but after that playoff game it was terrible. I remember Pee Wee said that it was the one game of his career that he refused to talk about afterwards. None of us wanted to talk to anybody after that."[23]

9

"I Couldn't Even See the Ball"

As bad as 1951 turned out to be, for the Dodgers and Furillo it was a collective loss. The following season was triumphant for the Dodgers, except for another World Series loss to the Yankees, but problematic for Furillo. The 30-year-old athlete faced the lonely challenge of failing eyesight. At the end of the season, Furillo's statistical totals included his all-time lows in nearly every category, except for the partial season when his career was winding down. Despite playing 134 games and coming to bat 425 times, he hit just eight home runs with 52 RBI, and his batting average was .247. His lifetime average dipped below .300. In retrospect, the year was an aberration, the only time between the 1949 season and the 1956 season when he hit fewer than 16 home runs, had fewer than 92 RBI and hit less than .289. Of course, at the time it was not quite so easy to Furillo to dismiss his daily failures.

"That year for me was downhill all the way," Furillo recalled. "For the first time in seven years, I didn't measure up as a major league hitter; my RBI, home runs, average and everything else was down. I figured that one mediocre season in seven wasn't the end of the world because maybe I had it coming to me. But the thing of it was that my eyes were bad all through the year. They had been getting worse ever since my nose was broken three years before, and so by '52 there were times when I went up there and I couldn't even see the ball. It was like there was a mist in front of my eyes and I'd see it coming, and then I would lose it in the mist, and then see it again when it was right on top of me.

"In a lot of places, I had to step out of the box and kind of wipe my eyes because they would get all teary. Or else I would have to pinch them like you do when they're strained. I would think it was my sinuses or my eyes going bad or something, and I was even trying glasses for reading, and a couple of times I tried them in practice. But I didn't want to use my eyes for an excuse. Sometimes you go into a slump and you can't buy a hit. You shouldn't be going out and buying eyeglasses to alibi for it. I got a little worried because this was a slump I couldn't come out of. But I was just glad the rest of the team was doing okay and we won the pennant anyway."[1]

The off-season included a trade rumor, Furillo to the Phillies for pitcher Howard Fox, who could replace Don Newcombe, drafted into the Army, in the Dodgers rotation. More notably, however, Furillo did not hold out. Instead, he signed on January 16 after a brief meeting with Bavasi in Brooklyn. The contract was for about $22,000. The following month, as he packed for spring training, which was scheduled to begin Feb. 27, Furillo told *The Reading Times* that he did not expect a repeat of the 1951 season. "'Just say this for me, the Dodgers are going to win the pennant this year and no doubt about it,' he snorted. 'Just forget about that dismal finish in 1951. Charge it off as one of those things. It won't happen again.'" Although the Dodgers lost Newcombe to the draft, Furillo noted that other teams also lost players to the draft and that Andy Pafko would play the entire season.

As for himself, Furillo declared, "No reason why I shouldn't hit around .300. I slumped the last few weeks of the season. I hope Manager Chuck Dressen doesn't start me at leadoff again. I prefer to hit in the fifth or sixth position. But he's the boss."[2] Dressen was apparently of the same mind, however. By March, a *Times* story with a Daytona Beach dateline proclaimed, "Carl Furillo is happy. He's getting his hits and he has been told that he won't be asked to bat leadoff."[3] Furillo predicted he would hit above .300 and added, "Man for man, we are the class of the National League. We won't make the same mistakes again and you can lay to that."[4]

Despite his initial optimism, Furillo, by the end of May, was mired in a slump. In late May, he told Gordon Williams that his batting average "just dropped, instead of going up. Just one of those things. Can't buy a hit. But I must say I haven't been banging the ball very hard, so I can't alibi that way. My health is good, weight stays around 194. Nothing wrong with my appetite." Asked about his vision, he responded stoically, "I don't want to say anything about that. I have been wearing glasses to read on advice of a specialist. I have been losing the ball on fast breaking stuff. And I wouldn't be surprised if he recommends that I wear them in ball games. I have tried them in batting practice.

"I figure I will snap out of it soon," Furillo said. "This may be the only slump I'll have this year. Usually mine come near the end because I never miss a game unless I am injured and we all get tired after the hot months of July and August."⁵ Furillo had told Dressen that the manager could put him in or take him out at any time, as long as it helped the team. In fact, Furillo was benched May 17, after making one hit in 39 at bats. He had played in 255 consecutive games. Dick Williams played left, while Pafko shifted to right. Nevertheless, on Sept. 21, Furillo got his 1,000th major league hit, doubling in the eighth inning at Boston.

As the season started, the Dodgers pitching was clearly diminished. Newcombe had been drafted, Roe was 36 and Branca hurt his back. But once again, the team had the benefit of Rickey's early move to sign black players, as Joe Black, a former Negro Leagues player, stepped to the front as a relief pitcher. Black pitched 142 innings, won 15 games, saved 15 more, and recorded a 2.15 ERA. At the end of the season he was named Rookie of the Year. Ironically, by that time his future was already past. Over the rest of his career, which extended into the 1957 season, he would win just 15 additional games. Some blame Dressen, who tried to force Black to learn a third pitch in 1953. Unable to do so, Black lost his confidence and his control. But for one season, Black was unbeatable. Rickey had also signed a young right-hander named Billy Loes, who stepped into the rotation and won 13 games. Carl Erskine won 14, while Roe and Ben Wade each won 11.

Meanwhile, the Giants were weaker. Willie Mays had also been drafted, while Monte Irvin and Larry Jansen were injured for much of the year. The Dodgers played well early, running their record to 60–22 by late July. After that, they played .500 baseball for the rest of the season. The Giants, meanwhile, began to step it up. On Sept. 1, the Dodgers led by 9½ games. By Sept. 17, it was three games. History, it appeared, had decided to repeat itself. But this time, the Dodgers held on, winning the pennant by 4½ games. Once again, they found themselves facing the Yankees in the World Series.

After beating the Dodgers in 1941, 1947, and 1949, as well as the Phillies in 1950 and the Giants in 1951, the Yankees were heavy favorites. Dressen decided to take a chance and named Black his first-game starter. Black won 4–2, which raised some hopes, since he was in line to pitch two more times if the Series went to seven games. In the fourth game, Black allowed just three hits, but one was a home run by Johnny Mize, helping the Yankees to win 2–0 and tie the Series at two games apiece.

In the fifth game, Mize hit his third home run of the Series in the fifth inning, giving the Yankees a 5–4 lead. But the Dodgers tied the game in the seventh and pushed it into extra innings. The Dodgers scored a run in the top of the 11th, but in the bottom of that inning Mize hit one to the wall. "Mize really wanted to tie it up," Furillo said. "He already had a couple of home runs in that Series and he really slammed it out there. But I was able to see the ball this time and I got some height by pushing off the fence with one hand and reaching up with the glove, so that saved us the game." Erskine, who pitched all 11 innings, was the winner, and Furillo was a hero.

"That picture (of the catch off Mize) was on the front of *The Daily News* and in *Life* magazine and everywhere else," Furillo said. "So then they made up a story that some lady in the stands said, 'Furillo, I want that ball,' and I said to her, 'Lady, I need it more than you do,' or something like that. But all that really happened was when I caught it I heard this lady say something like "Gimme the ball, gimme the ball,' but I took the ball and I threw it in. The rest of it was just something the reporters made up. They used to put a lot of words in your mouth."[6] Loes and Black pitched well in the final two games, but the Yankees pitched better, and won in seven.

Not surprisingly, Furillo's name came up in trade talk following the season. One story had the Cardinals trading Stan Musial and pitcher Gerry Staley for Cox, Furillo and Hodges. Another had the Boston Braves offering Warren Spahn, first baseman Earl Torgeson, and a young catcher for Furillo, Hodges and utility infielder Bobby Morgan. "I can't see that one going through," Furillo told *The Reading Times*. "I believe it will be a man-for-man deal if it goes through." However, he acknowledged: "Brooklyn needs pitchers and the front office is willing to barter with any club in the National League, (and) I didn't have such a good season at the bat. For the first time in seven seasons, I didn't measure up as a big-league hitter. Maybe I had a slump coming to me. In other years, I always was near the top in driving in runs. Every ballplayer has a bad year. Look at Jackie Robinson, our ace. He was away off at bat and in the field. Duke Snider didn't show much until the latter part of the schedule. (And) how about poor Gil Hodges in the World Series? (He was 0 for 21.) Yet Manager Dressen can't complain about Hodges. He knocked in plenty of runs during the season."[7]

Trade talk was a constant throughout Furillo's career. "At one time or another, they had me with every other team in the league," he recalled. "At the end of '52, they had me going to the Braves; then in '54 there was this real strong rumor that Gilliam and I were going to go to Philadelphia for Granny Hamner. The Philadelphia players would be coming up to me and saying, 'Well, Carl, I hear you'll be with us next year.' But that same year, we would go to Chicago, and the players there would come up to me and say, 'Well, Carl, I guess this is where you will be next year.'

"It began to seem like every year I played there, they said, 'Oh, Furillo is going to be traded' and 'Well, Furillo, if I can get the right price for Furillo, then Furillo will be traded,' and stuff like that. And you would say to yourself, 'Gee, I'm working like a mule and I'm having good years,' and 'Do I deserve to be traded?' and 'Do I have to be here?' With all that trade talk, I still think the newspaper reporters had something to do with that, because they would ask questions like 'Is this guy available?' or 'Is that guy available?' Then Mr. O'Malley would say, 'Yeah, anybody's available.' And they would just blow it up.

"At first, I didn't mind it much because Brooklyn, as everybody knew, was paying lower salaries than most of the other clubs in the league. As far as I was concerned, it was all the same to me where I played; I just wanted to play my game. But after awhile, I didn't want to leave Brooklyn, because once I got to be settled down there I liked it. I had a lot of friends and everything else. But I don't know. Sometimes I wish that when we went to California, I would have asked to be traded, because then the friction would have never come up. It would have been a lot better for me as far as baseball is concerned. But I stayed with that ballclub for 14 years and I finally was released."[8]

After the 1952 season ended, the Dodgers urged Furillo to have an

Carl Furillo was portrayed on Bowman baseball cards in 1952 (left) and in 1954. The cards were popular because the Dodgers often played in the World Series. "I stayed with that ballclub for 14 years," Furillo said (courtesy Topps Company).

eye operation. When it took place on Jan. 8, 1953, at St. Clare's Hospital in Manhattan, the operation was big news. "Carl Furillo, rifle-armed Dodger outfielder who has been mentioned in recent trade talks, underwent surgery on both eyes yesterday at a Manhattan hospital," wrote Dick Young in *The Daily News*. He added, "There is hardly any question that the difficulty Carl suffered with his eyes caused the tremendous drop in his batting average in '52. His BA tumbled from .295 to .247. In '51 he played in 158 games, last season in only 134.

"Undoubtedly, Furillo's name will now be dropped from further trade talks, at least until the surgery is tested in spring training," Young wrote. He added, "Because of his batting slump, Furillo had to be benched at times last season. But he always took the benching by manager Charley Dressen with good grace."[9] A few weeks later, Young wrote that no one had realized how seriously injured Furillo's eyes were until after the surgery, even though Furillo would often step out of the batter's box and pinch both eyes, explaining that his eyes were tearing up and his sinuses were bothering him.

Years later, Furillo recalled: "They had to work on both eyes. They got 'foreign particles,' like sand or grit, from the right one, and they found a film on each eye, and then they put stitches in both of them. They had bandages on them for a couple of days, and when they finally took the bandages off I still had to spend the rest of the winter wondering if my career was over. You couldn't tell if the operation was a success or not, as far as baseball was concerned, until you got into the season. Of course, for the same reason, the Dodgers couldn't be trying to trade me because nobody wanted to take that kind of a chance. I just had to wait and see, and when spring training started the next year I would be out to prove myself all over again."[10]

10

Batting Champ

In 1953, Furillo had his best season, leading the National League in batting and tying Game 6 of the World Series with a dramatic ninth-inning home run. But 1953 also had its downsides. In September, a conflict with an old nemesis cut Furillo's season short, injured in a fight with Leo Durocher on Sept. 6, he had to sit out the last three weeks of the season. And in the Series, although they made it to the seventh game, the Dodgers lost again to the Yankees.

Shortly after he was discharged from the hospital following eye surgery, Furillo agreed to terms for his 1953 contract. While some reports indicated that Furillo took a small cut, perhaps because the team did not want the truth known, it appears that Bavasi increased his salary to $23,000. "In past years I always had a little trouble, but not this time," Furillo said. "Bavasi made me an offer slightly in excess of my last year's salary, and I accepted. It was over, just like that. (He) didn't say much about my .247 batting average. After all, it really was the first bad year I've had with the Dodgers. But I'll have to hustle more than ever this year if I want to hold down a steady job. That George Shuba was coming along like a house afire at the end of the 1952 season."[1]

As he headed to Florida for spring training in February, Furillo was nervous about his eyesight. Even in early March, he declared, "I don't know whether the operation helped or not. It will be a month or more before I can tell. I probably won't know until we are well into the regular season and I'm up against tough pitching every day. One thing I do know, I sure can't be much worse."[2] A month later, he was around .300 and predicted he would hit at least that high. But he added, "I look at my batting average once a year, on the last day of the season. I figure that's the average that counts in the paycheck."[3]

As it turned out, "I had nothing to worry about," Furillo recalled. "I started hitting when I got to camp and I didn't stop. I had the best season that I ever had, I won the hitting championship and I won the Comeback Player of the Year award and went to the All-Star Game. But it ended up I won the batting title sitting on the bench because Durocher broke my little finger in that fight.

"I got hit by pitchers quite a few times that year, twice in the head, and naturally I was getting pretty tired of it. In April I went after Maglie because he almost hit me. I figured he was throwing at me, so I threw my bat at him. Then I started charging out to the mound and the umpire and the catcher had to hold me back. I had just started hitting after my bad year and I didn't want anybody to interfere with that, especially one of Durocher's pitchers."[4] During the 1953 season, Giants pitchers threw at Furillo twice.

The first incident came in an April 25 game that "turned into one of the nastiest contests ever played" between the Giants and Dodgers, wrote Judith Testa in *Sal Maglie: Baseball's Demon Barber*. With the Dodgers leading 5–2 in the bottom of the third, Furillo came to the plate. "Maglie loosed a fastball that buzzed just over the Dodger right fielder's head. It is difficult to believe that Maglie intended to bean Furillo with a pitch that—had it been a few inches lower—could have killed him, but there is no doubt he intended to frighten Furillo, who had already been beaned five times in his career. The two men glared at each other for a moment before Furillo loosed a string of loud profanities at the pitcher. Sal said nothing, but his next pitch was his contemptuous answer, the classic Maglie follow-up to a brushback, a curve low and outside. Furillo took a vicious cut and missed by two feet."

At that point, the bat slid out of Furillo's hands and "sailed toward the mound like a whirring helicopter blade at the level of Maglie's knees. He avoided it successfully, but a dramatic photograph in the *Herald Tribune* suggests a near miss. (Then) Furillo advanced slowly toward the mound, where Maglie stood his ground, glowering. Catcher Sal Yvars hurried to Furillo's side, trying to assure him that Maglie had not meant to bean him. Furillo ignored the distraction and kept advancing on Maglie, but before he could reach the mound, umpire Larry Goetz and players from both teams blocked his path. The umpire managed to restrain Furillo, but he nearly broke away when he spotted Durocher. It took an arm lock applied by the powerful Gil Hodges to keep Furillo from charging the Giants' manager. Furillo was persuaded back to the plate, and Maglie struck him out to end the inning."[5]

In an interview after the game, Furillo insisted the bat "just slipped out of my hands." He added that when he approached Maglie, "I was just going out to pick up my bat."[6] It may be that Furillo did not publicly admit to throwing his bat at Maglie until the 1970 interview. In any case, Testa wrote, after the game Walter O'Malley sent Furillo an envelope containing $50, and explained facetiously, "It's for catching the largest bass in Vero Beach this spring."[7]

On July 20, during a game at Ebbets Field, Furillo was beaned by Cubs pitcher Bob Rush, and had to be carried off the field on a stretcher. "I wasn't hurt too bad," he said. "I was just lucky that I had been wearing some padding under my hat. I didn't think Rush was really trying to hit me in the head; I think he was trying more to knock me back. He might have wanted to hit me in the ribs or something, but like I said before, you tend to fall back, and when I did there was the ball in front of my face and no way that I could get out of the way. But I think it was an accident."[8] Two years after he brushed off the impact of the Rush pitch, Furillo declared that it was the worst beaning he ever suffered. "The time I got hit by Rush, that was the hardest shot of all," he said. "It gave me a real burning sensation."[9]

Following the Rush beaning, a comment by umpire Larry Goetz provided additional insight into Furillo's overall approach. Throughout his career, Furillo maintained a positive relationship with umpires. Said Goetz, "Nobody said anything. I don't think Rush was trying to hit Furillo. Rush doesn't throw at hitters." Then Goetz added, "You hate to see nice guys get hurt. Furillo is a really nice guy—and so is Rush. When Jake Pitler told me a little later that Furillo was all right, I told him, 'That's the best news I could hear. Makes me feel a lot better.'"[10] Two years later, umpire Babe Pinelli underscored the comment in a story about his career. "Some players gripe a lot at the plate, but stars like Stan Musial, Carl Furillo and Ted Kluszewski never complain," Pinelli said. "They let the umpire call the plays."[11]

Then on Sept. 6 came one of the baseball's most famous beanball incidents, which triggered one of the worst on-field brawls in the game's history. Ruben Gomez was pitching for the Giants against the Dodgers, when Furillo came to bat in the second inning. "Here I was having the greatest season of my life and leading the league in hitting and close to a hundred RBI and it's my first time up in the game and Gomez hits me right in the hand," Furillo recalled. "Right away I knew why he did it, and like with Maglie I went for the mound but they held me back. So there was a little rhubarb there and I didn't reach Gomez.

"So I took first base and Billy Cox came up. He looked at a few pitches, and I was looking into the Giant's dugout and I caught sight of Durocher and his mouth was moving. I couldn't hear what he was saying, but then he signaled me with his finger to come in there. So I saw red. I went for him then. It wasn't much of a fight because I didn't get a chance to hit him. I would have paid a thousand dollars for that chance because it would have been worth it. But he sort of came out of the dugout to meet me, and we wrestled around for a little while and we both went down. Then both teams started pouring out of the dugouts. And just as I wrapped one arm around his head and got ready to let him have it, somebody grabbed me.

"I don't know who it was, but I do know one thing, it was Durocher who broke my little finger. The doctors and everyone were saying that somebody must have stepped on it and broken it. But after the fight I looked at it and there were no spike marks or anything like that from somebody stepping on it. So then I realized what had happened. I knew that Durocher had grabbed my finger and twisted it when we were wrestling, so as to put me out for the year.

"People said to me afterwards, 'Well, Carl, how come you went into the Giants dugout? The players might have jumped you.' But I knew they weren't going to jump in for him because they hated his guts. Durocher didn't know the half of it. He was a man that was never able to get along with his players, no matter what team it was. From the day he took over the Dodgers to even with these Cubs (in 1970), Durocher has had his problems."[12]

The front page of next day's *Daily News* was devoted to the incident. A large photo showed Furillo being restrained by Joe Black and Cookie Lavagetto, while Dodger pitchers Erv Palica restrained Durocher and, separately, Duke Snider scuffled with Jim Hearn. Afterwards, as Furillo walked across the field toward the clubhouse, Giants fans hurled debris at him, and one swung an umbrella that grazed his cap. Two policemen had to disperse demonstrators so that Furillo, flanked by the Dodgers physician and trainer, could reach the clubhouse door.

In the Dodgers clubhouse, Furillo spoke through gritted teeth as he underwent treatment for what turned out to be a broken metacarpal bone in his left hand. "There was deep-seated hate in every word that Carl Furillo spat as he spoke of Leo Durocher in the shower room at the Polo Grounds," Dick Young wrote.[13] Said Furillo, "I'm gonna get him. The first time I see him. The next time we come face to face. I don't care where it is: on the street, or anywhere. I've had enough of that——. He has crossed me once too often."[14] For his part, Durocher denied saying anything to Furillo or beckoning to him, saying, "Herman Franks yelled to me to watch out. Then I saw him making a beeline for me. So I went out to meet him. What was I supposed to do? Sit there and let him take a punch at me?"[15]

Two days later, back home in Stony Creek, his left hand in a cast, Furillo discussed his troubled relationship with Durocher. "Durocher never has liked me, even when he was manager of the Dodgers. I can think back and recall several times when he yanked me from the lineup when I was hitting the ball. Just because I was having my best season, Durocher was sore. I had four-for-four the day before his pitcher, Ruben Gomez, hit me. Believe me, that pitch was close. I fell back, but it still struck me." Asked why Durocher disliked him, Furillo responded, "That's more than I can tell you. I played for Leo the same as I have for other managers. I never criticized him in public or to a newspaperman. But he always took delight in telling the press that I couldn't hit right-handers and that my average was made off southpaws."[16] Another possible explanation was offered by Charlie Dressen, in a remark published in 1954. "Durocher knows that there are two guys on the club that don't hit when they have been knocked down—Campanella and Carl Furillo."[17]

Later, baseball broadcaster Ernie Harwell would describe the fight as his biggest thrill of the 1953 season. "It was one of the strangest sights in baseball to see Furillo racing from first base and then charging toward Durocher in the Giants dugout," Harwell told *The Sporting News*. "Leo came out to meet the on-rushing Carl and both fell to the ground as Furillo missed with a wild-swinging right. In the fracas, Furillo suffered a fractured metacarpal bone in the left hand, an injury which might have cost the Dodgers a World Series victory. The Durocher-Furillo battle enlivened an otherwise dull season for the Giants. And it prompted this telegram from Rocky Marciano, world heavyweight champion, to Leo Durocher: 'Don't fight for nothing. Come see me and I'll put you on my sparring staff.'"[18]

The Dodgers had an extraordinary season in 1953, winning 105 games to just 49 losses as Campanella and Snider both hit more than 40 home runs, Campanella won the league's Most Valuable Player award, rookie Jim Gilliam led the league in triples and Furillo won the batting championship. Erskine notes that Furillo "should have been a top candidate for MVP, but in the fight his wrist was broken (and) he didn't finish the season."[19] However, Furillo was named *Associated Press* NL Comeback Player of the Year and earned a spot on various post-season all-star teams. As for pitching, Erskine was 20–6, Russ Meyer was 15–5, Billy Loes won 14, and Preacher Roe and Clem Labine each won 11. In the MVP voting, Furillo and Erskine tied for ninth. Meanwhile, the second-place Braves, in their first season as the Milwaukee Braves, finished 13 games behind the Dodgers. The Braves, the first major league team to relocate in half a century, drew more than 1.8 million fans, a National League record. Although the Dodgers drew 1.2 million, it was clear they needed a new ballpark.

It was also the second year of a famous slump by Hodges, who at the time was Furillo's roommate. After his average dipped to .254 in

Carl Furillo recovered from an eye operation in 1953, enabling him to add 97 points to his batting average to reach .344 and to lead the National League in hitting. He also hit 21 home runs, up from eight the previous year (National Baseball Hall of Fame Library, Cooperstown, New York).

1952, Hodges went 0-for-21 in the World Series, and his problems continued into 1953. After 28 games, he was hitting .181 with one home run and five RBI. But the fan support remained. "The people in Brooklyn loved that team and they loved Gil too," Furillo said. "He was having an awful slump and didn't start hitting for two months, but the fans would still be cheering for him every time he came to bat. There was even one Sunday in Brooklyn that the priest at a Mass said it was too hot to preach, so he said, 'Go home and observe the Commandments and pray for Gil Hodges to come out of his slump.'

"It was really bothering Gil. I know because we roomed together on the road for five or six years, and I never saw him so upset as he was then. He used to sit up for half the night worrying about it, smoking cigarettes, and he would say, 'I don't know what is wrong' and 'I don't know whether to swing at it or not.' So I would tell him not to pay any attention to everybody that was telling him 'change your stance' and 'think about this and that.' I would tell him to forget all that and just to play his game. But let's face it; nobody could help Gil too much at that time except Gil and some luck."[20] On May 24, Hodges got two hits, which seemed to turn around his season, as he batted .325 from then on to finish with 31 homers and 122 RBI. Hodges' average, .302, was the second best of his career.

Joan Hodges said it was very rare for her husband to talk about his slump; she was unaware that he discussed it with anyone. "Gil was not that type of a man" to discuss such things publicly. In fact, she said, when he slumped, "his biggest concern was for the fans. When he came home, he felt so bad for them."[21]

The timing of the Durocher fight was unfortunate. The day before it occurred, Furillo had a perfect day at the plate, with a single, two doubles, a triple and a walk against Giants pitchers. Afterwards, Furillo recalled, "I was supposed to be out for ten days, but it turned out I

Gil Hodges (left) and Carl Furillo were roommates and friends who fished and hunted together. They are shown here with their children in Florida during spring training. Furillo's two boys are on the right (Furillo family photograph).

missed the rest of the regular season (23 games). So I was raring to go for the Series, and it was against the Yankees again. They let me play with a special bat with a sponge rubber end because my hand still hurt, and I had to wear a bandage on my hand besides that. I figured it was about time that it was the 'next year' when the Dodgers would win one, but it only went six games and they beat us again."[22]

Despite his injury, however, Furillo performed well in the Series, batting .333 with eight hits and four RBI in 24 at bats, including one of the best moments in his career. It came in the sixth game after the Yankees, who were leading three games to two, scored three runs in the first two innings to go up 3–0. The Dodgers scored a run in the sixth, making it 3–1, and in the top of the ninth Furillo came to bat with a man on base. Facing Allie Reynolds, he hit a home run that created a 3–3 tie and gave the Dodgers a moment of hope before the Yankees came back to win it in the bottom of the ninth.

Later, long-time Dodgers batboy Charley DiGiovanna picked the home run as his greatest thrill in baseball "That one sent chills through me," DiGiovanna said. "You should have seen Furillo. His hand was broken and it was all wrapped up in bandages. He had a sponge on the bat, and how he even gripped the bat, I don't know. Then he hit that home in the last game off Allie Reynolds to tie it up and give us another chance. We lost in the next inning, but that didn't take away anything from what Furillo did."[23] DiGiovanna's selection was made the year before the Dodgers' 1955 Series victory, which no doubt replaced it in his memory rankings.

"Thought we might grab that (game) after my homer," Furillo said afterwards. "But it wasn't in the cards for us to win.... If you remember, I fouled one into the stands just before the homer. That stung my hand good and I had to blow some feeling into the fingers. It was pretty cold, around 60, and that didn't help. I don't want to offer the damaged hand as an alibi, but I might have gotten a few more safeties if I could have used all my power." The pitch from Reynolds was "a fastball, letter-high on the outside, just where they try to pitch me at Yankee Stadium," he added. "This time, however, Allie hit the corner a little too full. I got plenty of wood on the pitch and I figured it was high enough into the stands to escape Hank Bauer's clutches. I wasn't aiming for the home-run sector. I wanted to get on base to give Billy Cox another crack at bat. But with the count three and two, I swung hard on Reynolds' best pitch and away she went. It was a grand feeling. Never hit a sweeter homer. We lost anyway."[24]

11

Next Year Finally Arrives

DURING THE WINTER FOLLOWING the 1953 season, Furillo went hunting with his roommate, Gil Hodges, and Hodges' brother. One night, sitting around the campfire, they talked about the team's new manager, Walter Alston, who had replaced Charlie Dressen.

"Gil's brother says, 'Well, how about this Alston, what do you hear?'" Furillo recalled. "We all knew that he had been the manager at Montreal and he had been with Bavasi there, but not much else, so I said, 'Nothing much—pretty conservative, I hear.' But then Gil says, 'Next to Dressen, anybody but Durocher looks conservative.' And then he says, 'Maybe the real reason they got him is to win the Series—I'm getting tired of not winning one.'"[1]

Hodges' hopes were to be fulfilled, with Alston at the Dodgers helm, but not in 1954. For his part, Furillo, although he welcomed Alston to the team, also expressed regrets over Dressen's departure. The two men always got along well. Even when Furillo stopped hitting during the 1952 campaign, they jointly resolved a potentially disruptive situation because Furillo offered to sit out games and Dressen continued to praise him and, often, to play him. Dressen "wouldn't take one of O'Malley's one-year contracts, which Alston has been taking since that day," Furillo said in 1970. "Dressen wanted a longer contract because here he had won two pennants and finished second in three years. But he just got fired for it."[2]

Furillo's stellar 1953 season brought him a raise to $30,000 in 1954, an increase of $7,000. (Press estimates put Campanella at $36,000 and Robinson at $40,000.) Furillo's deal was sealed in January, at the annual dinner of the New York press photographers in late January. Bavasi came over to sit at Furillo's table. A short time later, Walter O'Malley joined them. "They began talking contract to me and they asked me what I wanted," Furillo said. "I told 'em I was worth a few dollars more than before. Then O'Malley left, and Bavasi and I had the conversation all to ourselves. He shoved a contract at me. I looked at the figures and signed. That's all there was to it."[3] Early in the offseason, Furillo turned down an offer of $6,000 to barnstorm, preferring to allow his finger to heal. In February, he headed to Vero Beach with his family—his boys were about to turn three and five—for spring training, in a good mood after his stellar year and a substantial raise. Later that month, he and Fern went fishing with O'Malley; photos from the time indicate that their take included two large speckled trout.

The 1954 season brought disappointment for the Dodgers, while everything went right for the Giants. Willie Mays returned from the Army and led the team with 41 home runs, 110 RBI and a .345 average. Right fielder Don Mueller hit .342 and Johnny Antonelli won 21 games. The Giants went 24–4 in June and did not have to mount a late-season surge. Instead, they won the pennant by five games. The Milwaukee Braves, meanwhile, drew 2.1 million fans, eclipsing the National League record they had set the previous season, as a young outfielder named Hank Aaron joined the team. The Dodgers finished second and attendance drooped to just over a million, its lowest level since 1944. On the cover of the 1954 Dodgers yearbook, the Brooklyn bum drawn by Willard Mullin stood in a thoughtful pose, a saw and board in his hand and a cigar in his mouth, while encapsulated above his head was a picture of his dream, a modernistic stadium labeled "a new home." That September, the team signed an 18-year-old pitcher, Sandy Koufax, as a bonus baby. He would go on to win just nine games over three years during his career as a Brooklyn Dodger, before he blossomed in Los Angeles.

Furillo's average fell by 50 points, but he still hit .294 with 19 home runs and 96 RBI. The falloff reflected a slow start; after 33 games, Furillo was hitting .217. He failed to hit a home run until June 5, and he drove in only 48 runs in his first 102 games. But in the next 48 games, he drove in 48 runs. On June 26, he hit his fourth homer of the season, the 100th of his career, against the Cardinals. After the All-Star game, Furillo batted .308 and drove in 61 runs in 69 games. The season included another incident involving Giants pitcher Ruben Gomez. On July 8, Furillo complained to home plate umpire Dusty Boggess after a close pitch by Gomez, and became embroiled in a dispute with Giants catcher Wes Westrum. Afterwards, newspaper photos showed Boggess restraining Furillo, while Giants captain Alvin Dark restrained Westrum.

Later that month, Furillo was hit by a pitch from Chicago Cubs pitcher Johnny Klippstein, but he was not seriously hurt. A high point

11. Next Year Finally Arrives

In Vero Beach, Florida, Duke Snider, Carl Erskine, Carl Furillo and Al Campanis (left to right) look over the new book, *The Dodgers' Way to Play Baseball*, which was written by Campanis (courtesy Carl Erskine).

came Aug. 14, when Furillo's sixth grand slam enabled the Dodgers to defeat the Giants 6–5 and reduce the Giants' lead to 1½ games. A day earlier, Furillo had hit a game-winning two-run homer against the Giants, in a 3–2 Dodgers victory. But it was not the Dodgers' year. In the end, 1954 was a prelude, nothing more.

"The team had a lot of trouble," Furillo said. "Like Gil said, Alston was hired to win the Series, so when we didn't even win the pennant different people were sort of blaming it on him. Some of the guys were beginning to get a little older then and they weren't hitting too well or able to play every day. Cox and Robinson didn't do too much, and Campy injured his hands and was out part of the year and wasn't hitting when he was in. I guess that sometimes we played a little sloppy. And the pitching wasn't what we expected; a lot of guys fell down. Besides that, we didn't steal bases like we had been used to. We played a little more conservative baseball, and a lot of blame went to the new manager. People were saying that the Dodgers were getting old and had lost their spark and all of that, and we just didn't go anywhere that year."[4]

The following year, 1955, was the apex of the Brooklyn Dodgers experience, the year when "next year" finally arrived. The Dodgers won the World Series for the first time since Series play began in 1903, even though they were an aging team playing in a deteriorating ball park and neighborhood, with the search for a new ballpark in Brooklyn beginning to gather steam.

"They were calling us 'old men' by then," Furillo said. "Cox was gone, Roe was gone, and Robinson couldn't even play regularly, but he came through when it counted. I guess we all came through that year because winning the pennant was a cakewalk for us. I'm not saying we weren't getting old. In fact, Alston even started this program of rest for the regulars after it looked like we were sure to win. I didn't take part in it because I was trying to pull my RBIs up to a hundred for the season. But we knew we were getting on, and maybe we wouldn't have another chance, and besides all of that we were awfully tired of losing to the Yankees every year. I guess Pee Wee said it right before that '55 Series. He had played in one more (Series) then I had, and he said, 'I'm the only guy in history that ever played in five World Series without winning any of them, and all against the same team.' He said, 'How long can this last?'"[5]

In January, Furillo signed for $29,000 and prepared to play his tenth season with the Dodgers. Furillo signed in mid–January after meeting with Bavasi in Brooklyn. "We just sat down, talked about a little bit of everything and then he asked me if I'd be satisfied with a contract which called for [about] the same salary as last year," Furillo said. "I said that would be fine with me and that's all there was to it.... When the conference was over, I called Doc Silva (sports editor of *The Times*), told him I had signed, and it was all over."[6] Furillo added that Bavasi had told him the Phillies had offered Del Ennis and Smoky Burgess to Brooklyn for Furillo and Jim Gilliam, but the deal fell through when Bavasi insisted that Curt Simmons be included.

Furillo reported early to Vero Beach, enabling him to pass the time running on the beach to get his legs in shape and fishing with Hodges, who had spent the winter selling automobiles in Brooklyn. By this time, Furillo was very much a fan favorite; on March 8, Brooklyn Borough President John Cashmore was in Vero Beach to present him with a cake in honor of his 33rd birthday. As the season began, Furillo was one of just nine National League veterans with a lifetime average above .300. The Cardinals' Stan Musial headed the list at .344 in 1,834 games: Jackie Robinson was second at .319 in 1,160 games, and Furillo was ninth at .300 in 1,218 games. In May, he proclaimed, "My one ambition is to improve my lifetime batting average of .300 to build up some surplus points for my declining years. I want my kids and their kids to be able to boast the old man was a .300 hitter in the big leagues."[7]

Despite being an old pro, Furillo made a mistake during an April 24 game, neglecting to try to throw Alvin Dark out at the plate because he miscounted Giants outs. Instead of making the throw after catching a fly ball hit by Hank Thompson, Furillo headed for the dugout. Then, realizing his mistake, he threw out Don Mueller, running from first, at second. The mistake was costly as the Giants won the game, 11–10. Never one to alibi, Furillo declared, "I'm stupid. You don't have to tell me. I fouled that play up, period. I thought there were two out."[8]

But nothing could stop the Dodgers in 1955. They opened the season by winning 10 straight games. By May 10, their record was 22–2. One of the most dramatic victories came on May 2, when Carl Erskine and Milwaukee Braves right-hander Gene Conley were locked in a scoreless tie in the 12th inning of a night game at Ebbets Field. Because the Braves had a train to catch, the decision was made that no inning would begin after 11:15 P.M. At 11:13, Furillo came to bat with a man on base and hit Conley's second pitch into the lower left-field stands—this from a hitter who once was benched against righties. The hit came at the height of the Davy Crockett craze. "Even Davy Crockett would have doffed his coonskin cap to Carl Anthony Furillo at 11:13 P.M. Monday, May 2," wrote Roscoe McGowan.[9]

Later that month, *The Daily News* published a story focusing on the frequency with which Furillo was hit by pitched balls. "Scungilli is a hard-shelled sea creature which finds considerable favor among Italian gourmets, but you don't have to be Italian to appreciate the likes of Carl Furillo, who, because he's hard-headed like this mollusk, is called 'Skoonj,'" wrote Peter Coutros.[10] Said Furillo, "I can't figure out why I've gotten hit so often, but I'll tell you something: It ain't fun. I still get headaches from those beanings. About every month or so, my head acts up."[11] The occasional headaches would bother Furillo for the rest of his life. Weeks after the story appeared, on June 17, Furillo showed his anger when he approached the mound with a bat in his hand after St. Louis Cardinals pitcher Brooks Lawrence threw too close to him. Players from both teams rushed onto the field, but Furillo turned back before reaching the mound, and was restrained by umpire Lon Warneke.

As the team entered the latter part of the season, Alston introduced a "rest for regulars" program in order to help his aging team prepare for the World Series. Furillo declared that he wanted no part of it, telling Dick Young in mid–September that he wanted to play "in every game, at least five innings' worth."[12] While the Dodgers were clearly aging, they were hardly doddering. Robinson, who had his differences with both

Carl Erskine (left) and Carl Furillo walk to the clubhouse on May 2, 1955, after a dramatic, late-night 2–0 victory. Furillo homered in the 12th inning with the game slated to be called when the inning ended (courtesy Carl Erskine).

11. Next Year Finally Arrives

Alston and O'Malley, was obviously past his prime; in just 317 at bats, he hit .256 with eight home runs and 36 RBI. But Snider hit 42 home runs, batted .309 and garnered 136 RBI, to lead the league. Campanella had hit just .207 in 1954 after chipping a bone in his left hand in spring training, but after the season he had an operation and came back in 1955 to hit .318 with 32 home runs and 107 RBI, winning the Most Valuable Player award for the third time in five years. Furillo suffered a mid-season slump that saw his average fall to around .270 in mid–July, but he still ended up with a .314 average, 26 home runs and 95 RBI. As for the pitching, Newcombe found himself after a disappointing 1954 season; he went 20–5 with a 3.20 ERA. Labine won 13, Erskine won 11, and Billy Loes won 10. Additionally, the Dodgers got nine wins from Johnny Podres, who did not turn 23 until Sept. 30, the same day he claimed his first World Series victory in the third game. The Dodgers won the league championship by 13½ games over the Braves.

The Braves won a different battle. Their attendance totaled just over two million, about twice what the Dodgers drew. In the American League, the sixth-place A's, in their first season in Kansas City, drew nearly 1.4 million fans, 45 percent higher than the attendance during their last season in Connie Mack Stadium, which they had shared with the Phillies. The concept was emerging that perhaps it was not so wise for two teams—let alone three—to share the same aging city, when so many highly populated, faster-growing cities outside of the East and Midwest had no major league baseball teams at all. Another result of the Braves' move to Milwaukee was that the National League schedule required more flying between games. But some players initially declined to fly, and would travel between games by train. By the 1957 season, the Dodgers' no-fly group included Furillo, Junior Gilliam, Sal Maglie, and Don Newcombe. By then they were old-timers, clinging to a bygone America.

In the first game of the Series, Furillo homered in the second inning; he had also homered in his previous Series at bat, against Allie Reynolds in 1953. Nevertheless, the Yankees won the first game and the second game, both played at Yankee Stadium. Then the Dodgers won three straight at Ebbets Field. In the fourth game, Furillo did something he had not done since 1947, hitting the outfield sign that said "Hit Sign, Win Suit" with a line-drive single. "As soon as I got to first base, I got umpire Bill Summers and Coach Jake Pitler sworn in as witnesses," Furillo said afterwards. "Later on, I got Rizzuto. I think I'll probably get myself a brown summer suit. I did win one before, you know. Back around 1947, I hit the sign during the regular season and the GGG people (the firm's name) gave me a very fine suit."[13] Furillo's single was the second of his two hits. The Dodgers had 14 hits in all and beat the Yankees 8–5 to even the Series at 2–2. They also won the fifth game, 5–3, to take the

Series lead as the teams returned to Yankee Stadium for the last two games. When the Yankees won Game 6, the Series went to a decisive seventh game.

The 23-year-old Podres, who had a complete-game victory in Game 3, was again the Brooklyn starter. The game hinged on a sixth-inning play, which was preceded by Alston's fortuitous defensive maneuvering. At the start of the bottom of the sixth, with the Dodgers winning 2–0, Alston inserted Sandy Amoros in left to replace Junior Gilliam; Gilliam moved to second, replacing Don Zimmer. The first Yankees hitter, Billy Martin, walked, and the second hitter, Gil McDougald, got a bunt single. The Yankees had two on, nobody out. "Then Berra came up and he sliced it right down along the inside of the left-field foul line," Furillo said. "It looked like it was going to drop for extra bases. But Amoros turned around and took off like a shot after it, and at the last minute he stuck his glove out in front of him and he grabbed it. Then it was such a surprise that he had caught it that he threw to Pee Wee (who) threw to Hodges and they doubled the runner off first. That play really broke the Yankees' back, and we held them after that and won the game."[14]

In the ninth, Podres pitched to three hitters. Moose Skowron hit back to Podres, who ran towards first and then flipped to Hodges. Bob Cerv hit a pop-up to Reese. Then Elston Howard came up with two out. "I was the most tense I had ever been in a game or watching one," Erskine said. "I was crouched down at the inside front edge of the dugout. All my career I tried never to be superstitious but somehow at that moment, while Podres was facing Howard for the last out, I couldn't move a muscle. Jackie Robinson, who didn't play in that game because he was hurt, was on the bench behind me. He was as nervous as a cat. Howard kept fouling off pitches. Finally Johnny threw him his outstanding change-up and Howard hit a weak ground ball to Reese. PeeWee's throw was low but Hodges dug it out. We always kidded Pee Wee about the bad throw. He always said it was waist-high."[15]

Recalled Furillo, "I saw quite a few strange things when I was in Brooklyn, but I never saw anything like the celebration they had that night. If there was ever a baseball-crazy town, it was Brooklyn, and if they ever had a celebration, that was the time. The Dodgers had a party at the Hotel Bossert and we were all loaded, and I was so happy that I kissed Robinson. I never since the war heard so much noise, from all those horns and cowbells and firecrackers and everything else. People would be leaning out of the windows banging on pots and pans to make noise, and they would be yelling too. And there were all kinds of parades with automobiles and people walking, and everybody on the street and everywhere would be smiling, and all the bars and restaurants and delis were giving away drinks and hot dogs and stuff like that.

11. Next Year Finally Arrives

"There wasn't a man on that team or a fan in Brooklyn that didn't have their greatest thrill in baseball that day. I was here when the Mets won last year (1969), but I have to go with the Dodgers' win because baseball was more important then. Besides that, the Mets had only waited maybe ten years but Brooklyn must have had that team over 50 years, with all those pennants that they won, before they finally won the Series."[16]

Furillo's heartfelt move to hug and kiss both Jackie and Rachel Robinson has been cited by onetime Dodgers reporter Lester Rodney as an important symbol of Robinson's acceptance, even by players who once had doubts. "I remember the victory party at the hotel," Rodney said. "When Jackie and Rachel came in the door, Furillo was the first to jump out of his chair and run up and hug them."[17] The scene provided one in a long series of indications that Furillo and Robinson became loyal teammates who respected each other. Another indication occurred that December, when Robinson traveled to Reading to appear at a banquet in his honor given by the Reading Round Table of the National Conference of Christians and Jews. Of course, Furillo was in attendance.

In addition to the emotional satisfaction of finally winning the Series, the Dodgers players received winners' shares of about $9,700, giving Furillo a total of about $28,000 for his five World Series to that point. The day after the Series ended, he told *The Reading Times* he was ready to return home. "I'm going to do plenty of fishing and hunting as long as the weather permits, and then I'm going to hibernate for the winter," he said. "It's been a long season and I've had enough baseball—until it's time to go to Vero Beach next spring."[18] Early in 1956, Alston paid tribute to Furillo, declaring, "There's a fellow who doesn't give anybody a bit of trouble. He plays hard, never gripes, and does a helluva job. Nobody wanted to win the World Series more than he did. He's a real competitor."[19]

Was the seventh game of the 1955 World Series the greatest baseball game ever played? The case is certainly arguable, given the historic context of an iconic team with a lineup that featured three future Hall of Famers, including Pee Wee Reese, finally winning a Series after six tries against the Yankees, with a taut 2–0 game punctuated by a miraculous defensive play as the clock ran out in Brooklyn.

The game was not quite the Brooklyn Dodgers' last hurrah. They would go to the seventh game of the World Series again the following year, and they would play one more season in Brooklyn in 1957. But they had reached their peak in 1955.

12

"We're All Dagos in Here"

THE 1956 SEASON BROUGHT EVENTS that no Dodgers fan ever expected to see. The aging team managed to eke out another World Series appearance, and even came within a game of a second consecutive Series victory. It made two once-unimaginable trades with the Giants, acquiring aging nemesis Sal Maglie and later dumping Dodger icon Jackie Robinson. It played in yet another game from the list of the greatest games ever played, this one the only perfect game in World Series history. And it played home games away from Ebbets Field for the first time since 1913, as the end of its run in Brooklyn came clearly into view.

Within weeks of the 1955 World Series win, Walter O'Malley unveiled his plan for a new domed stadium. It would be located in Brooklyn and paid for by the Dodgers, and O'Malley displayed potential designs conceived by Princeton students overseen by renowned architect Buckminster Fuller. Meanwhile, as O'Malley had announced the previous August, the team was planning to play seven home games in Roosevelt Stadium in Jersey City. But the effort to secure a new Brooklyn stadium to replace aging Ebbets Field faced an implacable foe, powerful New York City building czar Robert Moses, and O'Malley eventually came to see a move to Los Angeles as the only viable outcome. For decades, O'Malley had been excoriated; more recently, however, Moses' preeminent role in the Dodgers' departure has been more fully explored, and much of the blame seems to have shifted. Still, after the first Jersey City game, on April 19 against the Phillies, "the players were mad as hell because it was a real slap in the face to Brooklyn," Furillo said. "We were just ballplayers though, so we had to play those games whether or not we liked it. To be

12. "We're All Dagos in Here"

honest with you, at that point I don't think that any of us even saw the handwriting on the wall. If you had been there, you just couldn't have been able to dream that the Dodgers would leave Brooklyn.

"The last year that all of the old Dodgers were together was 1956, because Robinson got out after that year. We were really a bunch of 'old pros' by that time. All of us who had been with the team all those years were over 30, and some like Robinson and Reese and Campanella were over 35 and getting toward the end in baseball. And then in May we got Maglie on waivers from the American League and of course Sal was no spring chicken either; he was pushing 40 by that time. I never thought I would live to see the day that Sal Maglie was pitching for the Dodgers, but he joined us that May. He and I posed for a picture with him cutting my hair, because he was 'The Barber.'"[1]

Maglie's move from the Giants to the Dodgers was extraordinary, not only because the teams were rivals, but also because Maglie's persona involved throwing close to hitters, particularly Furillo. Over the years, the two players had disliked one another, and it seemed impossible that they could co-exist on the same team. Yet on May 16, 1956, Maglie made his appearance in the Dodgers clubhouse. Tom Villante, executive producer of the Dodgers television and radio broadcasts in the 1950s, recalled that he "happened to be in the Dodger clubhouse having my pre-game sandwich and soda, compliments of Charley 'The Brow' DiGiovanna, former Dodgers batboy and now assistant clubhouse man."

"We were the only ones there," Villante recounted. "As Charlie and I were kidding around, in comes Furillo from batting practice. He goes to his locker and lights up a cigarette. His back is to the door. A few seconds later, in walks Sal Maglie carrying a white equipment bag. He stops at the entrance as he spots the big number six on Furillo's back. The Brow and I are frozen numb as we watch this scene unfold.

"Furillo turns around and sees Maglie. They glare at one another. It is a scene from 'High Noon.' The silence is frightening. God knows what's going to happen next. Suddenly The Brow yells out, 'Don't do it! We're all dagos in here!' Furillo breaks up. So does Maglie. I'm too nervous to laugh. However, the tension is broken. Furillo puts out his hand. Maglie takes it. They shake hands. From that moment on, they were the best of friends. They even became roomies."[2]

Maglie recalled the meeting with Furillo in a 1969 interview. "For some reason, he detested me and I guess I detested him and the rest of the ballclub," he said. "When I joined the Brooklyn ballclub in '56, the first fellow I met going into the clubhouse was Carl Furillo. He shook hands with me and he welcomed me to the ballclub. And he said, 'I'm very happy that you're on our side now.' It turned out that we were really close buddies on the Brooklyn ballclub."[3]

Bavasi had his own scheme to assure that the two men got along. He gave Furillo $200, a lot of money in 1956, and told him to take Maglie out for a meal at Toots Shor's, the famous Manhattan watering hole that was both a men's club and a restaurant. Furillo's initial reaction was negative. "But after Furillo concluded that dinner for two would cost only about $20 and he could pocket the remainder, he agreed to Bavasi's request," wrote Judith Testa in *Sal Maglie: Baseball's Demon Barber*.[4] According to Carl Furillo, Jr., "Bavasi said to my dad, 'I know, there's bad blood between you two, but you're taking him out to lunch,' and he handed my dad $200."[5]

Testa, who interviewed Bavasi, and Furillo have slightly different versions of the story of the meal. According to Testa, "Bavasi called Shor and told the owner to put the two men's meals on his own tab but to let the players think that Shor himself was paying for their dinners. Neither man ever learned about Bavasi's tactic, and Furillo spent the rest of his life thinking he had taken the Dodgers' general manager for an impressive sum of money."[6]

Carl Furillo, Jr., said his dad told him the meal was lunch, and Bavasi joined the two ballplayers. "When Bavasi handed Dad the $200, he said, 'Here, we're going out for lunch with Sal Maglie. You're going to pay for it, that's what the money is for.' They had lunch and Toots Shor came over; he knew who they were. When they asked for the bill, he said, 'There is no bill, it's on me.' Then when they were finished, Buzzie said something to Dad about the $200 and Dad said, 'What $200?' Buzzie laughed and told him to keep it."[7]

Testa questioned whether Maglie and Furillo ever really hated each other. As for Maglie, she writes, "It is unlikely that Maglie hated Furillo. Sal always insisted there was nothing personal in his treatment of the Dodger right fielder. He did not brush him back—or throw at him, depending on one's point of view—any more often than any of his other favorite Dodger targets, such as Reese, Hodges, and Campanella, and he liked to remind reporters that he had never hit Furillo with a pitch (although he had once, in 1950). Moreover, Maglie was a man who did not bring his on-field animosities with him into his off-field life."[8]

Did Furillo, before the trade, hate Maglie? Probably he did. Furillo was a passionate man, known to hold a grudge. Additionally, "Sal used to throw at my dad's head—that can end a ballplayer's career," said Carl Furillo, Jr. "So they were not friends, even though they were both Italians. At first, when Dad heard the rumor that Sal was coming to the Dodgers, he asked Buzzie, and Buzzie said, 'It's true,' and Dad wasn't too happy about it."[9] Testa writes that Furillo phoned Bavasi to express his displeasure when he learned of the deal. Villante says that Furillo "was greatly influenced by his old-time Italian heritage. He was suspicious of outsiders, tight-lipped, single-minded, and he did not forgive or forget."[10]

Yet once he encountered Maglie in the Dodgers clubhouse, Furillo was forgiving. "At the end of the year I went up to Sal's home in Niagara Falls for Sal Maglie Night, because we were good friends by then," he said.[11] Furillo also gave Maglie full credit for helping the team get to the World Series. "Maglie kept us on our toes," he said." He talked World Series all the time, and whenever it was his turn to pitch he said, 'Don't worry gang, I'll get them.' And he did. We couldn't have won the pennant without him."[12] Recalled Carl Furillo, Jr., "They became very close friends. When Sal threw at my dad's head, it was because he was ordered to throw at his head. When Dad passed away, Sal Maglie's wife got in touch with my mom and told her Sal wanted to be there, but he was really ill."[13] Maglie was confined to a nursing home at the time.

Furillo signed his 1956 contract in January for a slight raise, estimated to bring his salary to $33,000. (Press estimates of salaries for the top Dodgers ranged from $25,000 for Newcombe to $45,000 for Snider.) As usual, the Furillo family vacationed in Vero Beach, preceding the start of spring training in February. Furillo forecast another Dodgers pennant, and the Reading writers extolled his accomplishments. "As time goes on, the name of Carl Furillo becomes more indelibly engraved in the baseball annals of Brooklyn," wrote Bill Reedy. "With an 11th successive season for him in Flatbush coming up, the son of Stony Creek is destined to add to a mountainous list of contributions to the cause of the Dodgers."[14] By then, on a list of the all-time Dodgers leaders in ten different hitting categories, Furillo was named eight times. He was the fourth-most prolific home run hitter with 141. His .458 slugging average also ranked fourth, while his 1,490 base hits ranked third. (On April 29, he would reach 1,500 base hits.) In most cases, the players ranked ahead of Furillo in key categories were future members of the Hall of Fame. Also during spring training, Furillo, who had always swung one of the heaviest bats on the team, moved up a notch to 37 ounces, thinking he could get more hits off the lower end of the bat. Told that the extra weight could diminish his home run total, Furillo responded, "Homers don't mean money to a hitter like me—batting average does."[15] Additionally, Furillo predicted the Red Sox would "walk away" with the American League pennant and would face the Dodgers in the Series, and praised young Dodgers pitcher Don Drysdale. "Drysdale is another Ewell Blackwell, when the Whip was in his prime," he said. "The ball is up on you before you know it. I'm glad he's on our side."[16]

Maglie wasn't the only Dodger to perform well in 1956. "Newcombe had a great year, and Snider and Hodges with the home runs," Furillo recalled. "Campy had been MVP in '55, but he didn't do too much in

This Gulf Stream fishing trip in the spring of 1956 included, from left, Carl Furillo (seated), Dixie Howell (standing), Karl Spooner (seated), Carl Erskine (kneeling), Randy Jackson (standing) and Roy Campanella (kneeling at far right). The other two men are unidentified crew (courtesy Carl Erskine).

1956. I think his hand was hurting him again, but he was there when we needed him. I had a strange year. I had a 20-game hitting streak, which was my longest ever, but then I got a virus and I was out for a few days and then I played a lot more days when I should have stayed in bed. But when September came I got going. In fact, the whole team got going. I think we proved that there is nothing like experience when the chips are down."[17]

Newcombe pitched to a 27–7 record with a 3.06 ERA and became the first National League player to win the MVP and the Cy Young award in the same season. Meanwhile, Maglie was 13–5 for the Dodgers, Erskine was 13–11 and Roger Craig was 12–11. The hitters were led by Snider, who batted .292 with 43 home runs and 101 RBI. After the season ended, Furillo revealed that his performance had suffered due to a virus that raged for three weeks, during which his average fell to .228, as well as to a late-season injured elbow, after he crashed into the right field wall at Ebbets Field. Moreover, he was subject to stomach pains, which turned out to be early symptoms of appendicitis. Still, he finished with 21 home runs, 83 RBI and a .289 average. Meanwhile, Junior Gilliam played second and hit .300, while Hodges hit 32 home runs and batted .265. On the downsides of their careers, Campanella hit .219 with 20 home runs and 73 RBIs, batting just 388 times, while Robinson, by then a utility player, hit .275 with 10 home runs and 43 RBI. The team averaged .258, fourth in the league.

"They were calling us 'the hitless wonders' and they counted us out in August, but in September we hit when we had to," Furillo said. "We were in a hell of a race. It was between us and the Braves and the Reds, and that was another pennant that we won on the last day. It was because of guys like Robinson, even though he couldn't play every day and he was calling himself 'just an old gray fat man.' That year I was nothing if I wasn't a September hitter. I was glad when they said, 'Furillo is still a September hitter' and 'Furillo is still a money player.' I think that's what I will be remembered for in baseball, coming down the stretch over the years and breaking open some of those games that would mean a big game or a pennant or whatever it was for Brooklyn."[18]

This is one wish that came true. In a Sept. 11, 1969, column in the *New York Post*, Pete Hamill made the connection between Furillo and the Mets, who had just passed the Chicago Cubs and led the National League East by two games. The Cubs were managed by Furillo nemesis Leo Durocher. Wrote Hamill, a Brooklyn native, "Don't talk to me about Biafra today. Don't explain to me about General Thieu. Don't call me at home to say that Con Ed is raising its rates or that Blue Cross is going to make its third fortune or that Mario Procaccino has given up his limousine. Today, I don't want to hear anything. The Mets are leading the league.

"I don't really care whether John Lindsay is supporting Democrats, or whether the F train will be air-conditioned, or that there is a strike at the Metropolitan Opera. Will Ted Sorensen run for the Senate? Will Nelson Rockefeller make the Long Island Railroad run on time? Will the sewers of Queens survive the winter? Today I don't care. It's the month of September and the Mets are leading the league.

"Tell me where Carl Furillo is today and maybe I'll answer the phone. I'd like to take him where I'm going, to talk about all the sweet Septembers of our poor gone Brooklyn. I'd like to tell Furillo how much Tommie Agee reminds me of him, coming down that August stretch, playing it for every ounce of energy and desire and ability, breaking up ballgames, hitting in the clutch, making the old sweet dream of baseball into something real. That's a call I'll take."[19]

The Brooklyn Dodgers made their final successful stretch run in September 1956, going 18–10 for the month, and Furillo played a big role.

The team started the month in second place, 2½ games behind the Braves, with the Reds in third, 3½ games back. During the month, the Dodgers took five of eight games from the Giants, six of ten from the Pirates and two out of two from the Reds. On the last day of the season, they beat the Pirates to win the pennant by one game over the Braves. "Carl Furillo, Brooklyn's chips-down old pro, banged out his 20th home run to lead off the 10th inning tonight to give the National League-leading Dodgers a 5–4 victory over third-place Cincinnati," *The Associated Press* wrote, following a Sept. 17 game.[20] The game-winning homer came after Furillo had driven in two runs with a first-inning single; the victory was the fourth in a row for the Dodgers and gave them a full-game lead over Milwaukee with 11 to play. "The clutch-hitting old pro has been in the headlines these past two weeks as the Dodgers battle to retain their National League championship," wrote *Reading Times* columnist Doc Silva a few days later. "Five of the World Champions' last 11 triumphs have been decided by Furillo's clutch bat."[21] Those wins included a game where Furillo broke up a 1–1 tie with the Cubs with a two-run, eighth-inning double, and another where he hit a two-run, 11th-inning homer against the Giants.

The following spring, Furillo told Dick Young that had he not become ill with the flu in August, he would have won the NL batting title. "I was hitting .320—and that was climbing—when I got the virus, and then the appendicitis pains," he said. "Not much more than that won it, did it?" (Henry Aaron led the league with a .328 average.)[22] Wrote Young, "Furillo ran into a series of misfortunes during the last six weeks. First, he was bitten by the virus bug. Then he felt 'gas pains' that turned out to be a festering appendix which led to a post-season emergency operation. Toward the end, Skoonj cracked into the right field wall and injured his left elbow.

"'I shouldn't have been playing then,' said Furillo, 'because I couldn't swing a bat, it hurt so bad. Alston asked me if I could play the outfield and I told him I could. He said then he wanted me to play, because he needed me out there, and if he got to the point where a hit would mean the game, and I was up, he'd put a hitter in for me.' So virtually a sure out, Furillo played—and his average dwindled to its ultimate .289. 'Then, when it's all over,' Furillo said with a sarcastic grin, 'they tell me I've had a bad year, and I hear how I'm old and slipping and not so good anymore.'"[23] Furillo's point that spring was that he was he was not too old to play for the Dodgers. "What's all this talk about trading me because I'm getting old?" he sniffed. "That's all I keep hearing. I'm so old that I would have won the batting title if I didn't get sick in August."[24]

In the World Series, the Dodgers again faced the Yankees. In a ceremony before the first game, Furillo and other members of the team

12. "We're All Dagos in Here"

Carl Furillo returns to the dugout after a key play (in 1956 or 1957). Greeting him are Don Drysdale and an unidentified teammate (back, left to right), Johnny Podres, Sandy Koufax, Rube Walker and Walter Alston (front, left to right) (National Baseball Hall of Fame Library, Cooperstown, New York).

shook hands with President Dwight Eisenhower. "He sure is a nice gentleman," Furillo said. "He just had time to say hello to most of us, but he warned Campanella to be ready for his pitch from the box seats, on account of he might not reach (him)."[25] The Dodgers won the game 6–3, as Maglie beat Whitey Ford and Furillo got his 28th World Series hit in 100 times at bat.

The next day, *The Reading Times* reported that Furillo had put his Stony Creek Mills home on the market. He and two longtime friends, both godfathers of his sons, planned to open a restaurant and cocktail lounge called "Carl Furillo's" on Jericho Turnpike in Long Island. "I've decided it's time I began planning for the future—I can't stay here forever," Furillo said. "No, I have no intention of quitting baseball—at least while I'm a major leaguer, and I figure I've got three or four years ahead of me." In the end, the planning yielded no return; it was years before the house sold, and the restaurant never opened. Furillo also said he would quit the game "when I leave Brooklyn. I wouldn't consider playing minor league baseball. I'd be a fool to go down to the minors. When a ballplayer does that, after years in the majors, he knocks down any reputation he might have earned."[26] Less than three years later, in a heated conversation with Buzzie Bavasi in a Los Angeles office, Furillo would in fact refuse to go to the minors, triggering his decade-long exile from baseball.

The Dodgers won the second game even though Newcombe gave up six runs in the first two innings, and the Yankees won the next two. In the fifth game, Maglie pitched even better than he had in the first, giving up just five hits and two runs. But he faced Don Larsen, who was perfect. "Maybe that sort of broke our backs," Furillo said. "We won the (sixth) game 1–0 on a single by Robinson in the tenth, but in the seventh game they murdered us."[27] It was a 9–0 rout. After seven Subway Series in ten years, New York would not see another one for 44 years.

Later, Furillo said the tough September pennant race simply took too much out of the aging Dodgers. "Our guys were beat when the Series came," he said. "We had all been under terrific strain. After we won the first two games, I thought we might make it, but it didn't turn out that way. We were just too tired to be real threats." Still, "we got a pretty good check from that Series," Furillo recalled. "The amount had been going up every year. I got about $4,000 and some in my first three, and then $6,000 in '53, but by '55 and '56 you were getting $9,000 to $10,000. I always used to save that World Series money for a fallback when I hung up my spikes, and I could see that my time was coming. I had no intention of quitting baseball or anything like that, I figured I had a few more years ahead of me, but I also thought by that time that I ought to begin planning for the future."[28]

Two days after the Series ended, the Dodgers left Idlewild Airport for Los Angeles, from where they would fly to Japan on a good-will trip. During the layover, O'Malley met with a Los Angeles city councilman who was seeking to facilitate the team's move. The trip lacked appeal for many players, and nine stayed home. They included Maglie, Charlie Neal, Sandy Koufax, and Furillo. Furillo offered various explanations for not going. During the season, he declared, "I want no part of it. I've seen Japan (during the war) and there's nothing there that I want to see again."[29] Later, he would add that his wife had a medical procedure scheduled, and that he disliked flying because it provoked air sickness. Weeks later, on Dec. 4, Furillo went to the hospital in Reading for an emergency appendectomy, making him particularly glad he refused to make the trip. "I might be in a Tokyo hospital right now, if I had made that trip," he said, a week after the operation.[30] Later, Furillo recalled, "It turned out that I had been slowed down considerably the year before because of my appendix, that I had some of those poisons running into my system during the season, which did a lot to slow me up. In fact, I set the Dodger record that year for grounding into double plays (27), and the reason was that I just couldn't run. I didn't have any power in my legs by the end of the season. I was hitting the ball a lot, but I didn't get what I could from it."[31]

Despite the benefits that accrued from staying home, "I think O'Malley took some offense, and they were talking about trading me again," Furillo said. "And sometimes looking back I wish they had traded me, especially at that point" because of the friction that developed in his final days with the team.[32] A trade was discussed that would have sent Furillo, Gino Cimoli and others to the Phillies for Richie Ashburn and Harvey Haddix. After the report surfaced, Furillo received a letter of encouragement from Roscoe McGowan, a sports writer for the *New York Herald Tribune*. "Every spring or summer, the Dodgers put you up for sale, but when the chips are down you are the one player who contributes most to the club's success," McGowan wrote. "Have no fear. I don't believe Brooklyn has any intention of trading or selling you. The Dodgers need you in right field."[33]

But the Dodgers were not averse to trading veterans. On Dec. 13, 1956, the team announced it had traded Jackie Robinson to the Giants for Dick Littlefield and $30,000. Robinson told Giants owner Horace Stoneham that he was not sure he would play. It turned out he had made a deal with *Look* to announce his retirement in the magazine and planned to go to work as an executive for the Chock Full o' Nuts restaurant chain. In January, the magazine article came out, Robinson announced his retirement from baseball, and the trade was voided.

13

"I Should Never Have Moved Out There"

THE SAD END OF THE BROOKLYN DODGERS FRANCHISE followed quickly on the 1957 season, which was largely a walk-up to an all-but-foregone conclusion. The march was inexorable, consisting of dozens of events including the 9–0 loss in the seventh game of the 1956 Series, the trade of Robinson, the games in Jersey City and the team's disappointing play in 1957. A common response, among those who lived through it, or played through it, was numbness. For the first time since 1948, the Dodgers did not finish first or second, and were not involved in a September pennant race. Their attendance was about one million, which included crowds at several games played in Jersey City. For the last game the Dodgers ever played in Brooklyn, when they beat the Pirates 2–0 on Sept. 24, attendance totaled just 6,702.

During spring training in 1957, O'Malley announced that he had bought Wrigley Field in Los Angeles as well as the Los Angeles team in the Pacific Coast League. "Once O'Malley made that announcement, there came to be an unhappy feeling that ran all through the team," Furillo said. "We were all getting on in years and we didn't play baseball as well as we used to, but I wouldn't say that the idea of moving was any help to us. We were in the race for a while, but then around August everybody but the Braves starting losing steam, and they went way out in front. I had a good enough year, I hit over .300, but I missed quite a few games. Pee Wee and Campy didn't play them all either, and Robinson was gone and Maglie was sold to the Yankees that year. So the team was changing—not just the place, but the players too. And a lot of the younger players who were coming up weren't ready to fill in yet."[1]

On May 28, 1957, the Dodgers and the Giants received permission from the National League to move, contingent on their moving together. On August 19, the Giants announced that they would play in San Francisco in 1958. O'Malley, however, waited for an October 7 vote by the Los Angeles City Council, enacting a city ordinance enabling the city to turn over a 300-acre Chavez Ravine site to the team for a new ballpark. On October 8, the Dodgers issued a brief press release, which read, "In view of the action of the Los Angeles City Council yesterday and in accordance with the resolution of the National League made October first, the stockholders and directors of the Brooklyn Baseball Club have today met and unanimously agreed that the necessary steps be taken to draft the Los Angeles territory."[2]

That season, Furillo signed for $33,000 in early January, and headed to Florida early for his 12th season with the Dodgers. "He believes the Dodgers can make it three pennants in a row if the pitching improves," Silva wrote. "Johnny Podres certainly will aid the staff, according to Furillo."[3] Furillo also told Silva he expected to have a big season, though he realized that he had to start slowly following an appendectomy. "He figures that with a break here and there he will satisfy himself and the Brooklyn front office with his play," Silva wrote. Yet Silva also wrote, ominously, that Furillo's "many friends ... are concerned over the 34-year-old outfielder's future."[4] Their concern, it turned out, was warranted. For the season, Furillo hit .306, but batted just 395 times, hitting 12 home runs with 66 RBI. It was clear that he, along with most of his contemporaries, was slowing down.

Still, the season had its high points. On May 14, Furillo hit a single and a double at Milwaukee, giving him 1,667 major league hits. That placed him tenth among active players. The other nine, in order, were Stan Musial, Mickey Vernon, Enos Slaughter, Ted Williams, Pee Wee Reese, Red Schoendienst, George Kell, Del Ennis, and Richie Ashburn.[5] It is worth noting that seven of the nine are now in the Hall of Fame. In his first 27 games of the season, Furillo had 29 RBIs. By early June, he led the league in RBI. But later that month, Furillo was on the bench, diagnosed with anemia in the middle of a 2-for-53 hitting slump.

In August came an interesting juncture, as Furillo mended the fence with Leo Durocher. "Leo Durocher and Carl Furillo, arch-enemies since they clashed in a brawl at the Polo Grounds late in 1953, patched up their differences on television, August 3," read a report in *The Sporting News*. "The former Giant manager, now NBC 'Game of the Week' telecaster, interviewed the Dodger outfielder on his pre-game show. After the pair shook hands, Durocher asked why Furillo had 'charged' him to set off the celebrated rhubarb. 'I had been hit by the pitch and I saw fire,' Furillo replied.[6] When Furillo died in 1989, Durocher was quoted as making kind remarks.

Toward the end of the season, Furillo ramped it up once again. Furillo "has been swinging the hottest bat on the club for more than a month,"[7] wrote Roscoe McGowan in *The Sporting News* on Sept. 18, following a night when Furillo went three for four with a home run. By hitting .401 during August and September, Furillo managed to maintain his lifetime batting average at .300 for 12 big-league seasons. But this was a September when the Dodgers were not really in the race. They began the month seven games behind first-place Milwaukee and never got closer than six games out. "A little bit of everything happened to the Dodgers, but mostly it could be traced to deterioration of a ballclub which stayed together too long," *The Sporting News* summarized on Oct. 6. "They seemed to miss the leadership of the retired Jackie Robinson. Gil Hodges was the only season-long hitter. Carl Furillo hit a terrible slump in June and July, finally banged out of it but too late. Roy Campanella no longer is an iron man. The failure of Don Newcombe and Sal Maglie to win even half as many games as they did a year ago was the final touch to the collapse."[8]

Overall, Snider hit 40 home runs and 92 RBI while batting .274, and Hodges hit 27 home runs and 98 RBI while batting .299. Campanella slumped to .242 and Reese hit .224; each batted 330 times. The pitching staff was led by Don Drysdale, who went 17–9. The only other double-digit winners were Podres, who was 12–9, and Newcombe, who was 11–12. Sandy Koufax was 5–4, while Maglie won six games before being traded. Drysdale, a California native who would flourish in Los Angeles, had joined the team in 1956, going 5–5 his first year. He retired in 1969. Recalled Furillo, "When he retired, I read they asked him, 'Well, Drysdale, what was your biggest thrill in baseball?' and he said, 'Just being on the field with Reese

Don Drysdale, Fern Furillo, Carl Furillo and Ann Meyers Drysdale gather in a post-career reunion. Drysdale once said his biggest thrill in baseball was to be on the field with the Brooklyn Dodgers greats, including Furillo (Furillo family photograph).

and Snider, Campanella, Erskine and Furillo and all of them that first time I got to Vero Beach—that was my biggest thrill.'"[9]

The Dodgers finished third, 11 games behind Milwaukee and three games behind the St. Louis Cardinals. "Most of what we talked about during the year was moving to Los Angeles, and it didn't seem as if anybody wanted to go there too much, except that a few of the boys who lived in California sort of liked the idea," Furillo said. "Mostly the players were used to Brooklyn and New York and liked it there. A lot of us had business or friends there. Hodges married a Brooklyn girl and lived there year-round, Campy had his liquor store and a home that he had just bought on Long Island, and I was going to move in. Whenever we had one of those discussions about it I would end up saying, 'What's the sense of worrying about it now? We don't know what's going to happen next year.' And there was a joke going around that if we won the World Series again they would give us Yankee Stadium and we wouldn't have to move.

"The final announcement came that October while the Yankees and Braves were playing in the Series: the Dodgers were leaving. So you ask yourself, 'What can you do?' but there was nothing. I went home and went hunting the same as ever, and I signed my contract for $33,000 just like always, and I (prepared to go) to Vero Beach for spring training, and then to go to Los Angeles to play baseball."[10] Longtime Dodgers writer Dick Young wasn't sure how well that would go for Furillo. On Oct. 16, he wrote, "Skoonjy is one of the real pluggers that The Faithful will miss. He's a bit earthy for the Los Angeles hoop-tee-doo, and you may hear about an occasional flare-up in print when Carl answers stuffy questions with his four-letter pungencies."[11]

On Jan. 27, 1958, as the Los Angeles Dodgers prepared for their first spring training, things went from bad to worse. That evening, a car driven by Roy Campanella, who was on his way home to Long Island from his Harlem liquor store, skidded on the ice and crashed into a telephone pole, leaving Campanella paralyzed. It was hard to miss the symbolism.

Furillo was close to Campanella. They fished together, their families knew one another and before each game they would warm up by playing catch. During the 1958 season, Furillo said, "We went to cheer him up at the hospital a few times, like one day we were rained out in Philadelphia and a bunch of us went to see him. It really hit you when you went in there. He didn't have too good of a season that last year in Brooklyn, but in 1957 he was the Dodger catcher and in 1958 he was not, after being the catcher, day in and day out, for ten years. And here is a man that loves to play baseball and everything else and he finds out he can't move, and he has to teach himself everything he knew all over again. But the thing about Campy was he was a guy that never got discouraged. He would always be cheering up other guys in the clubhouse, and he was able to stay that way enough to get himself moving again after he had that accident."[12]

During spring training, Dick Young caught up with Furillo in Vero Beach. "Furillo is a realist," he wrote. "There is small sentiment in his makeup. He has often said he is in baseball for the buck, but now, in the last days of his career, he is not ashamed to show his emotions: not extremely, just a bit. 'It's funny to say Los Angeles Dodgers,' he said. 'I find myself saying Brooklyn Dodgers most of the time, and people correct me. You know who it's gonna be hardest on? The kids. The kids in Brooklyn. Just before I left, I was talking about it with my wife. We wondered about the kids who used to come to the games, and what they're going to do now. What's going to become of the Knothole Gangs?'"[13]

Adjusting to Los Angeles was difficult. "In Los Angeles, we were strangers," Furillo recalled. "The cops and the kids and the writers and the people on the street didn't know us like they did in Brooklyn." The team missed Campanella. "And the Coliseum we played in was a football stadium. It was not a baseball park.

"You take someone like Duke Snider. He couldn't stand the place. Snider was a left-handed hitter and he used to hit to right center for home runs. He must have had 40 every year for the five years before we moved. Then we got out there and right center was over 400 feet away, so he couldn't get but ten or 15 home runs all year. He was calling it 'the snake pit' and he began to wonder about did they want him on the team or didn't they. And he said, 'I'm just one of the hired help' because it seemed like they didn't care. One day he even strained his arm trying to throw a ball out of the Coliseum, because he was beginning to think that was the only way he could ever get one out.

"The left-field fence in the Coliseum was just the opposite; it was about 250 feet and the shortest one I ever saw in the major leagues. To keep you from bunting the ball into the seats they put this screen up there, called 'the Chinese fence,' to raise the height. But it didn't help much, and it bothered the pitchers because it was so easy to hit a home run over it. That would give them all high earned run averages, which hit them right in the pocketbook. So then everybody expected the Dodgers' right-handed power hitters, I mean mostly Hodges, to hit about a hundred home runs over the damn thing. That put a lot of pressure on Gil. When he didn't come through as much as they wanted, they booed him, which was something that in his whole career had never happened before in his home park."[14]

Nevertheless, in May, Furillo defended the Los Angeles Dodgers from Jackie Robinson's charge that the Dodgers had "deteriorated." Robinson also "claimed that Walter O'Malley has lived off Branch Rickey's team and that the Dodgers had now 'deteriorated.'"[15] The charges were triggered when O'Malley accepted an award from the Urban League. "Robinson's quotes had scarcely hit the newspaper before an old teammate, Carl Furillo, answered the rap. "I don't see where he gets off calling us a deteriorated team," said Furillo, who broke in with the Dodgers a year before Robinson. "He'd blow his stack if anybody said that about us when he was with the team."[16] A few days after making the charges, Robinson apologized, and Rickey issued a statement saying it was appropriate for O'Malley to accept the award in behalf of the team.

Of course, the Dodgers had deteriorated. They finished seventh in the eight-team league. Their 71–83 record made 1958 the team's worst season, and its first time below .500, since 1944. "It was the lowest I ever finished in baseball," Furillo recalled.[17] But the Los Angeles fans didn't seem to mind. Attendance rose 80 percent to a little over 1.8 million from a little over 1 million in 1957, partially because the Coliseum had a capacity of around 92,000, compared to about 32,000 at Ebbets Field.

On the field, just four regulars—Snider, Hodges, Gilliam and Furillo—were left from the Brooklyn days, and Furillo and Reese were the last Dodgers remaining to have played for Larry MacPhail. In his last good season, Furillo led the team in RBI and had the highest average among the players with more than 400 at bats. He hit .290 with 18 home runs and 83 RBI, played in 122 games, and came to bat 411 times. Snider hit .312, batting 327 times, but hit just 15 home runs. Hodges hit .259 with 22 home runs, tying him with second baseman Charlie Neal for the team lead. A young shortstop, Don Zimmer, hit .262 with 17 home runs. Junior Gilliam batted 555 times and played outfield, third base and second base, while Reese played in just 59 games, batting 147 times and hitting .224. Johnny Roseboro was the primary catcher. Among the pitchers, Podres was 13–15, Drysdale was 12–13, Koufax was 11–11, and Stan Williams was 9–7. Erskine, nearing the end, went 4–4 with a 5.13 ERA, while Labine was 6–6.

"The move west was a mixed bag," Erskine said. "The old guard 'Boys of Summer' had already had their best years, so it was a real challenge to go to L.A. and be the kind of team and players we had been for a decade in Brooklyn. On the other hand, players like Drysdale, Podres, and particularly Koufax were on the brink of greatness and were younger with much of their career ahead of them, so their feeling was quite different.

"We all, however, felt a sense of history to be playing for the first time on the West Coast. Much history had happened already to this team: we went from day baseball to night baseball, trains to planes, radio to TV and had been a part of the Jackie Robinson experience all in the previous decade, and now were the first team West. I was honored to be chosen to pitch the first game in Los Angeles and get the first win."[18]

As the first season in Los Angeles came to an end, Furillo planned a return to his home in Stony Creek Mills, where his house was still unsold. But when Bavasi approached him about remaining in Los Angeles and working for the team, which planned to mount a marketing offensive, Furillo's financial preoccupation was fully engaged. It is important to remember that during the 1970 interviews, his conflict with the Dodgers was very clearly in Furillo's thoughts, and so he seemed to recall in particular detail the conversations that preceded it.

"One day that fall, before the season was over, Bavasi comes up to me and he asked me, 'What do you intend to do when the season is over?'" Furillo recalled. "'Nothing much, except do a lot of hunting and that back home,' I said. 'Loaf around, that's all—keep myself in shape.' And that's what I should have done. I should have gone back to Pennsylvania and stayed there. But he said to me, 'How would you like to work for the ballclub?' 'Well,' I said, 'That sounds all right too, providing the pay is pretty good, because you know you have to consider that my family is in Pennsylvania and I'll be living here.' 'Well,' he said, 'Why don't you move your family out?'

"I should never have listened to him. I should never have moved out there. But I did, and I didn't go hunting or hiking or stay in shape over the winter, and that was how my legs softened up. At the time I just didn't realize what had the potential to happen, or I never would have done it. But I wasn't thinking, and I said to him, 'Who's going to pick up the tab?' I said. 'That's a long haul to get everything ready and move the family out here and all.' And he said, 'Don't worry about it. I'll work something out with you.'

"So all right, my wife and I get the kids ready and everything else, and we get a big moving van. And in the meantime I had found this place in Manhattan Beach and bought it. We still had the home in Pennsylvania, and we kept it. But we moved out there and I went to work for the Dodgers organization in L.A., and they used us as good will ambassadors. There were about four or five of us and we went around to different factories and different hotels where they had big functions. We were trying to sell baseball there."[19]

14

Number Six Passes On

AT THE START OF SPRING TRAINING in 1959, Furillo revealed a side of himself that no one had seen before. He called Ron Fairly, the rookie who was his heir apparent as the Dodgers' right fielder, and asked him to go fishing. "I got a phone call from Carl prior to spring training, and he said, 'Do you like to fish?'" Fairly recalled. "I said 'Yeah,' and he said 'Do you want to go to spring training a couple of weeks early and do some fishing and work out?' So I went early—How can you say no?"[1] Throughout the season, Furillo mentored Fairly, offering clues on how to play right field, analyzing pitchers, signaling where he should play during games, and talking to him afterwards about his performance. Fairly was so grateful that he later wore Furillo's number six in tribute.

Fairly was a hot prospect who had played for the University of Southern California in the spring of 1958, signed with the Dodgers immediately afterward, played briefly in the minors and was called up by the Dodgers at the tail end of the 1958 season. One day he arrived at Connie Mack Stadium in Philadelphia to join the Dodgers. "When I got there, I was in awe of the names: Furillo, Hodges, Snider, Erskine, Labine, Bessent, Newcombe, Pee Wee Reese," Fairly said. "I was in awe of these guys and yet I was wearing the same uniform." On Fairly's first day with the Dodgers, he watched the brief conclusion of a suspended game in the afternoon. "I sat in the dugout, Philadelphia at the plate with the bases loaded, Larry Sherry pitching and Wally Post hit the first pitch on the roof to end the game," he said. "I said to myself, 'Oh my god, one pitch— what did I get myself into here?'"

The next evening, Fairly went out to right field to warm up, and had his first extended conversation with Furillo. "Only the two of us were there," he said. "Carl says to me, 'Ron, I want you to know one thing here. They tell me you're pretty good. I don't know. I haven't seen you enough. I am the right fielder on this team. You can have right field when I'm finished with it, but I'm not finished with it yet.' That was my introduction to Carl Furillo. It scared the hell out of me. Carl was very strong. I said, 'Yes, sir.' During the remaining few weeks of the 1958 season, I got to know Carl just a little bit. He told me a few things about certain ball parks, like how the ball caroms off the wall. Obviously, I paid attention to him."

In the spring of 1959, both men arrived early at Vero Beach, per their agreement. "Carl and I would work out in the morning and fish in the afternoon," Fairly said. "In the workouts, he would hit me ground balls in the infield and talk to me about how to field. The idea was to get your feet in position to throw. I would throw them to the batting cage area. Little by little, he would hit harder and harder, and I would throw the ball, and he would say, 'You have to read the ground ball, read the bounce.' Once he thought I could do the foot work, he said, 'Now go to the outfield. Now you have twice the distance to figure out the bounce of the ball, the speed of the ball, do the timing, so you can get yourself in position to make the throw.' Apparently, after I went fishing with him, he decided I could play a little bit. He said here's a young kid that I can help a little bit. He ended up being a very good friend of mine."[2] In a spring training report in *The Sporting News,* Joe King wrote, "Warmest story of the training season, east or west, is the friendship of the 37-year-old pro, Carl Furillo of the Dodgers, and the 20-year-old rookie, Ron Fairly, who hopes to take Carl's job."[3]

Fairly was not expected to stick with the Dodgers in 1959, although he was on the April roster when the team carried 27 men before being required to cut back to 25. But that month, Furillo pulled a calf muscle, Snider had water on the knee and Fairly emerged as one of the league leaders in hitting. The combination of events enabled Fairly to remain on the Dodgers roster, and to continue to absorb Furillo's wisdom. "When he found out that I could play, he was a mentor," Fairly said. "He would say, 'Okay, this guy you're hitting off today, here's what he likes to do,' and he would give me an idea of what the pitcher was going to do. In the outfield, he would say, "There are two guys in the lineup that spray the ball around, hit to right center, you may want to shade that way a bit.' And when certain guys came up, I would look into the dugout, and he would signal to me to move.

"Carl always used to say that when you had runners in scoring position, the more RBI you could get and the more money you're going to make. He kept talking about that. He was one heck of a competitor, and when he wasn't playing, he was always concerned about World Series money and about whether I was helping to win ballgames so he could get it. He came up to me one day, around the batting cage, and he said, 'You're in the lineup today. You're dealing with my money. Do something about it.' The thing is he wasn't kidding. I played that day and I made a very good defensive play. I went 0 for 4, but twice in the game I came to bat with nobody out, and I advanced runners from second to third. When I got back to the clubhouse when the game was over, Carl came up to me. He patted me on the back and said 'Nice going' and he meant it. He knew that even though I was 0 for 4, I had made a good defensive play and I had moved runners along. They both scored. I had good at-bats, and we won the ball game.

"So he would compliment me if I did something well, and if I didn't, he would say, 'Listen, we talked about this, here is something you should do.' He probably talked to me the most about playing the outfield. One thing he said was 'Don't try to get too smart. When the ball is hit to you, a ball down the line that bounces off the fence and you have to throw to a cutoff man, just get it back to the infield as quickly and accurately as you can. Throw it accurately to the cutoff man and let him try to figure out what to do with it. Then you've done your job.'

"Carl didn't like that I was taking his job, but he was injured. He wasn't fast anyway. His nickname was Skoonj—he was a snail. He knew his career was winding down, but he was like an old warrior. He was not going to give up. That's how tough of an individual he was. I could see it in him: 'I might be older, but that doesn't mean you are better, just because you are younger.' He was a tough man—like he said, 'You can have right field when I'm finished, but I'm not finished yet.' He used to call me 'the college hot dog.' He would say 'Let's see what the college hot dog has to say.' He had a good knowledge of baseball. Maybe he wasn't educated in school, but he was nobody's fool. He had a lot of street smarts, a lot of common sense."[4]

If the principal reason the Dodgers drew fans in Los Angeles in 1958 was because they were a novelty, the situation changed dramatically in 1959, when they became World Series champions. They also became the first team to finish seventh one year and win the Series the next. The stunning reversal caused a transition in the perception of the team, from the former Brooklyn Dodgers to an entity that belonged to Los Angeles, complete with new stars such as Wally Moon, Larry Sherry and Fairly, as well as emerging stars like Drysdale and Koufax, who had played only minor roles in Brooklyn. Attendance totaled 2.1 million, twice what the team drew to Ebbets Field in 1957 and about 265,000 more than the Ebbets Field record of 1.8 million in 1947.

By 1959, the old Dodgers were fading fast, although some played a role in the march to the World Series, including Hodges and Snider, the two leading home run hitters. An inspiring tribute to one of the old gang came on May 7, when the Dodgers and Yankees staged an exhibition game to honor Roy Campanella. The game, attended by 93,103 fans, provided a moving tribute to the great catcher. But Furillo paid a price because during the game he was hit in the ribs by a fastball thrown by Yankee pitcher Ryne Duren, and was out from May 7 until June 11. Later in the season, he injured and reinjured his leg, and he played only 50 games during the season.

In the post-season, however, the 37-year-old veteran returned to provide two of the most glorious "old pro" moments in baseball history. First, he clinched the victory in the final game of the National League playoff between the Dodgers and the Braves, who finished the regular season tied for first. In the second game of the best-of-three series, with the Dodgers up by a game, Furillo had two key at-bats: a sacrifice fly to tie the game in the ninth and a 12th-inning single to win it. Then, in the first World Series game ever played in Los Angeles, he had a pinch-hit, two-run single with the bases loaded and two out in the seventh, breaking up a 0–0 tie and driving in enough runs to ensure a victory.

By the time he arrived in Los Angeles, Carl Furillo was an "old pro" on the Dodgers. Here he is shown on Topps 1958 (left) and 1959 baseball cards (courtesy Topps Company).

14. NUMBER SIX PASSES ON

Taken together, the impact of Furillo's moments approached the impact of the most stunning old-pro moment of them all, when 39-year-old Grover Cleveland Alexander entered the seventh game of the 1926 World Series, striking out Tony Lazzeri with the bases loaded in the seventh inning and then getting the Yankees out in the eighth and ninth to win it. Furillo's hits provided a last hurrah not only on a personal level, but also for the Brooklyn Dodgers, a team that had played in six World Series in ten years and knew something about rising to the occasion. Along with a game-winning eighth-inning home run by Hodges in the fourth game of the Series, they represented the last moments in the sun for everyday players from the team's glory decade, 1947 to 1956, although a trio of pitchers who got their start in Brooklyn—Koufax, Drysdale and Johnny Podres—went on to star for the Los Angeles Dodgers.

At the start of the 1959 season, "I figured I still had something left," Furillo recalled. "I wasn't ready to hang them up yet, and I saw where they made Reese a coach that year. I figured I would still hit okay, and I wanted to keep my lifetime average at .300 because you end up with very few that hit .300 for their lifetime average, especially with all the years I put in. I was never a home run hitter, but I still ended up with 192 and I guess I would have liked to get maybe another eight home runs to make it 200. But to my sorrow I hadn't kept my legs in shape that winter, and it came back to haunt me early that season one day at first base.

"At the time I was going to the outfield and I ran across first base and I stepped out there where the grass and the ground combine. There was a water puddle or something there; I hit that and my leg went down. That's when I tore the main muscle in my left leg. Afterwards, I could only do mostly pinch-hitting that year, and I could only play about a quarter of the games. And a lot of times I could only go as far as first base and then they would have to put in a pinch runner for me. But most of the hits I got were clutch hits that won ballgames."[5] Among the hits was a ninth-inning double on Sept. 20, when Alston summoned Furillo to pinch-hit for Snider in a game against the Giants. With two out, the Dodgers were leading 4–2; at the time, they led the Braves by a half-game and the Giants by a game. Furillo's hit drove in a run and triggered a four-run rally for an 8–2 pennant-race victory. For the full season, Furillo played in only 50 games and went to bat 93 times. His average was .290 and he had 13 RBI, but for the first time as a Dodger, he failed to hit a home run.

Unlike the preceding season, in 1959 the Dodgers sought to use the Coliseum to their advantage. They came to rely on strikeout pitchers and on left-handed batters who could hit to the opposite field, rather than home run hitters. At the end of the 1958 season, they traded Gino Cimoli for Wally Moon, who managed to perfect an inside-out swing that let him take advantage of the short left-field porch and hit .302 with 19 home runs. They were called "Moon Shots."

Reese had retired at the end of the 1958 season after 16 years—and seven World Series—to become a coach. Although they led the team with 25 and 23 home runs respectively, Hodges and Snider were playing in fewer games. Prospect Norm Larker often spelled Hodges at first. Given Furillo's frequent absences, Fairly and Snider played right, as Snider sometimes moved back to his original position so that Don Demeter could play center. Generally, Neal played second and Gilliam played third, while a young Maury Wills came up from Spokane in June to replace Don Zimmer at shortstop. Johnny Roseboro was the primary catcher.

The pitching staff was led by Drysdale, who went 17–13, Podres, who was 14–9, Danny McDevitt at 10–8 and Roger Craig at 11–5 and a 2.06 ERA. Koufax was 8–6 with 173 strikeouts in 153 innings, while Labine had nine saves to go with his 5–10 record. Sherry, who would become a World Series star, also came up from the minors during the season. Don Newcombe had been traded to the Cincinnati Reds in 1958. And Carl Erskine would voluntarily retire on June 15, with the team languishing in fifth place.

By then, it had become clear to Erskine that the Brooklyn Dodgers era in general, and the era of Carl Erskine and Carl Furillo in particular, was coming to an end. "Newcombe was traded, Reese was retired, and we were old guys," he said. "We were the boys of summer, but it was late winter for both of us. The nucleus of the team that won the Series in 1959 was in the minor leagues the first part of the season. Wills, Sherry, and Roger Craig all came up in mid-season, took us out of fifth place and won the Series. So there was a psychological change happening; the old guard was passing."

Erskine had pitched 15 seasons, counting minor league time, in a career filled with arm problems. "I knew in the spring of 1959 that my arm trouble was not going to let me be the pitcher I had been," he said. "I had a poor spring and, after the season started, I was sure it was time for me to hang 'em up, but my teammates kept insisting that I should stay, so I continued to pitch and not win. That was a mistake because I ended up giving up runs that increased my final ERA to 4.00. I had pitched ten seasons in Ebbets Field and had a respectable era of about 3.80, so my instincts were right."

By mid–June, Erskine had an 0–3 record and a 7.71 earned run average, and he went to see Bavasi. "I knew the club had to make changes," he said. "So I said, 'I can't throw in the bullpen, my arm can't take it. What can I do?' Buzzie said, 'I don't want to release you.' At first he said, 'Go to Spokane, and I will bring you back up at the end of the season. You've got almost 10 years of credit (in the pension plan); you are 28 days short, and if you go to Spokane, then when I increase the roster I will bring you back and you can get 28 days.' I was short because I had come up midyear in 1948, but I had an arm injury in 1949, and I went back to Fort Worth and had to pitch my way back. Then I went to Montreal in 1950. So I had broken up my time, and didn't get credit for it. But still, I said, 'Buzzie, if I go to Spokane, (manager) Bobby Bragan is going to pitch me, he probably needs pitching, and if I could pitch, I want to pitch here. But I can't pitch; my arm won't let me do it, so why should I go there?' So then he said the only real opportunity for me is to voluntarily retire, 'but if you do I will keep you around the rest of the season as a coach and I will pay your salary.'

"When Bavasi went out of the room for a minute, I had a meeting with myself. I said, 'Two years from now, will you say, 'I could still pitch some?' You have to be honest with yourself: you can't pitch. You can't say two years from now that you could still have pitched.' I had no plans for a post-baseball life; I had started at 19 and I was 32, I had four kids, one with Down's Syndrome. But I decided to retire. I retired on June 15, and I stayed through the end of the year. They brought Roger Craig up to replace me, the Dodgers won the World Series against the White Sox, and I got a check and a ring. So I have the only World Series ring for the Brooklyn Dodgers, and the first World Series ring in Los Angeles."[6]

The story of Erskine's decision is pertinent because 11 months later, Furillo would be in the same position, faced with the end of his career. It appeared he would have the opportunity to reach an accord with Bavasi, who seemed predisposed to help ease the path out of baseball for veteran Brooklyn Dodgers players. But Furillo, not convinced he could no longer play, would approach the decision-making differently. No doubt Furillo's starring postseason role, when he was once again critically important to key Dodgers victories, just as he had been throughout his career, indicated he could still hit and made it all the more difficult to accept that he no longer fit in the Dodgers' plans.

After a tight three-way pennant race, the Dodgers ended the season tied with the Braves. The Giants were third, three games out. Again, the Dodgers prepared for a best-of-three playoffs, eight years after their dramatic playoff loss to the Giants. Again, the Dodgers won the coin flip. But this time they elected to play the first game on the road with the next two at home. In the first game, they beat the favored Braves 3–2 in Milwaukee.

In the second game, in Los Angeles, the Braves led 5–2 with Lew Burdette pitching as the game entered the ninth, and many fans departed early, in a pattern that came to characterize Los Angeles Dodgers baseball. Then the Dodgers struck, running the score to 5–4 with Hodges and Larker both on base. Warren Spahn came in from the bullpen to pitch, and Furillo pinch-hit for John Roseboro. Furillo hit a sacrifice fly to deep right field on a low, outside pitch, scoring Hodges to tie the game at 5–5.

In the bottom of the 12th inning, with the game still tied 5–5, Furillo came up again. This time, Hodges was on second, Joe Pignatano was on first and Bob Rush was pitching for the Braves. Said Furillo, "I hit a hard ground ball right over second base, between the shortstop and the second baseman. The shortstop (Felix Mantilla) moved way over and got it behind the bag, but his throw from there was bad and it went past the first baseman and into the dugout. It would have been a hit anyway, but this way Hodges ran all the way home from second and the game was over. Reese was coaching at third then and he was so happy he was running down the line with Hodges. That was the only playoff we ever won."[7]

In the World Series, the Dodgers faced the Chicago White Sox, making their first appearance in the Fall Classic since the 1919 Black Sox scandal. It would be another 46 years until they returned. Furillo, by contrast, was playing in his seventh World Series in 14 years in the majors. He, however, would never return. The teams split the first two games in Chicago before moving to Los Angeles.

The third game was the first World Series game to be played in the Coliseum, and an all-time Series record crowd of 92,394 showed up. (The record was eclipsed by a few hundred in each of the next two games.) In the bottom of the seventh inning, with a scoreless tie, the bases loaded, and two out, White Sox manager Al Lopez brought in Gerry Staley to pitch, and Alston brought in Furillo to face him. "I took the first pitch and then I hit the next one to the same place as (in the second playoff game), right over second base where the shortstop couldn't get to it," Furillo said. "I thought he was going to reach it, but it must have taken a hop over his glove or something because the next thing I knew it was out in center field and we had two runs, and that was enough to win the game."[8] Each team scored a single run in the eighth inning, making the final score 3–1.

The next day, *The New York Times* termed Furillo "the game's hero" in a cutline for a story that began "Carl Furillo, once again the 'man who' in the clutch for the Dodgers, admitted afterwards that he thought his tie-breaking single was going to be gobbled up by Luis Aparicio.[9] 'I hit (Gerry) Staley's sinker pretty good, but it looked like Aparicio was going to get it,' Furillo, the eldest of the active Dodgers, told a dressing room audience. 'Then I guess it took a hop over his glove.'"[10]

The story quoted Alston as saying he chose Furillo to pinch-hit with the bases loaded because "I needed a man who doesn't strike out and can get the line-drive single" and said that Furillo "virtually duplicated the pinch hit he got in the 12th inning to beat Milwaukee 6–5 in the final National League playoff game last Tuesday."[11] Furillo was given one more chance to star in the bottom of the eighth inning of the fifth game. With the Sox nursing a 1–0 lead, he pinch-hit with the bases loaded. Dick Donovan came in to face him, and he popped out, enabling the White Sox to stay alive for one more game.

Years later, Furillo recalled the aftermath of the third game. "Those fans in Los Angeles went crazy. They were up two games to one in the Series and they had just won their first game at home. And naturally, you feel real happy after doing something like that, breaking open a big important baseball game with a base hit at the right time."[12] The Dodgers lost the fifth game 1–0 despite a strong outing by Koufax, but won the sixth game 9–3 in Chicago. It took the team 65 years to win a World Series in Brooklyn, but in Los Angeles, it had taken just two.

Fairly, meanwhile, recalls the post–Series meeting of Dodgers players, called to decide who would get full Series shares and who would get less. Furillo objected to paying full shares to players who had not made a full contribution, saying they should get "oogatz." It was customary for Furillo to utter the rarely used word, which means "nothing" or "nada," during such meetings, Erskine said. After the 1959 season, Fairly saw little of Furillo. Fairly went into the Army Reserve, returned for a few days of spring training in 1960, and then spent the 1960 season in Spokane. When he returned to the Dodgers in 1961, number six was available. "I asked (clubhouse man) John Griffin if I could have it, to wear it in honor of Carl and to show the respect I had for him," Fairly said.[13] Ironically, when Furillo learned that Fairly had taken his number, he was angry, thinking that the Dodgers had arranged it as a slight. But soon afterwards, Carl Furillo, Jr., recalled, Sandy Koufax called and said, "Carl, don't be upset with Fairly—he asked for that number as a sign of respect."[14] Afterwards, Furillo felt honored.

15

The Game Turns Sour

In 1960, Furillo returned for his fifteenth and final season with the Dodgers. He lasted only until May 12, when he was released in an ugly separation that provided an unfortunate conclusion to an outstanding career and, sadly, came to define his post-baseball life. Furillo might have spent the next three decades as a veteran from an iconic team who went on to another career in baseball when his playing days ended. It is not difficult to imagine him as a coach teaching hitting, fielding, and work ethic. Not only was he a lifetime .299 hitter, but also, because of a strong right arm and hard work, he made himself into one of the best right fielders in baseball history. One can easily picture him coaching third base for the Dodgers, or perhaps for the New York Mets, where former roommate Gil Hodges was the manager, providing another link to an historic legacy as he judged the capacity of an opponent's right fielder to throw out a runner at home, just as he had often done. Had Furillo been with the Mets in 1969, as the team captivated New York with its run to a World Series victory, everybody would have benefitted: Furillo, the Mets, the baseball fans of New York and baseball itself. Instead, he became an exile, working his way through a variety of unglamorous, more difficult occupations: co-owner of a kitchen cabinet business, co-owner of a delicatessen, construction worker, deputy sheriff and security guard.

The most unfortunate thing about this chapter in Furillo's life is that it need not have ended the way it did. Neither Furillo nor Buzzie Bavasi behaved wisely as the end of Furillo's career played out in the spring of 1960. Their most important failures occurred at critical meetings on Monday, May 9, and Tuesday, May 17. At the first meeting, Bavasi did not want to tell Furillo directly that his release was imminent two days before it occurred. When Furillo formally learned of the release on Friday, May 13, he allowed his displeasure to escalate, and moved too quickly to mount a legal challenge. Then, at their most crucial encounter on May 17, both men were angry, to the point that the confrontational environment precluded the possibility of agreement. At both meetings, Furillo actually seemed to reject the very sort of opportunity he later sought. Various factors contributed. He could not bear to see his career ending, the new opportunities may not have been made clear to him, and financial barriers hindered his ability to accept them. In retrospect, these barriers were not insurmountable.

To reiterate, Furillo had concluded the 1959 season as a hero, the old pro who had won both a playoff game and a World Series game with late-inning clutch hits. On Jan. 18, the team signed Furillo for the same $33,000 he had earned the previous year. That spring, "I went to spring training camp at Vero Beach long ahead of time on my own to get my legs in shape," Furillo recalled.[1] In fact, he arrived in camp nearly a month ahead of the Feb. 29 report date, and he worked out every day after arriving. Still, his legs were giving him trouble. After pulling a calf muscle in his left leg during the 1959 season, he favored the left leg and the right one got hurt too.

Despite his spectacular postseason, his new contract and his eagerness to prepare for the season, Furillo was battling the odds as he sought to make the Dodgers roster. At 38, he was the fourth-oldest player in the National League, eclipsed by only Bud Byerly, Stan Musial and Dave Philley, according to a story in *The Sporting News*, which reported that "Carl Furillo at 38 is making the last stand after an unhappy season with injury, but one capped by old-time clutch hitting at the close."[2] He was the oldest player on an aging team, at a time when Dodgers management wanted the team to get younger. "Furillo Fights to Keep Dodger Job" was the headline on a *Los Angeles Times* story on Feb. 28. The story began, "The day of reckoning is at hand for Carl Furillo, one of the noblest Dodgers of them all."[3] It quoted Bavasi as saying, "'Furillo is the biggest question mark in camp. I know it's a hard thing to say of a man who has done so much for the club, but Carl will have to produce to stay with the Dodgers. We've got some fine young outfielders coming up and we can't afford to carry Furillo—or anybody else for that matter—out of sentiment and loyalty.'"[4] Furillo grinned in response. "I've gotta bear down and battle these kids," he told reporter Frank Finch, as he mopped his brow after a long session in the batting cage.[5]

Quietly, Bavasi was seeking to trade Furillo. Had Bavasi succeeded, Furillo might have concluded his career with the New York Yankees or the Boston Red Sox. On Feb. 24, Bavasi wrote to Roy Hamey, assistant general manager of the Yankees. The letter, written on Atlanta Crackers stationery, said, "I am headed for Vero Beach but meantime I thought I would drop you a line regarding Carl Furillo. I have in mind trying to go with two young outfielders which would of course make Furillo available. As we discussed Carl before, I thought perhaps Casey (Stengel, Yankees manager) might still be interested." Bavasi went on to say that he also intended to talk with Red Sox General Manager Bucky Harris about Furillo, "due to the fact that (outfielder Jackie) Jensen seems to be serious about his retirement," and concluded by saying "I will be in Dodgertown next Monday."[6]

Hamey responded in a March 7 letter, saying, "Have your letter at hand regarding Furillo. At present we do not have any interest as we are going to try to give one or two of our young outfielders a real good shot." Hamey went on to say that he was still seeking players for the Yankees' minor league team in Richmond, naming some available minor leaguers including outfielder Bob Martyn, who "wants to play on the coast."[7] Four days letter, in a March 11 letter to Bavasi, Bucky Harris wrote, "Not interested in outfielder Furillo. However, would be interested in Hodges, Howard and Davis."[8] Needless to say, Bavasi had little interest in trading Frank Howard and Tommy Davis, who were future stars. It is unclear why he did not deal Hodges, who was made available to the Mets in an expansion draft at the conclusion of the 1961 season. In any case, Furillo remained with the Dodgers. In a March 9 story in *The Sporting News*, Bob Hunter wrote, "Carl Furillo's status was a problem, but the ol' pro seemed to be solving this for Alston and Buzzie Bavasi by hitting and running as though he never had a bad leg that limited him to 50 games last season. 'I wish I knew what to do with Carl,' said Bavasi. 'Perhaps this would be the time for a youth transfusion. If Furillo stays with us, he must play. He can't sit on the bench with a bad leg and do us justice. Besides,' continued Bavasi, 'to keep Furillo means a year longer delaying the promotion of the Tommy Davises, the Frank Howards and the Carl Warwicks.'"[9] Alston, meanwhile, said Furillo was hitting the ball better than anyone in the camp.

Though he may not have known specifically of the letters to the Red Sox and Yankees, Furillo was well aware that something was up. That spring, he discussed his feelings with Jimmy Cannon, a veteran columnist employed by *The New York Journal-American*. In a column that was not published until after Furillo was released, Cannon wrote that Furillo felt "the Dodgers were through with him."

Cannon described an encounter with Furillo. "I met Furillo outside of the mess hall of the renovated Navy base where the Dodgers train in Vero Beach," Cannon wrote. "'Let's get out of here,' Furillo said. 'I got something I want to tell you.' He led me into the parking lot. 'They're giving it to me,' Furillo said. 'Who?' I asked. "Buzzie Bavasi,' said Furillo. 'He wants to get rid of me.' 'What about Walter Alston?' I asked. 'What's he got to do with it?' Furillo said, bitterly. 'He just does what they tell him to. Buzzie wants to get rid of the old-timers. I can still play, but you know this cheap outfit. They want the kids not getting the money.'"

Furillo told Cannon that he wanted to be traded to Milwaukee, where Charlie Dressen was the manager, and he asked the writer to communicate his wish to Dressen. "I told Dressen what Furillo had told me," Cannon wrote. "'They won't deal with us,' said Dressen. 'But I hear Furillo can't walk.' He changed the subject." Cannon summarized it this way: "I carried the message, but Dressen ignored it."[10]

Furillo's son Carl Jr. recalls that, as late as April, Dressen and the Braves appeared to be interested in his father. He recalls a day when his father came home and said to his mother, "'Do you want to go to Milwaukee?'(and) Mom said, 'If that's what you want to do.' She left it up to Dad.

"But the whole thing kind of blew up," said Furillo Jr. "After that Dad came home furious because the Braves wanted Dad, but Bavasi had told them the Dodgers were not letting Dad go because he's too valuable. This was about three weeks prior to his release."[11] Bavasi's apparent reluctance to deal with the Braves is understandable, given that the Dodgers and Braves had just played in the 1959 National League playoffs and might again have become competitors for the National League pennant. In a *Sporting News* story on April 6, Hunter reported that Giants coach Hank Sauer had made an inquiry about Furillo, but that Bavasi said he would not trade Furillo to the Giants under any circumstances. Added Alston, "It makes me feel better just to look down the bench and see Furillo sitting there," given his pinch-hitting abilities.[12]

Still, it did not take long for Furillo's season to turn sour. On April 19, playing against the San Francisco Giants in the Dodgers' sixth game, Furillo tore his calf. "I hit a triple against the Giants and I went into third standing up, and right away I felt the leg tightening up again," Furillo recalled. "I could hardly stand up."[13] He was removed by Alston in the seventh inning. The next day, April 20, Furillo made his last appearance as the Dodgers right fielder. He was hitless in two at-bats before coming out of the game because the pain was too severe for him to continue. He sat on the bench for a week before returning as a pinch hitter, but went hitless in pinch-hitting appearances on April 28, April 30, May 2 and May 3. In the May 2 game against the Reds, the 16th game of the season, he pulled a muscle in his right leg while running to first base. Sometime during the next several days, Furillo declared that his leg was so painful that he couldn't get out of bed, but then "I rested it for about a week and I think it was coming around again," he said.

On Saturday, May 7, in the eighth inning of a game the Dodgers were losing 2–1 to the Phillies, Furillo pinch-hit for Norm Larker with two men out in the bottom of the eighth inning. He singled to center field, enabling Wally Moon to score from second base. The game remained tied until the 11th, when the Dodgers scored again to secure a 3–2 victory, which meant that fittingly, in his final major league appearance, Furillo got a clutch hit and an RBI that enabled the Dodgers to win a game. For Furillo, RBI were by far the most important baseball statistic, the ones that most heavily influenced the number on his Dodger's contract each year. "They pay off on RBI," he would say. For the 1960 season, he would record two hits and one RBI in ten at-bats.

On May 8, Furillo injured his leg again, this time during the pre-game warm-up. "I could hardly move (the leg) anymore," Furillo said. "I went to the clubhouse and I told Alston and the doctor, that my leg was hurt pretty bad." He was examined by Dr. Robert Kerlan, the Dodgers physician. "All that doctor bothered to do was touch it with his finger, he didn't even take an X-ray, and he said, 'This leg is shot,'" Furillo recalled. In fact, Kerlan determined that both of Furillo's legs showed extensive wear and tear as a result of a 15-year major league career.

On May 9, Furillo was called to the office to see Bavasi. He said his leg was "coming around and that in about another week or so I'd be ready to play." According to Furillo, Bavasi responded, "What I would like you to do is take it easy and make sure it's all right, but I would like to have you for June and July." At the end of the conversation, Furillo recalled, Bavasi said, "If you can't do it, let me know and we'll find something else for you."[14] Furillo, who said Bavasi told him several times that he would have a lifetime job with the Dodgers, assumed the promise was still in place.

Bavasi had little interest in keeping Furillo on the active roster. Rather, he was preparing to release him and to provide him—as promised—with a job in the Dodgers organization. The Dodgers record had dipped below .500 on May 3, and was 11–12 on May 9. By then Bavasi had "decided to bring more youngsters to the club," he wrote, in a 1961 letter to commissioner Ford Frick. "Carl was unable to run and throw the way he used to and he was not pulling the ball at all," Bavasi wrote. "I talked to Carl. I told Carl what I had in mind. I told him I would use him as a swing man in our scouting department. I would name the players I wanted him to look at—Tommy Davis, Carl Warwick and other outfielders—and I thought he could help them in their defensive play. This would have eventually worked into something that Carl could do for us in the future. Of course, it would have been impossible for me to pay him $33,000. He would have received his release, his month's severance pay and then we would negotiate a contract on the basis of a scouting

In his final season as a Los Angeles Dodger, Carl Furillo came to bat just 10 times. In his final at bat on May 7, he got a clutch hit and an RBI that enabled the Dodgers to win a 3–2 game against the Phillies (National Baseball Hall of Fame, Cooperstown, New York).

job."[15] At the time, the annual salary for scouting jobs was in the $7,500 to $10,000 range, representing a precipitous drop in income.

It is not entirely clear what was said in the May 9 meeting. Of course, a man hears what he wants to hear, and it may have been that Furillo did not want to hear what Bavasi was saying. Or it may have been that Bavasi chose not to say exactly what he was thinking, which is that he was about to place Furillo on waivers for the purpose of giving him his unconditional release. No doubt Furillo was reluctant to concede that his skills had diminished to the point that he could no longer play for the only major league team that had ever employed him. The history of sports is replete with painful tales of athletes who could not discern the end when it arrived. Somewhere in Furillo's mind, it no doubt seemed only yesterday that he was a young star in Montreal, 20 years old, with money in his pocket, handsome as could be, his innocence not yet contaminated by four years of combat, making head-first slides and adored by fans who read about him in two languages. "All in all, those were the years I really loved," Furillo said, long afterwards.[16]

Given his obvious failure to communicate on May 9, Bavasi sought to enlist newspaper writers to carry out the unpleasant task of making it absolutely clear to Furillo that his playing career had ended.

On the evening of May 9, Furillo returned to the ballpark and ran into Bob Hunter of *The Los Angeles Examiner*. Furillo recalled, "Hunter said, 'I hear you were up at Buzzie's office.' So I was sort of stunned, and I said, 'What are you talking about?' He said, 'I called Buzzie right after you left, and Buzzie said you were out. He mentioned something about he would like you to go into voluntary retirement.' So I got mad, I got really hot, and I said, 'He told me not to say a word about it.'"

Soon afterwards, Red Patterson, the team's vice president of public relations, appeared and spoke with Hunter about Furillo's retirement. "Red Patterson says (to Hunter), 'This is something new to me,'" Furillo said. "So I didn't say anything. I went back and I went out and I pitched batting practice that night. Afterwards, Red Patterson called me and says, 'Buzzie wants to talk to you.' Then Buzzie said, 'The newspaper writers are trying to stir something up here.'" Bavasi compared the situation to one earlier in the season, when word had leaked out about his plans to release Sandy Amoros and Rip Repulski. According to Furillo, he said, "Look, I didn't say nothing. As far as I am concerned, nothing happened. You just go about your business."

The following night, May 10, Bavasi asked Furillo how he felt, and Furillo said, "I feel pretty good. The leg is coming around good, I'm running better and everything else." On May 11, the third night in the sequence, Bavasi again approached Furillo, who reiterated the favorable prognosis, but "it dawned on me then that there's something in the wind,"

Furillo said. Then Bavasi mentioned that *Los Angeles Times* sportswriter Mel Durslag wanted to speak with Furillo after the game. During that conversation, Durslag asked Furillo what he intended to do as far as his career, and Furillo responded, "I intend to keep playing ball because my leg's coming around good, and I have another few years to go."

"And he says, 'Well, I'm supposed to talk to you about it.' I said, 'Who asked you to talk to me about it?' 'Bavasi,' he said. In other words, Bavasi wanted somebody to feel me out and see what was what." When Furillo inquired what Bavasi had said on the topic, Durslag responded that "he would like you to go on voluntary retirement."[17] According to the transcript of the hearing, Furillo responded, "Well hell, I've been talking to him for three days. All he said was 'Be ready for June and July.' Then he says, 'If you can't do it, then I will put you on voluntary retirement.'" But when Furillo said he wanted to keep playing and asked for Durslag's opinion, Durslag responded, "I think you're foolish to quit. If you feel that way about it, keep going."[18]

Midnight on May 11 was the deadline for National League teams to reduce their rosters to 25 players. That evening, Bavasi notified the commissioner's office that he was asking waivers on Furillo. This was not immediately made known to Furillo or to the public. Instead, on Thursday May 12, an off day for the team before a road trip to San Francisco for a weekend series, Furillo went to the Coliseum to work out. "I worked out in the outfield and I was running real good," he said. "Joe Becker was there and Bobby Bragan. So Bobby says to me, 'Hey dago (they called me "dago"), how is your leg?' I said it feels so damn good I feel like playing up at Frisco because they were (starting Mike McCormick) on that Friday."[19] But Furillo received a series of mixed signals from team officials, including Alston, who told him he didn't need to be there because the workout was for players who needed batting practice, and coach Joe Becker. When Furillo told Becker he planned to ask Alston to play him Friday night in San Francisco, Becker said that would not be necessary, that he would tell Alston that Furillo felt he was ready to play. That Thursday marked the last time Furillo would suit up for the Dodgers as an active player.

The next day was Friday the 13th. That morning, Furillo received a phone call from Lee Scott, the Dodgers' traveling secretary, who told him not to pack for San Francisco and to await a call from Bavasi. Later on, Bavasi called. "He says, 'I've decided to release you,'" Furillo said. "I say, 'Thanks.' He says, 'Be in my office Tuesday.'" Within two hours, a group of reporters, photographers and television cameramen had converged on Furillo's house, saying they had heard he had been released.

"My living room looked like a studio," Furillo said. "All the lights were shining and everything else, and as I told you I would get a little uneasy feeling from the lights and the television camera and all of that." A television reporter kept insisting that Furillo had gotten "a dirty deal," and some of the reporters recommended that Furillo hire an attorney. As the interviews continued, "they were all trying to put words in my mouth," Furillo said. "And they asked me, 'What do you intend to do if they don't offer you a job and all, if they just drop you?" He responded honestly, if not discreetly. "They can't, because I'm injured. The contract says that when you're injured, they're responsible for it, they have to take care of all the injuries." It wasn't long before Furillo had retained Redondo Beach attorney Arthur Cowan to advise him.[20]

As in any dispute, the suggestion of an attorney's involvement altered the emotional landscape. "Words led from one to the other and it got a little bitter," Furillo said. "Then the following day, there comes a statement in the paper, Bavasi with a nasty remark about Furillo. He says, 'Well, if that's the way he feels about the whole thing, he's finished.'" So this went on until I saw him on (May 17) Tuesday nasty stuff going back and forth. And when I went up to see him on Tuesday, there was a cold reception all the way around." Furillo maintained that during the time he was in Bavasi's office, Dodgers attorney Harry Walsh, stationed in an adjoining room, listened to the conversation. Walsh was the brother-in-law of Walter O'Malley.

"The first thing that happened was that Bavasi got a little nasty. He said, 'Well, of all the goddamned bullheads you take the cake.' I said, 'I didn't start this. You started it.' And he said, 'Well, you're going to get exactly what's coming to you. Here's your release and $5,000, and that's all you're going to get.' That $5,000 was just the salary that he owed me and my 30-days' pay for severance, which I was entitled to under the contract if he was giving me my unconditional release.

'But I had prepared myself for this. I had a letter in my pocket from my attorney which was to notify Bavasi of an injury, which the contract calls for. So I said 'Wait a minute, Buzzie. Before you go any farther I got a piece of paper here for you.' That piece of paper stated, 'We are notifying you of injury.' So that's when he hit the ceiling. That's when he offered me a job to go and play with Spokane, Washington, which is Triple A. And I said, 'Yeah, I'll go. I'll go on one condition.' He says, 'What's that?' And I said, "That you abide by my contract first.' The contract specifies that in case of injury the ballclub is responsible for medical and for the year's salary. If he did that, it would have given me the full 15 years on my pension. And that pension is strictly major league; if you go in the minor leagues you are dead."[21]

Honoring the contract for the full year would have meant medical coverage, a full-year major league salary and inclusion in the pension plan at the 15-year level. At 14 and a quarter years, Furillo said in 1970, the pension was worth about $680 a month, compared with around $750 a month at 15 years. But a 1968 report in *The New York Times* said the difference was just $30.[22]

"Bavasi was real bitter then, because of the press and everything building the whole story up. And he said to me, 'I'm giving you what's coming to you and that's it.' That's when Mr. Walsh stuck his head through the door. 'I want him to sign this paper,' he says. It was releasing the Dodgers from paying anything more to me. But I said, 'I won't sign nothing. You abide by my contract first. Then I'll sign.' So Bavasi says, 'You know I can't, since I've already given you that release. You've got what you're getting from me and that's it.' So I said, 'All right then. From now on if that's the case, then you'll hear from my attorney.'"[23]

As Bavasi remembered the meeting, "I returned to the office on May 17 and Carl came in to see me. He did not feel he should accept the job of scouting for the club at a lesser salary than he was receiving as a player. I then offered to send him to Spokane as a player at the same salary he received from the Dodgers. Carl refused due to the fact I could not guarantee his pension, which of course I had nothing to do with. He then threw the enclosed copy of a letter from his lawyer on my desk."

Bavasi went on to deny the suggestion that he could have put Furillo on the disabled list. He said that was impossible, "first, because I already had one man on the disabled list and I didn't want to take on a second man as I might need the space later on (and) secondly, I doubt very much the commissioner would permit me to place a man on the disabled list, as the day (May 7) I talked to the commissioner about this, Carl got himself a base hit and drove in a run, which of course does not make the theory that Carl is disabled stand up."[24]

On May 19, provocative Furillo stories ran in three L.A. papers. In *The Los Angeles Examiner*, the headline read: "Furillo Considers Suing Club." The story quoted attorney Cowan as saying that under his contract, Furillo could be released only if "he violated the rules of good citizenship, his playing was below standard or he refused to play." Additionally, Cowan said, "the contract provides that if a player is injured while playing for the club, he will receive his full salary and be entitled to the player pension benefits." Cowan said Furillo had refused to accept the release Bavasi offered and had instead handed Bavasi a letter saying he injured his right leg while running to first base on May 2. He said the next move would be to seek a hearing before Commissioner Ford Frick. Cowan also told *The Examiner* that "the contract provides that if a player is injured while playing for the club, he will receive his full salary and be entitled to the player pension benefits."[25]

Furillo told the newspaper he had spoken to Dressen, and that Dressen had said, "I'd like to have you, but I can't take you now. I just cut down to the player limit." Furillo said he was bitter that he had been placed on the waiver list just hours before teams had to cut their rosters to 25 players. "That's a helluva way to treat a player who has given a club 14 years of service," he said.[26]

That same day, under the headline "Mrs. Furillo Prefers to Have Carl in Outfield, Not Home," *The Los Angeles Times* ran a story about Fern Furillo's reaction to her husband's release. From her words, her husband's shock and pain at the end of his career are clear.

"To say that Carl's release came as a surprise would be putting it mildly," she said. "He was stunned. Only last Monday, May 9, Buzzie Bavasi had assured Carl, 'Don't worry; you'll stay on the club. We'll use you to pinch it. Just so you're ready by June or July. When you feel you can't do it any longer, come to me.'

"Carl isn't bitter; he's hurt at the callous treatment. I think he feels the Dodgers just wanted to get rid of him, for some reason. Maybe he didn't see eye to eye with the management. He hasn't said much about it, but I know that the only time Walt Alston has spoken to him in the last three weeks was when he wanted him to pinch hit. He sat on one end of the dugout bench and Carl on the other, and when he wanted Carl to hit, he'd just call 'Furillo!' Sometimes, Carl didn't hear and one of the other players would tell him. The first time Mr. Alston had anything to say to Carl in three weeks was Thursday, May 12, when he said, 'If I'd caught you last night, I'd have told you there was no need to come down to practice this morning.'

"There was no outright disagreement about anything. But Carl has said all along that this club is a changed one from last year. There are others getting the cool treatment. Look how they forgot Chuck Essegian until he hit that home run. Baseball people have short memories. Carl was a hero in the World Series but you're a hero today—and a nothing tomorrow." Essegian hit two pinch-hit home runs in the 1959 Series, then hit an 11th-inning home run to win the 1960 opening day game in Los Angeles, but he came to bat only 79 times for the 1960 Dodgers.

Fern Furillo also referred to the Spokane offer, saying her husband "had 14 good years with the team. I'd hate to see him go to Spokane, that's humbling himself. He says, 'If I felt 38, I'd shut up. But I feel good.' He's working out on a playground now to keep in shape. He's the type who'd play on crutches, just to play. He loves baseball. It's his life."

Despite everything that was happening, Fern Furillo's words also made clear another side of her husband's personality, his innate capacity to accept whatever life brought him. She described his words after the phone call from Bavasi telling him that he was being released and need not make the trip to San Francisco, when his first words were: "Guess I'll have to watch that San Francisco series on TV, honey."[27]

15. THE GAME TURNS SOUR

A third Los Angeles newspaper, *The Herald-Express*, published the column in which Jimmy Cannon at last felt free to reveal the discussion he had with Furillo during spring training. In one section, Cannon wrote about Furillo's distrust of management, a working class perspective that on occasion, particularly after Rickey left the Dodgers, seemed to boil over in Furillo. Cannon seems to have somewhat overstated, however, when he wrote, "It started wrong for Furillo and ever since he came to Brooklyn, he has been a hostile man who worked for people he mistrusted.

"The same attitude prevailed during Furillo's 15 years with the Dodgers. He despised the people he worked for, but his hate didn't influence his playing. They won a pennant with him leading off and another when he batted fourth. But nothing ever diluted Furillo's resentment against his bosses. Of all the managers he played for, Dressen is the only one he regarded as a friend."[28]

Perhaps Cannon, a long-time New York writer, allowed his city's resentment over the Dodgers' departure to influence his view. In fact, in another story the same day in *The Los Angeles Times*, Furillo was quoted as saying that Dressen and Shotton were his two favorite managers. (He played three and a half years for Shotton and three for Dressen.) In any case, Cannon also said of Furillo, "Any club could have hired him, but they all passed. If his legs hold up, Furillo is worth a shot. No one plays baseball harder than this bitter man."

One additional point in Cannon's column highlighted the personal resentment that had arisen between Furillo and Bavasi, whose decade-and-a-half-old cordial relationship had totally deteriorated. Cannon wrote that Furillo charged Bavasi with not providing a winter job he had promised. He quoted Furillo as saying that Bavasi "promised me a good job with the club in the winter. I moved from Pennsylvania to Los Angeles. I figured I'd make good contacts working for the club in case I want to go in some business. I moved my whole family out. But Buzzie didn't give me the job. All he wants to do is get rid of me."[29]

On May 23, Bavasi sent Furillo a letter, objecting to the allegation in the Cannon column that "you came out here with the understanding you were to have a job—and you did not get it. You know this is a downright lie. You worked for the club the first year we came out and last year you told Red (Patterson) you had a job with an electrical company and could not work for us.

"I not only gave you a job but gave you $2,000 to pay for having your furniture sent out here," Bavasi wrote. "I do not mind your criticizing the organization, but I think you should tell the truth. If I did not give you a job and you did not work for the club, then you should be fair with me and return the $5,100 you received during the winter 1958-1959. I have the cancelled checks showing you received this amount."[30]

If it is difficult in hindsight to ascertain exactly what happened that May, that should not come as a surprise. It was also difficult at the time. "Carl said he had been mixed up from the start," wrote Bob Hunter in 1961. "I can understand that because when he was released by telephone on May 12, 1960, I had been told four different stories too."[31]

Carl Erskine, a friend to both Bavasi and Furillo, regretted what he saw happening. "To me Buzzie, and I dealt with Buzzie for ten years or more, was sort of like one of us," Erskine said. "He was a paid employee. I don't think he had a history of playing favorites. I feel like the Dodgers played it straight, the ownership at that time was sensitive about their players. I can name several guys who fell on hard times, and the Dodgers took care of them." The circumstances of Erskine's own release, 11 months earlier, indicated that Bavasi was eager to arrange a mutually satisfactory separation from the team. "I knew the Dodgers, and how they treated me, and Bavasi was consistent in how he took care of players," Erskine said. "Carl Furillo was a solid Dodger history guy, and they were going to treat him right."

Nevertheless, it was a different time in baseball, when teams felt they had no obligation to consider players' wishes or their emotions. "In those days, there was usually no diplomacy to releasing a guy," Erskine said. "The elevator guy might tell you. The club didn't want it to leak out, so they wouldn't say anything, even to the player. I was on the elevator once with Enos Slaughter, and somebody told him in the elevator that the Cardinals had just traded him to the Yankees (in 1954), and he was devastated."

"What happened with Carl, and I felt I knew him as well or better than anyone on the team did, he was so upset they were going to release him. His emotions got to him, more than his head. He exacerbated the situation. He and Bavasi, with whom he had worked a number of years, had a couple of quotes in the paper. I don't know which started what. But it was a newspaper fight, and once it got out in the open, Carl got entangled in what he believed. He was a strong-willed guy, but he was also a sensitive guy, and he thought he was being pushed out.

"It's just a fact of life; careers only last so long. Carl was taken with the fact that he could still hit, and that was a problem. His legs were gone, he couldn't run and he couldn't play defense, but put him at the plate, and he was a great hitter." Had the designated hitter existed at the time, Erskine said, Furillo would have been a natural.

Erskine even sought to advise Furillo in a letter: "I said to him, 'the Dodgers have a history of taking care of their own. So cool it; work with them; don't go public anymore.' But it didn't register with him. He felt that he'd been jilted, that baseball had turned its back on him. I didn't want to see his strong-willed side make him do things to taint his outstanding career. To take it to the level of suing baseball, I didn't want to see that."[31]

16

Outside Looking In

SUDDENLY, AFTER A LIFETIME IN BASEBALL, Carl Furillo was on the outside. The next 13 months would be consumed by an ugly fight against the Dodgers and eventually against Major League Baseball, even though, within a few months of his release, the Dodgers agreed to pay his full 1960 salary. (Unfortunately, $5,500 went to attorneys' fees.) Furillo was particularly embittered by his inability to find a job in baseball. He came to believe that this failure resulted from an organized effort by the 16 major league clubs to blacklist him, and he raised the charge publicly. He also believed that his continuing injuries ought to require the Dodgers to pay him for 1961 as well as 1960. On June 16, 1961, the various charges were heard by commissioner Ford Frick at a New York hearing. Frick, who of course was employed by the owners, found that Furillo was neither injured nor blacklisted, although he noted that his findings "are not to be construed as prejudicing any compromise or settlement that may have been heretofore offered."[1] The Dodgers, it seemed, had sought in their way to find a compromise. But Furillo went into exile, largely because he was as always unwilling to compromise when he felt he was right. For the next decade, he had almost no contact with baseball.

On May 31, two weeks after Furillo was released, attorney Arnold Cowan wrote to Frick, advising him of the dispute between Furillo and the Dodgers. In responding, Frick "suggested that Cowan explore the possibilities of settlement of Mr. Furillo's differences with the Los Angeles club."[2] On June 10, Cowan responded, saying a settlement was out of the question. On June 22, Cowan followed up. According to Frick's testimony, he "posed the question whether or not I felt I could undertake to resolve this dispute as an impartial arbitrator (since) an appeal may be taken to the commissioner on disputes between player and management."³ Frick assured Cowan that he would be able to act impartially.

Shortly thereafter, Furillo severed his relationship with Cowan, paying him $500. In Cowan's place, he retained Paul Caruso, a high visibility Los Angeles sports attorney who had represented the Los Angeles Rams when they went on strike in 1956. The change reflected Furillo's determination that he needed an attorney who was more aware of the specifics of baseball contracts, combined with a friend's recommendation of Caruso. A few other factors may also have figured into the change. For one, Bavasi would tell author Bill Ninfo years later that, in trying to assist Furillo, "I even got him the second lawyer."⁴ One other thing Furillo mentioned later, in an indication that Cowan was not such a good fit: "All I can see is this guy knows a lot about sailing and all that kind of stuff."⁵

On his first meeting with his new attorney, Furillo said, "I'm having some trouble with the ballclub (and) I'd like to go through this contract," which he had in his pocket. Caruso responded, "No. I don't want the contract. I know that contract inside out." Caruso went on to say, "You're in the right, 100 percent. You were injured and you're entitled to a certain amount of money which they're supposed to pay you." Furillo also told Caruso that if the injuries he incurred while playing baseball continued into a second year, then he should also be paid for that year. "By common sense, if the injury goes into '61 then they have to pay me for '61 too," he said. "And Paul said to me, 'We can draw a two-year salary from them.'"⁶ Although the concept was counter to all existing precedent, it was not illogical.

In an early conversation between Caruso and Bavasi, Bavasi said Furillo had refused to go to Spokane and therefore was not entitled to any money. But in July, Caruso went to the Dodgers' offices to meet with Bavasi and quickly worked out a deal. Furillo was visiting family members in Pennsylvania when Caruso called to say that Bavasi had agreed to pay the full year's salary for 1960 in two installments, one in 1960 and the other in 1961.

In retrospect, the agreement was hardly surprising. Despite the illwill surrounding Furillo's release, it seems clear that Bavasi never envisioned cutting him off with nothing more than one month in severance pay. Bavasi had consistently sought to keep Furillo in the Dodgers organization, either as a scout or as a player in Spokane. Unfortunately, neither offer was made at a time when the likelihood existed that Furillo would accept.

The Erskine precedent offered a template. But closing out Furillo's career presented far more obstacles than closing Erskine's. First, Furillo's performance in the 1959 postseason, followed by his clutch hit in the May

16. OUTSIDE LOOKING IN

7 game, seemed to indicate he could still play—or at least, he could still hit. Additionally, Bavasi and Erskine sat down to talk before the player's release was sought; this courtesy was not extended to Furillo. Moreover, Furillo's release was tainted by Bavasi's indirect approach and poor management of the sequence of events, particularly the delay between the release and the conference with Furillo and by intensive press coverage, which led to Furillo's unrestrained remarks and eagerness to quickly hire an attorney. Bavasi said later, "I wanted to do as well for Furillo as I did for Carl Erskine and Ed Roebuck but he would have no part of it."[7] Bavasi said he gave Erskine a job pitching batting practice, at his regular salary, and employed Roebuck as a coach and scout. Had he accepted either of the jobs offered to him, Furillo would likely have had similar opportunities. At worst, scouting would have kept him in the organization, and might have led to coaching or a higher level of player evaluation. A Spokane job might have enabled him to act as a player/coach, helping young players while continuing to play. Had he played well, the Dodgers or another team might have taken a renewed interest—or he might have come to realize that his on-field career was over.

Furillo's perception of the Spokane offer was clouded by various factors. For one, "Dad was being sent down to the minors, and he took that as a slap in the face," recalled Carl Furillo, Jr.[8] In addition, the offer required a series of financial calculations ill-suited to being made in an emotionally charged setting. Furillo's reaction was that he wanted to remain on the Dodgers payroll in 1960 before going to Spokane in 1961. He felt that his right under the contract, as an injured player, was not just to be paid his salary but also to retain his full benefit package. "I would be on the ballclub for one solid year and then I would go to Spokane," he recalled in 1970.[9] To Bavasi, who had already released Furillo, this was inconceivable.

In any case, following the July agreement with Caruso to pay the full 1960 salary, Bavasi wanted Furillo to spend a few weeks working as a counselor at the Dodgers' Vero Beach boys' summer camp, signaling to the public that the problems were resolved. According to Furillo, Bavasi told Caruso, "this way it would look good as far as baseball as concerned, as far as Furillo and the Dodger organization: everything would be smoothed over."[10] Bavasi also indicated that Furillo would be back in the good graces of baseball afterwards, Furillo said.

In mid–August, Furillo flew from Pennsylvania to Vero Beach. He spent two weeks working at the camp, helping to school youngsters in baseball fundamentals. Then he returned to Pennsylvania, gathered his family and returned to his home in Manhattan Beach. Responding to another suggestion by Caruso, he visited the Los Angeles Coliseum before a game in order "to show my face, which would look good amongst the ballplayers and the fans and the sportswriters and everyone; this would show that everything was all patched up."

"I walked down to the clubhouse and I talked to the boys and everything else," Furillo said. "They asked me what Vero Beach was like and I told them, 'It's a nice little spot; they have a lot of kids there; the kids are having a ball.' Pee Wee and I were doing most of the talking." Furillo was miffed, however, that none of the Dodgers executives spoke to him. "I stayed there for the full game," he said. "And then I left and I went home. And I still haven't heard from them yet."[11] This indicates that Furillo was still bitter during the 1970 interviews, before Peter O'Malley reached out to him.

Furillo remained in Manhattan Beach that summer but, he said, "I didn't do nothing. I had a few dollars put away, not much, but enough to hold me over for a little while. And that was when I wrote letters out to different ball clubs, trying to get employment in baseball. In the letters I asked about coaching and scouting, or work with kids, and I also put in there 'to play.' The first reports we would always get back were, 'How is your leg?' As for the others, they would just say, 'We have no openings at the present time.' It was just more doors being slammed in my face. And that was all I was doing out there on the West Coast, and I began to get kind of fed up with everything that had happened out there. Besides that the weather was always the same; the seasons never changed. So the next year (1961) I sold everything I had out there and I moved back to my home in Pennsylvania."[12]

Despite more than a decade as a mainstay of the legendary Brooklyn Dodgers teams of the 1950s, Carl Furillo found himself on the outside looking in when his playing days were over (National Baseball Hall of Fame Library, Cooperstown, New York).

Before returning, Furillo went public with his frustration at not finding a job, accusing baseball of blacklisting him, initially in an interview with the *Los Angeles Examiner* in March of 1961. The bold headline "Furillo Fires Blacklist Charge" was bannered across the top of the page, with the story labeled as an exclusive. "I have contacted almost every club for a job, playing, coaching or scouting," Furillo told the newspaper. "Most of them haven't even given me the consideration of an answer."

Furillo continued: "Frankly, I don't know whether I could play again. I started working out last winter and my knee caused me some trouble. I want to remain in baseball in some capacity, but nobody wants me." He cited several examples of baseball executives he had contacted without success. One was Charlie Dressen, who "gave me the brush off." Another was Los Angeles Angels general manager Fred Haney. The Angels were awarded an American League franchise on Dec. 7, 1960, and stocked the team with an expansion draft on Dec. 14. An eager Furillo called immediately after the franchise was awarded. "Naturally, I contacted Fred Haney when his group received the franchise in the American League," Furillo said. "At first, he was interested, but would have to wait until after the draft. I called him after the draft and he said he couldn't use me as a player. He said Roland Hemond handled the scouting assignments, but Hemond, when I told him I intended to return to the East, said he had a man in Ohio who would handle scouting in the East. Then, a couple of weeks later, I read where they signed a fellow in Connecticut to scout for the Angels."[13]

Later that week, Angels owner Gene Autry denied that Furillo had been blacklisted. "I have a high regard for Furillo," Autry said, in a report by United Press International. "He was a fine player, but he isn't what we need. Unless we can get young players who fit into our future plans, we're pretty well set." Autry went on to say, "Our coaching staff is complete, so I don't see how we could use Furillo" and to say that he had talked to other owners in recent weeks and the topic of a Furillo blacklist had never come up.[14]

In June 1961, Furillo moved back to Stony Creek Mills. "Carl Furillo, the disappointed Dodger who found California a dead end instead of the Promised Land, moves back to Reading, Pa.," proclaimed a *Los Angeles Times* story. "His three-unit Manhattan Beach dwelling is up for sale (and) on June 16, he has an appointment in New York with Commissioner Ford Frick that may write a new twist to baseball arguments."[15]

On June 16, Frick convened a hearing at baseball's office in New York. Furillo attended, along with Caruso, his attorney, Harry Walsh, the Dodgers' attorney and Paul Porter, baseball's attorney. "We went in trying to collect on '61, because Bavasi had already promised Caruso that he would pay me my $33,000 for 1960," Furillo said. "He hadn't done it (all) yet, I was still waiting—he had paid about $20,000 of it."[16]

Additionally, Furillo made the case that he had been blacklisted by baseball; on that subject, he had written a letter to Sen. Estes Kefauver, D.–Tennessee, who was chairman of the Senate Anti-Trust and Monopoly Subcommittee.

In fact, the hearing was largely theater. The Dodgers had already agreed to pay the 1960 salary and, judging from the transcript, even Caruso did not seem convinced of the claim he made that Furillo was also owed his 1961 salary. At least, he did not present a particularly strong case. Thus, in terms of the outcome, Frick had nothing to consider seriously, other than the validity of Furillo's charges. "Baseball owners are always at each other's throats, but when they get in trouble, they stick together," Furillo said later. "And the commissioner is hired by the owners and paid by the owners. So whose side do you think he was on? When he came through with a decision it was just that Bavasi should pay me the rest of the $33,000, which he had already promised to do."[17]

In opening the hearing, Frick responded to Cowan's contention that he could not act impartially; not surprisingly, he assured that he could. First to argue was Caruso, who said that Furillo was injured in spring training, and then reinjured on April 19 in the game against the Giants. "Mr. Furillo hit a triple, ran to third standing up and felt his leg tightening again," Caruso said. "We allege this continuation of the injury incurred in spring training." Then, on April 20, Furillo played three innings and "had to withdraw because his leg was not operating properly." Between April 20 and May 7 or 8, Caruso said, Furillo "carried out his functions as a pinch-hitter. He ran in the outfield and finally on the last of these days, Mr. Furillo felt his leg tighten to such an extent that he could not play that night. Dr. Robert Kerlan touched Mr. Furillo's injured leg with his finger and said in effect, 'This leg is shot.'" After that, on May 17, Furillo was given his unconditional release. Caruso said Furillo was entitled to his 1960 salary, of which $20,357 had already been paid, and quoted from the contract: "Disability directly resulting from injury sustained in the course and within the scope of his employment under this contract shall not impair the right of the player to receive his full salary for the period of such disability or for the season in which the injury was sustained (whichever period is shorter) together with the reasonable medical and hospital expenses incurred."

Caruso then argued that Furillo should be paid for 1961 as well, saying, "Nowhere in this contract does it provide for a disability which lasts longer than one season. At least I haven't been able to discover it. (But) Mr. Furillo is still injured (and) has received medical attention as recently as his return to his home in Pennsylvania." Caruso said it is "clear cut" (that) the contract clause applied to the 1960 season. He added, "We are making a claim for the 1961 contract on the basis that Mr. Furillo was injured while playing baseball. He is still injured and that he has, to our knowledge, never been placed on the waiver list."[18]

Walsh responded for the Dodgers, saying the team does "not admit that the player was injured, and two, that there is no provision in the player's contract which would allow for recovery for the 1961 season." He said the contract could not have applied in 1961 unless it had been renewed, which is a matter of the club's discretion. "The intent of the contract over all of the years of baseball has been too clear to read into it an option on the part of the player to renew his contract," Walsh said. In fact, Walsh said, Furillo's contract had been terminated, and "I am at a loss to understand how an option can exist under a terminated contract." Walsh then revealed a fact Caruso apparently had not known, which is that on May 11 the Dodgers had in fact sought waivers on Furillo for the purpose of giving him his unconditional release. (Walsh was unclear on certain dates during the hearing; in this account, correct dates are provided.) Subsequently, the Dodgers received a telegram from the National League office declaring that waivers had been obtained, and the team informed Furillo verbally and by registered mail. "At this point, the Los Angeles Dodgers have fulfilled their entire obligation to the player under the contract," he said. This concluded the Dodgers' initial argument over whether Furillo was entitled to compensation for 1961.

Walsh then entered a second phase of his argument, insisting that Furillo was released not because he was injured, but rather because his skills had diminished. He said that on May 17, "Carl came into Bavasi's office and served on him a notice of disability." The Dodgers, however, had already given Furillo his unconditional release "on the basis of the fact that it did not consider the player of sufficient skill to play with the team." The issue is solely "a question of how much money he was to receive," Walsh said, since "there was no question of whether or not the contract was terminated."

As evidence that Furillo's skills had deteriorated even before spring training began, Walsh noted that the Dodgers sought to trade him in February, 1960. The letters Bavasi wrote to the Red Sox and Yankees indicate that "our release of the player was not predicated on an injury but on the then-expressed intent of management to use players whom they thought would make a better team." Walsh added that once Furillo was released, he was free to make a deal with any club, and that "he evidently attempted to do so." When Caruso responded that Furillo was "not in physical position to perform," Walsh said, "That is inconsistent with trying to make a deal." When Caruso asked whether the Dodgers were contacted by Charlie Dressen about a week before Furillo's release, Walsh did not respond.

From the arguments, it is clear that the Dodgers chose to interpret

Furillo's belief that he could still play as compelling evidence that he was not injured. Yet in reality, it cannot be known whether Furillo could still play or whether he was too injured to play. He never played again, and it is unclear whether other teams' presumption that he could not play resulted from his injury or from the deterioration of his skills due to age. Moreover, Furillo's insistence that he could still play reflects the view of aging athletes in every sport and in every generation. They invariably believe they can still play, whether they can or not. So the issue of why Furillo's career ended is murky, but it was also largely irrelevant to the hearing because the Dodgers had agreed to pay him in any case.

Walsh also reiterated his initial point that under a terminated contract, no option for 1961 could exist. Caruso responded, rather vaguely it seems, "There is mutual consideration in this contract. It isn't a one-way street at all." Later, Caruso said that providing disability for the second year of an injury, after a contract has been terminated, "is a question of interpretation by the commissioner." He also said, "All contracts are subject to modification, in accordance with the changing needs and the changing time," and that the baseball contract includes an option, one that is not mentioned, related to "the mutuality of performance."[19]

Furillo spoke next. Questioned by Frick, he said he had not been offered a job in baseball. He related the details of his various discussions, during the last five days of his career, with Durslag, Hunter, Bavasi, Becker and Bragan. Included was his description of what happened on Thursday, May 12, when he was running in the outfield and Bragan asked him, "'Hey dago, how is your leg?" and he responded, "It feels so damn good I feel like playing up at Frisco." Later, this abundantly enthusiastic self-diagnosis would be taken by Frick as an indication that Furillo was not precluded by injury from playing.

Furillo also discussed a phone call to Dressen in Milwaukee, in which he sought to pin down the answer to the lingering question, "Am I right or am I wrong that you wanted me for the Milwaukee club?" Dressen said, "Yes, Carl, I did want you if your leg was all right." Furillo responded, "At that time you wanted me, my leg was all right." And then, Furillo told Frick, "I just let it go then." Afterwards, he said, "I wrote my letters out to different ballclubs, trying to get employment, but I asked a lot of them for coaching and scouting or work with the kids and I also put in there 'to play' and the first reports we would always get back was 'How is your leg?'" When Porter, the attorney for major league baseball, asked about the job offer in Spokane, Furillo responded, "The only time Mr. Bavasi offered me Spokane was when I gave him that piece of paper stating what that contract read, that 'we are notifying you of the injury' and that is when he said to me, when he blew his top, he said, 'You go to Spokane.' That is when I said to him, I said, 'My lawyer told me not to refuse you anything providing you abide by that contract, the major league contract.' That is when he said to me, 'I am giving you what is coming to you, and that's it.' I said 'I won't sign nothing—I won't refuse you nothing providing you abide by my contract. But he did not offer me any employment until that letter was in his hands."[20]

As the commissioner's hearing came to a close, Furillo continued to field questions regarding the Spokane offer. It seems that Bavasi viewed Furillo's position as a willingness to go to Spokane in 1960 if he could accrue pension benefits, when in fact Furillo had proposed going in 1961 after accruing the benefits. First, Dodgers attorney Walsh asked Furillo if he had agreed to play in Spokane if there were no reduction in his salary, and Furillo said "Yes." In an aside to the commissioner, Walsh declared, "Under the rules we couldn't reduce his salary," and then said to Furillo, "Didn't you also say at that time that you wouldn't play there because you couldn't get your pension rights protected?" Furillo responded, "No, I did not. I did not say nothing about pension. No sir. I know the rules on pension. That is strictly major league." Walsh asked, "That was your concern?" Furillo responded, "No, I said all the benefits to go with it, that he would have to carry me for the rest of the year." Walsh said, "You would not only get your salary?" and Furillo said, "It would have given me 15 years; it would have given me the full 15 years. On the contract, if I am not mistaken, it says all medical and all benefits go through the period of the year in case of injuries. The only way I could receive that would be if I stay in the major leagues, not in the minor leagues, and I said, 'You can't do it.' I knew the score on the pension, if you went in the minor leagues you are dead. I did offer to go to Spokane, providing he abide by the contract first, and he wouldn't do it."[21]

Curiously, Walsh had written himself a note on May 23, 1961, three weeks before the hearing, in which he questioned the mechanics of the Dodgers paying Furillo had he gone to Spokane. (The note also indicates that Bavasi continued to seek a resolution even after the hostile meeting on May 17, 1960.) "Buzzie says he agreed to pay him his 1960 salary for doing odd jobs and not for 1961 (through Caruso). He offered him a job at Spokane. Can he be sent to Spokane after unconditional release without the major league club paying part of his salary? Normally if sent to lower classification, the major league club has to pay the difference in salary. But here the unconditional release intervened—what is the effect under baseball rules?"[22] It would seem that Walsh was preparing himself for questions that could have been raised during the hearing, but apparently they never were.

In any case, the remainder of the hearing was primarily consumed by Furillo's responses to a brief series of questions from Porter about whether he had received any income since leaving baseball. Furillo declared that he had some unspecified investments, but that as far as employment "I haven't done a thing since I am out of baseball. I am unemployed."

A month after the hearing, on July 13, Frick issued his findings. He found that Furillo signed a standard player contract with the Dodgers on January 18 and that as early as February 24, Dodgers management "had evidenced its intention to sever its contract with Mr. Furillo by assigning his contract to other Major League clubs (this was a reference to the letters Bavasi wrote to the Yankees and Red Sox)." Discussing Furillo's injuries, Frick found that Furillo had injured his leg three times during the 1960 season, on April 19–20, on May 2 and on May 6, 7 and 8, but that "these injuries were not shown to be sufficient to require the Dodgers to place Mr. Furillo on the disabled list."[23] In other words, in Frick's view, Furillo was injured but not disabled.

Frick then described the events of Furillo's release. On May 12, the Dodgers sent a telegram to the National League president to secure waivers on Furillo in order to unconditionally release him. Also on May 12, the Dodgers notified Furillo that he would be tendered his unconditional release. On or about May 17, the National League notified the Dodgers that waivers had been obtained. Also, on May 17, the Dodgers sent Furillo a letter releasing him. On May 18, Furillo received the letter, which included a check for one month of his salary plus unspecified travel expenses.

Also on May 17, Furillo notified the Dodgers of his injuries in a letter, but Frick found that "this letter incorrectly infers that it was these injuries which continued to prevent Mr. Furillo from carrying on his duties as a player." It was not injuries that kept Furillo from playing, Frick found, citing these facts: "Mr. Furillo's testimony that as of May 12, 1960, the injuries to his leg no longer impaired his playing ability; that he sought employment as a player with other major league clubs after receiving notice of his release; that he was willing to play for the Dodgers' Spokane farm team, and in view of the efforts by the Dodgers since 1960 to terminate their contractual relations with Mr. Furillo on the grounds of insufficient playing ability." Thus, Frick found that Furillo was terminated due to insufficient playing ability, rather than injury, and that the Dodgers had fulfilled their contract obligations. Therefore, Furillo's claim was denied.

However, Frick noted at the conclusion of his ruling that the Dodgers had offered to pay Furillo's salary and that his determination was "not to be construed as prejudicing any compromise or settlement that may have been heretofore offered. Indeed, it is my view that such an offer having been made, the Dodgers should fulfill this commitment and tender Mr. Furillo the balance of the compensation he would have received had he performed for the full season under the 1960 contract. The record in this proceeding established that the Dodgers are still ready and willing to do this."[24]

In the aftermath of the hearing and the Dodgers' agreement to pay Furillo his full 1960 salary, it has often been written in various online venues and newspaper stories that Furillo sued baseball and won. But that is not what happened. Furillo did sue the Dodgers, but the team—predisposed to seek an amicable settlement with a longtime player—quickly settled. Then, following a hearing, Frick simply endorsed a settlement that had already been reached.

Shortly after Frick issued his ruling, Hunter discussed it in a column. "The Carl Furillo/Dodger squabble is at an end, or will be as soon as the outfield star receives $12,600 and travel expenses, the balance due on his contract for 1960," Hunter wrote. The column, based partially on an interview with Caruso, reflected Caruso's view that the case had been brought to an equitable conclusion. For instance, Hunter wrote that "Furillo, who had to fight for this much, wanted to continue his case in Congress, but Caruso advised his client to forget about it and Furillo acquiesced."

In any case, Hunter summarized, "Frick based his ruling on a finding that Furillo was not injured, inasmuch as he wrote other clubs seeking employment. If Carl thinks he was the victim of a 'house' decision, he can be forgiven. But he also has agreed to forget." The column was entitled: "All's Well That Pays Carl Well."[25]

But all was not well, Furillo did not forget, and his bitter feelings would linger for two decades, occasionally provoked when he applied for baseball jobs—which he did repeatedly for at least a decade—and did not get them.

Immediately following the hearing, Bavasi turned over the balance of the money to Caruso, who collected his fee before turning over the remainder to Furillo. "That was the end of that case, because I had to sign the release before I got the money," Furillo said. "Then Caruso had said to me, 'Bavasi will take good care of you, so don't worry about it.' He said, 'he'll call you up and get in touch with you and he'll have something going, and this way you'll get back in the grace of baseball.' But the windup is I still haven't gotten the phone call. All I ever got was promises.

"Then one day I read in the paper that Caruso had invited Bavasi to a sports banquet in Los Angeles. And it had a quote from Paul where he said, 'Mr. Bavasi treated Carl more than fair.' And then I hear that Caruso is saying that I was misled by people, that I shouldn't have gone for the '61 salary, that 'Bavasi was more than fair.' Misled by people? Hell, I was misled by my attorney. I was never misled by anybody but my attorney."[26]

In December 1961, Furillo received a letter from Hub Kittle, general manager of the Honolulu-based Hawaii Islanders of the Pacific Coast League. Kittle asked whether Furillo was interested in managing. "I wired back an emphatic 'yes,'" Furillo said. "On Dec. 7 I got Kittle's offer: $10,000 plus my expenses out there. I wrote back asking for a little more money and expenses to include my family."[27] Furillo said he never heard from Kittle again. He later told the *Los Angeles Times* that he considered the offer "merely a 'gimmick' to settle his feud with the Dodgers."[28] Soon afterwards, the Islanders hired Irv Noren as a player-manager.

Curiously, it was the second time that Noren replaced Furillo. The longtime American League outfielder also joined the Dodgers as a pinch-hitter after Furillo's release. "They said they were looking for a left-handed pinch-hitter, and I knew Bavasi because he was an errand boy at Montreal and we went to the track together," Noren recalled. "I didn't do much, I just pinch-hit and I got my paycheck."[29] Noren batted just 25 times for the Dodgers and was released at the end of the season. He was a player-manager for the Hawaii Islanders in 1962 and 1963, and recalls that he was paid about $13,000, which would have been substantially more than Furillo was offered, perhaps because he both played and managed. As an aside, it is worth noting that Noren was in spring training with the Dodgers' minor league players in 1947. Occasionally, he ran into Jackie Robinson—who in 1946 had been a teammate on the Los Angeles Red Devils (part of the National Professional Basketball League, an NBA predecessor).

At some point in 1961, Furillo wrote to Sen. Estes Kefauver. At the time, Kefauver was one of the country's best-known senators, a crusader against organized crime and wealthy, monopolistic elites in a variety of businesses. He had been the Democratic candidate for vice president in 1956, after performing strongly in presidential primaries in 1952 and 1956. In his letter, Furillo described his efforts to get a job with a baseball team. "By the end I had written to all of them, and I could not locate a job on any major league ballclub as coach, player, scout, batting instructor or anything," he said. "Sometimes I would receive answers that such and such a club was all filled up but would keep me in mind, and then I would read in the paper of new additions to the same clubs for the same jobs I had applied for. It all goes to show that I was blacklisted or whatever you want to call it, which is against the law. Because baseball has a monopoly. If you can't get a job, you can't get a job anywhere. I wrote to Senator Kefauver but it was just like another baseball club, a 'we will look into the matter' is all I ever got from them."[30]

Furillo also pursued a job with another new team, the New York Mets. The franchise was awarded in 1960 and the team picked its first players in an October 1961 expansion draft. Furillo charged that the Mets had hired four new scouts after he had received a letter from the club saying the organization was "all filled up," according to a January 9, 1962, story in *The New York Times*. The Mets and Frick denied the charge. "There is no such thing as a baseball blacklist," Frick said.[31] Added Bavasi: "The trouble is Carl wants a job as a scout or manager. He should go to the minors to find out if he can, do these things. I have no animosity toward Carl. I thought we ended our relationship with good feelings."[32] In another example, cited in an *Associated Press* story, Furillo heard from the Phillies on Nov. 21 that no jobs were available, yet he read a month later that the Phillies had hired a new scout, Joe Caputo, who had spent the previous season scouting for the Indians.

Was Furillo blacklisted? No evidence exists that baseball maintained an organized blacklist, but it is entirely logical that a baseball team would not jump at the chance to hire the plaintiff in a lawsuit against another team. With so much demand for jobs in baseball, finding one can be challenging for a person who sued the organization and also engaged in a bitter public exchange, said Fay Vincent, commissioner of baseball from 1989 to 1992, in a 2009 interview. "If someone has the reputation for litigation and being very difficult, the others might avoid him. Look at the recent (Barry) Bonds case," Vincent said.

Still, Vincent declared, "I've never known anyone to be blacklisted" from baseball. In fact, he said, he had never even heard of the possibility that Furillo might have been blacklisted until this writer asked him about it. He responded, "You're the first person I've ever talked to about it."[33]

17

Back Home for Good

EVEN AS HE CONTINUED TO FIGHT with baseball, it became clear to Furillo that he needed to move on with his life. Today major league ballplayers, particularly 15-year veterans who played at Furillo's level, can easily accumulate sufficient wealth that they need not seek employment when their baseball careers end. But that was hardly the case in the early 1960s: ex-ballplayers needed to work to support themselves and their families. For Furillo, who had an eighth-grade education, that meant a succession of blue-collar jobs. None paid a high salary. But Furillo knew something about managing money. He was frugal, he saved much of his baseball income, he made various investments, he layered a second pension on top of his baseball pension, and he managed to live comfortably for the remainder of his life, partially because he realized that living in Stony Creek Mills provided both an enjoyable lifestyle and a low cost of living. How strange it seems, in light of what Furillo accomplished financially, to recall that in 1973 Harold Parrott felt it necessary to denigrate Furillo's financial acumen by describing his response, when Branch Rickey supposedly asked how many years earlier his father had immigrated from Italy, this way: "His lips moved and he counted on his fingers."

Early in 1962, Furillo sold his house in Manhattan Beach and moved back to Reading. He enrolled his sons in school, fished and hunted, and eventually bought into a kitchen cabinet business. He also had two operations, spaced a year apart, for a ruptured disc in his back. The problem resulted, he said, from the leg injury he suffered while playing. The operations were successful enough that in 1970 Furillo said, "To this day I have no complaints about my back, except when we get bad weather or dampness or something, I get a pain in my back. There is a world of difference between what I can do now and what I could do before the operation. As far as working, now I can work just like any other man.

"After those operations, I was anxious to go to work, because they ran into a pretty good chunk of money, and of course the Dodgers weren't paying anything on that medical,"[1] he said. After the second operation, late in 1962, he sold his share of the kitchen cabinet business and returned to New York. In the fall of 1963, he bought a home in Flushing, Queens, not far from Shea Stadium. In partnership with a friend, he opened Furillo and Totto's, an Italian delicatessen and grocery on 32nd Avenue in Queens. Furillo enjoyed the business, to an extent.

"I like to work when I'm in business," he said. "I like to be around the business. When you have registers you have to be near them because too many hands in the till does no good. So I did a lot of my own work when I was there, and I saved a lot of salaries because I did most of it myself with my partner. I had lots of different personal friends of mine come in to do their shopping. I was amazed that one day this woman and her daughters came in and she said, 'We just took a ride from Sheepshead Bay and we wanted to see your store and we figured we'd grab a hero here and then we're going right back.' I had quite a few people coming in to see me, and we were taking in as high as $350, $400, $450 a day, and when the holidays came it was as high as $600 and $700 a day."[2]

It's unclear how much of that income was due to the presence of a former Brooklyn Dodgers star behind the counter. However, the children of Furillo's partner came to believe they could generate as much money without him. Furillo was miffed, and also tired of the small business entrepreneur's lifestyle, which meant getting to work early and staying late. The business had been about $75,000 in the hole when he stepped in. "When the bill collectors found out that I was coming in, they were a little more lenient, and before you knew it we had the bills paid off," he said. "But once the bills were paid, the daughters were saying, 'We don't need him.' Besides, there had been a promise this partner had made to me, which was 'Come in for a year or two and then we'll have a real business together and we'll open up in the city.' The promise never came through, and after three years at that place I didn't want any more part of it. I sold out my share."[3]

In 1966, Furillo went to work as an assistant manager for the Big Apple supermarket, where he spent eight months and was on his way to becoming a manager when a friend asked him if he wanted to be an iron worker. He began taking jobs out of the union hall and by 1967 had worked his way up to a regular job with Otis Elevator Co., installing doors at the World Trade Center, which was under construction. The job paid well and Furillo sent his family back home to Stony Creek Mills to live; he joined them on weekends. "One day, one of the guys on the crew I work with, he asked me, 'With all the money you made, what are you doing here?' And I told him it was simple. I like to eat."[4]

In reality, Furillo's thinking was a good deal more sophisticated. In 1970, Furillo was 47; his plan was to work until he was around 50, save up the money he earned (to save money, he lived with a friend on Long Island) and then move back home, where he could live off his savings and his pension. "I'm going to stay here another four or five years, then I'm going to sell everything I own and, if the Lord is willing, buy myself a nice big farm in Pennsylvania or wherever my wife and I decide," he said. "Maybe we'll just build a little home on a ten-acre piece of land with nobody near to bother us. And then I'll be hunting all the time, which is what I love to do. I like to be alone, to walk, to be outside with nobody else around except for the dogs. I can stop when I get tired and lie down and go to sleep, because I'm my own boss then."[5] Furillo always had the capacity to find happiness within himself and his family. He was always a man who seemed to prefer the company of his wife and sons to anybody else. "I don't have to go to barrooms or nightclubs or places like that to enjoy myself," he said. "I enjoy myself right here with my family."[6]

Similarly, he was able to live within his means. "Actually, I'm pretty well off," he said. "A lot of people are always worried, and a lot of the time what they're worried about is financial. But I never worried too much about anything back when I was playing, and I don't worry now. I've always tried to work day by day. I've tried to save for a rainy day, but mainly I go from day to day and little things don't bother me. Major things bother me, but I try to disassociate myself from those kinds of things. Like with people, I take people at face value. I treat people the way I wanted to be treated, and then if I find that they're a lot different and that they want to be a god or whatever it is, then I just don't associate with them. I stay away from them."[7]

As for baseball, Furillo had not given up his hopes of getting back into the game. Carl Furillo, Jr., recalls that during Wes Westrum's tenure as manager of the Mets, from 1965 to 1967, his father and Westrum would occasionally talk. At one point, "Wes called dad to talk about Ron Swoboda, some problem he was having. Dad tried to give him some insight, and Wes said, 'Hey, if I can get you a job as hitting and fielding coach, would you accept it?' and Dad said, 'Yeah.' So Wes said, 'I'll get back to you.' But two weeks later, he called and said the front office told him no. He didn't give him a reason. It's too bad because my dad still loved baseball; that was his heart and soul."[8]

Nevertheless, Furillo participated in old-timers games. On July 24,

1965, he was among the Dodgers who played against the Giants at Shea Stadium, in what was billed as a replay of the famous 1951 playoff game. Again, Bobby Thomson hit a home run, but this time the Dodgers won, 4–2. In the second inning, Furillo hit a single off his old friend, Sal Maglie. Since he was operating the deli at the time, Furillo brought Erskine a hero sandwich so big that it fed a half-dozen ballplayers.[9]

Still, Furillo remained bitter into the 1970s. At one point, he was interviewed by Roger Kahn, who was writing *The Boys of Summer*, which examined what had become of the members of the famous 1950s teams. The book was published in 1972. Furillo's story was perhaps the most intriguing. For him, Kahn wrote, "The wine has soured" because of the conflict with the Dodgers. "There are not going to be any more hurrahs for Carl Furillo, and those that he remembers, if he truly remembers any, are walled from him by harsher, newer memories." Furillo, he wrote, was born to play baseball—but no longer had baseball in his life.[10]

In particular, Furillo was concerned that many of his teammates, not to mention former adversary Durocher, were still in baseball. No doubt his concern was fueled by New York's obsession with the Mets, who had won their first World Series in 1969. "There's Hodges, who's right over here with the Mets, and Reese, Koufax, Snider, Maglie, a lot of these guys," Furillo said early in 1970. "Sometimes I sort of wonder when I see all these guys that I played with who are still in baseball, especially a guy like Durocher," who in 1970 was manager of the Cubs. "He was barred from baseball, I should say thrown out of baseball, and then he gets back in. And here I am sitting on the outside looking in, watching all this. So then you say to yourself, 'What is the inside dope here?' because he was supposed to have been hanging around with bookies or racketeers or whatever it was down there in Havana. So I often wonder, 'What is fair, what is wrong, what is right?' I'm out of it just because there was a little bit of ill feeling with somebody I had a lot of faith in and I respected and then all of a sudden I got slapped in the face. So it had a little sour note there."[11]

Things began to change in 1971, when Furillo agreed to play in a Dodgers' old-timers game on June 6, after being invited by Peter O'Malley to attend. "The Dodgers were very surprised," according to *The Sporting News*. "Furillo recently has displayed a bitter attitude toward baseball."[12] In 1972, he agreed to play in an old-timers game in Philadelphia. It was billed as a replay of the 1952 game, which was halted by rain after five innings.

One thing that bothered Furillo about New York was the constant intrusions related to his celebrity. "I ride the subway to work in the morning and sometimes people will just keep staring at you, and then they'll come over to you sometimes and say, 'You sure got a bad deal in baseball' and all that stuff. And there's other times when people you work with will want to talk over plays or different things in baseball, and sometimes it's nice to talk about it when you don't have too much to do. But sometimes you get a little busy, and your boss is around and you have to have some work done, or something important has to be done, and they try to block you and try to talk to you. Well, that aggravates the boss a little bit.

"I've always been a guy that tries to please the fans, but you have to draw the line somewhere," he said. "Right now, even though it's been ten years since I left the Dodgers, I still have to have an unlisted telephone number. The Mets and the Yankees have my phone number, and so does *The Daily News* and some of the sports writers, but I try not to give it out because you get a hold of some cranks. I should have it listed because sometimes people would like to give you a decent job or whatever it is. You could make personal appearances; if you really wanted to you could spend more time making personal appearances than you could at home. But me, I'm a guy that would rather stay at home here with my family."[13]

When his work on the World Trade Center came to an end in 1971, Furillo did what he had planned: He went home. For two years, he did little beyond fishing and hunting, often with his sons, who moved back also. But by 1973, he was restless. The local sheriff was a friend and offered him a job as a deputy sheriff. His duties included accompanying prisoners to the state prison. When his friend died, Furillo chose not to work for the new sheriff. Instead, in July, 1976, he took a job as a security guard at a nearby plant. Meanwhile, during the mid–1970s, Furillo got a shock when he learned that he suffered from chronic leukemia. He did not publicly disclose his condition until four years later, when reporter Jack Lang called in August, 1980, to inquire why Furillo was one of the few remaining 1955 Dodgers who had not responded to the Mets' invitation to attend an old-timers game. During the call, Furillo was at first reticent to discuss his condition, saying only that he was busy canning tomatoes with his wife. But as the conversation with an old friend continued, Furillo acknowledged he was ill. "Tell all the guys I said hello," Furillo said. "Tell them I'm sorry I can't be there. Tell them I've got leukemia. I think I've got it beat. But you never know."[14] Furillo believed that a vitamin regimen helped him to fight the disease, and he worked through it. "He took it as 'This is God's will,' something he needed to fight off," said Robert Erb, a friend from the plant.[15]

Located in Birdsboro, Pennsylvania, the plant makes nylon resin pellets, primarily used in auto industry components. It has been operated for decades, under a variety of different names, by divisions of a French conglomerate now known as Arkema. Furillo enjoyed the ten years he worked there. "They treated him very well," his son said. "He didn't have to worry about anybody bothering him, although he used to say that people always asked him, 'Why are you busting your ass working as a guard, when all the guys you played with are still in baseball?'"[16] Furillo told *The Los Angeles Times* in 1985 that "it's a nice job. The benefits are beautiful."[17]

Jack Ferenchick, a longtime lab technician at what was then called the Rilsan plant, became a close friend. Ferenchick said the company initially offered Furillo a public relations job, but "he didn't want to travel—he was a homebody."[18] Additionally, the security guard's job was a good one, paying $40,000 or $45,000 annually. With only about 150 workers, the plant's staff was a close group; the working environment was generally positive, and Furillo was the plant celebrity, sought out for his baseball reminiscences as well as financial and interpersonal advice. His office was a guard shack, a small tin building between the parking lot and the main building, through which workers passed as they entered and departed. His hours—he worked a swing shift—fluctuated not only between various hourly schedules but also between assigned days; he worked five days on and two off, including a weekend every month. It was the type of schedule that can build rapport among those who endure it. Furillo wore a guard's uniform. Between rounds, which he made every hour or two, Furillo would sit at a metal desk. A second chair often accommodated friends who came to chat, particularly during Sunday shifts and night shifts when the workload was not quite so heavy and the supervision was not quite so intense.

Once, Ferenchick went to the guard shack to play a tape he had made of Duke Snider being interviewed on television. Furillo was amused. Often, Furillo would recall events involving Durocher, who was "not his favorite friend," or Sandy Koufax, who had been a friend, or his stint in Los Angeles, where "he thought they put the screws to him," Ferenchick said. But at other times, he talked of the pieces of property he farmed, or the tomatoes he grew, or his grandchildren. Furillo spoke like a man. He swore often, and "had a favorite expression, 'sumbitch,'" Ferenchick said. But when baseball fans he didn't know came to visit, he took on a more professional approach. "I took my father to see him once, and Carl's whole demeanor changed," Ferenchick said. "He was the athlete. He didn't swear. He acted like he was on TV."

Another distinguishing characteristic, which became evident in his comfortable surroundings, was Furillo's sense of humor. At one time, he would summon Ferenchick by calling, "Hey, Polack," until Ferenchick finally explained that he was a Slovak, albeit one who attended a Ukrainian church. So Furillo switched, and began to call him "Russian." Once, as Ferenchick stood in line for a flu shot, Furillo accosted him, "Hey Russian, how are you doing?" Said Ferenchick, "Carl was funny. He was always joking."[19]

Erb, a maintenance mechanic who spent 38 years at the plant, often visited Furillo at home, served as a pallbearer at his funeral, and visits his grave on Memorial Day. Born in 1946, Erb is approximately the age of Furillo's oldest son. Because Erb was on Furillo's crew, the two men had the same days off, and frequently fished the Schuylkill River from Furillo's boat or hunted for deer, pheasant or rabbit. Other times, they would work together on Furillo's 15-acre-plot, where he grew various crops including corn and Christmas trees, which enabled him to take advantage of tax benefits afforded to timber growers.

"Carl was a down-to-earth person," Erb said. "He spoke like a commoner, but there was a lot of stuff going on in his head. He was a good businessman. A lot of people would ask him for financial advice." Erb once asked Furillo where to invest his tax return, and Furillo identified some stocks he was following. Another time, when the company introduced a 401K with a 4 percent match, Furillo urged Erb to invest. "I was just 22, I couldn't see putting away 4 percent," Erb said. "He sat me down and said, 'Bobby, listen to what I have to tell you, have them take out at least 4 percent because they match. You can't beat that.' I argued. He said, 'Listen to what I'm telling you.' He talked like my dad. After that, when he saw me, he would say, 'You join that 401K yet? You're losing time.'" After about two weeks, Erb signed up. Furillo also offered advice to Erb and others on how to deal with plant politics. "I was highstrung, and he was more even-keel," Erb said. "He would calm my temper down. When I had trouble with my supervisor, he would recommend that I sit down and talk with him."[20] Essentially, Erb said, everyone in the plant chatted with Furillo, from front office managers on down.

Sometimes, when Furillo was between rounds, he would answer letters from baseball fans, who wrote constantly to request his autograph on photos, baseballs and baseball cards. He was extremely conscientious, Erb said. Once, when Erb wanted to make a copy of a photo that a fan sent, Furillo agreed but was adamant that there be no delay in returning the autographed picture to the fan. He also enjoyed going to card shows to sign cards and talk to fans. Typically, Furillo's son Jon would drive him to the card shows, and Jon's son J.J. often tagged along. "I never will forget a card show in a school auditorium in Brooklyn," Jon recalled. "I was standing in the back, leaning against the wall, and a lady was talking about my dad. She said, 'He is so beautiful, he talks to you like he's family.' I was on Cloud Nine. My dad was loved. He always said that when we were in Brooklyn, 'your mother would never have to cook a meal—so many people wanted us to come over for dinner.' A lot of times, people would send him money for his autograph, but he would always put it back in the envelope and send it back."[21] Furillo did not like the idea of selling his autograph to fans. He was once perturbed by a fan who requested him to sign a large number of baseball cards, but not to personalize them, Ferenchick recalled. That obviously would have allowed the fan to turn around and sell the cards. So Furillo personalized every one.

Furillo maintained a complex relationship with baseball. Sometimes Erb would bring his glove to work on Sunday afternoon, and he and Furillo would toss baseballs between the buildings. "He could still throw," Erb said. "His arm was still strong; his grip was still strong. You could tell because he would kid you, and grab your arm." Returning from his first fantasy camp in 1983, Furillo indicated he had thoroughly enjoyed it, and "he didn't seem to be as hard against the Dodgers as he had been when he left," Erb said. At times, the two men would watch baseball on television at Furillo's home. Furillo preferred to watch Yankees games, and was partial to announcer Bill White and second baseman Willie Randolph, because of "his athletic ability and the way he ran the bases." Furillo disdained the Dodgers and the Phillies and outfielders who wasted time taking a step or two before throwing the ball back to the infield when a runner was between bases. "'He would say, 'Don't they teach these guys anything?'" Erb recalled. As for his own career, Furillo proclaimed, "It all seems like a dream now; it doesn't seem real."[22] Furillo loved baseball, Erb said, but in his exile, he proclaimed, "I did what I had to do. I don't need baseball."[23]

During his final years, Furillo raised crops on his two lots, using his own tractor for cultivation. Typically, he would grow far more than he and his family could possibly consume, leading to frantic efforts to give away vast quantities of corn and tomatoes. Erb recalled a day in the early 1980s when he and Furillo's wife, sons, and daughters-in-law were all at Furillo's home, husking the corn they had just picked. "We had more than a thousand ears of corn," he said. "Carl was sending hundreds of ears home with each person."[24] Eventually, Erb and Furillo drove off to deliver corn to a Reading resident who had been Furillo's roommate in the hospital. "Dad had a green thumb," said Carl Furillo, Jr. "He loved growing things—corn, tomatoes, cantaloupes, watermelons." One winter, Furillo planted tomato seeds in hot boxes in the basement, and they all germinated. "So he tilled the land with the tractor, and we started to plant the tomatoes," his son recalled. "There must have been thousands of them, so after a while I said, 'I'll throw the rest on the compost pile,' and he said, 'You will not.' He got the tractor, tilled more land, and we planted the rest of them. I said, 'we can't make enough stakes for all these plants,' so they grew on the ground. After that, the whole family came to pick them, and we were down there three or four days picking them, and it still didn't look like we had touched them. Dad came from the Depression. He didn't throw anything away. He felt it was a sin to throw tomatoes away. But we didn't plant as many after that."[25]

Furillo retired from the plant in 1986 after ten years, which entitled him to a second pension in addition to his baseball pension. He would spend the next three and a half years enjoying life with his wife and sons. Besides hunting, fishing and gardening, he and Fern made frequent day trips to nearby attractions. "They were very close friends," said Carl Jr. "Everybody should have a marriage as good as theirs." His mother, he said, was grateful that her husband's life in baseball had enabled her "to see a lot of things she never would have seen," while his dad was pleased to have more time with his family after retirement.[26]

The couple often visited the Pennsylvania Dutch country or the New Jersey shore in Margate, where they would arrive early in the morning and walk along the beach, or Philadelphia and New York, where they would visit Italian neighborhoods to shop or dine. Needless to say, Carl was often recognized. Occasionally, they made longer trips to places like Cape Cod, Nashville, New Orleans and Las Vegas. Furillo "just wanted one long vacation," wrote Bill Ninfo, who interviewed Fern Furillo. "He promised Fern there would be one, and there was."[27]

18

The Right Way to Leave

For Peter O'Malley, the way Carl Furillo left the Dodgers was "the wrong way to leave."[1] Moreover, it was a wrong that he was in a position to right, and that is what he did, through a series of simple yet powerful gestures. As a first step, in 1971, O'Malley picked up the phone to call Furillo, who by then had been estranged from the Dodgers family for a decade. O'Malley's intent was to extend his hand, to welcome Furillo back into the fold. His initial offer was an invitation to participate in an old-timers game in Los Angeles. Subsequently, he employed Furillo as an instructor in the Dodgers' adult baseball fantasy camps in Vero Beach and invited him to attend the 30th anniversary celebration of the 1955 World Series champions. Additionally, in 1989 O'Malley attended Furillo's funeral in Reading, speaking graciously and even quietly offering to pay for the funeral. While his father was seen by some as an opportunist, Peter O'Malley staked out a course not only as a much-admired manager of a highly visible business but also as a conciliator, a generous guardian of Dodgers tradition, and as his father's defender. His gestures were welcomed by Furillo and his family, but they resolutely separated their warm feelings about him from their continued resentment over the circumstances of the separation from the Dodgers. In some ways, Peter O'Malley and Carl Furillo, Jr., play the same role, guardians of their fathers' legacies, seeking to provide facts and dispel unfavorable impressions that have been left by incomplete histories.

Peter O'Malley was groomed by his father to run the Dodgers. His involvement with the team began around 1950, when Walter O'Malley acquired a 50 percent stake, becoming majority owner and president. The son's earliest memory of Furillo dates from that time. "I was 13 when my dad became president, and that's when my sister and I started going to spring training in Vero Beach for spring break," O'Malley said. At Vero Beach, "everybody got to know everybody. We had the same dining room. We walked to the dining room, to the baseball fields, to the clubhouse. We passed everybody so it was impossible not to bump into and say hello to and get to know players, writers, managers, coaches, doctors and everybody—that was the beauty of the place."

The young O'Malley took to certain players—particularly Reiser, Campanella, Black and Furillo. "I seemed to connect with them," he said. "I felt they were friendly and nice to me so we talked." He recalls one day washing Joe Black's car. "I was a young guy and he said, 'Peter, what are you doing this afternoon?' I said, 'I don't know' and he said, 'My car needs a washing and I'll give you a dollar.' So I washed his car. He was a prince of a guy and I miss him." Regarding Furillo, O'Malley recalls, "We talked fishing. He was a big fisherman—that was kind of a common denominator." Like Furillo, Walter O'Malley had a lifetime interest in fishing, which he passed on to his son; in one photo from the time, Walter O'Malley is shown fishing off a small boat with Carl and Fern Furillo.

After graduating from the University of Pennsylvania and the Wharton School of Business, Peter O'Malley began to work his way up in the Dodgers organization, starting as director of Dodgertown in 1962. He took over as president of the team in 1970 and as owner in 1979. The Furillo case, seemingly closed out in 1961, was not initially a top priority. "Towards the latter days of his career, I'm in college, so I'm not involved at all," he said. Later, "maybe Erskine mentioned it to me, maybe my dad did," he said.[2] In any case, in 1971, he made the initial phone call.

One day, "I picked up the phone one day at home and it was Peter O'Malley," Furillo said. "He said, 'Carl.' I said, 'Yes?' He said, 'The organization and your friends out here all would like you to come out here for an old-timers game.' I said, 'I would enjoy it; I'd like to see the boys again.'" Furillo continued, "My wife was sitting at the kitchen table. I said 'Honey, would you like to go?' She said, 'If they pay my way.' Peter heard her and said he would."[3]

The fantasy camps started in 1983. "The two areas the Dodgers drew from were Brooklyn and LA, and the Brooklyn area," recalled Carl Erskine. "Of the Brooklyn-era guys, they asked me, Furillo, Duke Snider, Ralph Branca, guys that were still identified with Brooklyn. To my pleasant surprise, Furillo accepted the invitation to come and be on the staff, and he came in those first three or four years. We were all just thrilled that Furillo would come back and identify himself with the team."[4]

18. THE RIGHT WAY TO LEAVE

In 1984, Dodgers great Don Drysdale was inducted into the Hall of Fame. In Cooperstown that August for the ceremony, O'Malley had dinner with Carl Erskine; O'Malley made it a practice to stay in touch with several of the old Dodgers, particularly Erskine, Branca, Campanella, Newcombe and Snider. "Peter asked me to go to dinner, and we were chatting," Erskine recalled. "I had been player rep—I always felt some responsibility to the guys to keep them informed after our playing days—and I mentioned to Peter that as player rep, with the 30th anniversary coming up, I was thinking about contacting the guys and doing something. I said I might need to get the addresses from the Dodger alumni group. I wasn't prodding him to do anything, but he said, 'Oh no, that is something we should do.'"[5] Erskine had visited with Furillo a few months earlier, in June, when both men were inducted into the Brooklyn Baseball Hall of Fame. (Hodges was also inducted.) "Skoonj looks fine," wrote Dick Young in *The Sporting News*. "He seems to have beaten a serious back injury."[6] In an interview at the induction in Brooklyn, Furillo said, "It's funny. I spent three-quarters of my lifetime here, but I hardly recognize the place."[7] Furillo was "looking tanned and fit at age 62 and showing no visible signs of the leukemia (now in remission) that threatened his life a few years back," wrote Bill Madden.[8] Comparing the Dodgers' two homes, Furillo declared, "There was such a big difference when we left Brooklyn for LA. In Ebbets, the fans were right on top of you and even though they booed you, they were like family. Out in LA, where we played in the Coliseum, the fans were so far away it was like being at the opera."[9]

The following year, in February, 1985, in Vero Beach, the Dodgers staged a 30th anniversary reunion of the 1955 team. O'Malley wrote letters of invitation to every living member of the club. "It was a low-key approach, and we had a heck of a good turnout," O'Malley said. "Almost everybody was there. Carl came and everybody had a good time. There were no negatives or any issues or anything like that at all."[10] At the time, Furillo was in his tenth and final year as a security guard. He seemed to rejoice in the opportunity to see old friends, many of whom had not participated in the fantasy camps. "I haven't seen Pee Wee in 20 years, it might be a little longer," Furillo said in Vero Beach interview with the *Los Angeles Times*. "Hughes, it's been a good 20 years. Koufax—he used to be my roommate—I haven't seen in 15, 18 years."

Furillo said he was willing to forgive, but not to forget. "A lot of water has gone over the falls," he said. "But regrets? I don't regret nothin'. I have a lot of respect for human beings. I treat them the way I want to be treated. My wife used to say, 'dago, stick to your guns.' If I was wrong, or if I was trying to take advantage of somebody, I would have backed off. But my feeling was that I was injured, and they didn't give me medical (disability) or nothing. I would have been satisfied just to get the medical. Let bygones be bygones," he added. "I enjoy the organization. But when people ask me different things, I don't pull any punches."[11]

The newspaper story concluded with a segment about a dinner on Saturday night, Feb. 23, 1985, when Carl and Fern Furillo ate dinner with Bavasi, O'Malley and others. Furillo related a story about how one winter, after a good season, Bavasi offered him a $1,500 raise. When Furillo balked, Bavasi said he would throw in two steers, and Furillo, who owned a farm, accepted. But when the cattle were delivered, they turned out to be two young milk cows. Furillo had them returned, and never did get his steers. "After everyone had a good laugh, Bavasi turned to O'Malley. 'That's on the contract,' he said. 'You owe him two steers.'[12] Furillo smiled, 'What am I going to do with them now?'"[13] And it appeared, from the exchange, that the rift had been mended.

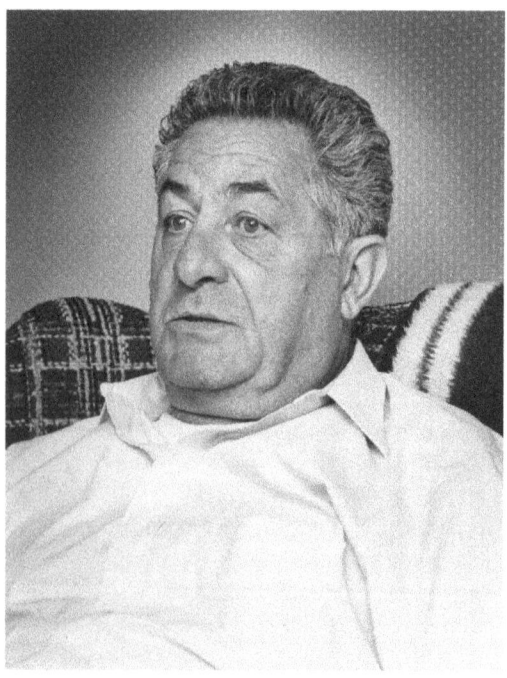

In his final years, Carl Furillo largely reconciled with the Dodgers. He said he was willing to forgive, but not to forget. "Regrets?" he said. "I don't regret nothin'." He is shown in a 1987 photograph (Reading Eagle Company).

O'Malley said he never familiarized himself with the minute details of Furillo's release or his hearing before the commissioner. But from what he knew, he concluded that Furillo's departure "was poorly handled. It was a sad chapter for any player to leave the Dodgers unhappy. Whether it was a misunderstanding, whether it was egos, whether both sides dug in or not, I don't know.

"My recollection of Carl is he was a very likable guy," O'Malley said. "There may have been different personalities on the team as there always are. I understand that. From my viewpoint, he was a man's man, a very likable, good person. Whether he and Buzzie clashed or whether Carl got bad advice, I don't know. You can fault Bavasi as well as Carl. There are no good guys or bad guys. Carl and Buzzie were close when Carl was a player for us. Buzzie was close to all of his players. And then boom, all of a sudden, they're not close. And that's sad. That's wrong. It was the wrong way for him to leave and for the chapter to be ended. If it could be repaired, if it could be mended, if the relationship could get back to what it was before, then (I felt) that would be a very desirable thing to do."

O'Malley stops short of accepting Furillo's contention regarding blacklisting, although he does acknowledge that circumstances may have led Carl to that conclusion. "For Carl to say that he was blacklisted by baseball, I can't buy that," he said. "But he said it, and knowing Carl, I can understand why he might have been frustrated or mad, and maybe a friend of his said to him, 'You know what, Carl, they blacklisted you, you can't get a job.' And Carl may have said, 'You know you're right, by golly, I am blacklisted.' I don't believe that, but I can understand why he said that or how he said that, and when he said that, that raised the whole level of the events."

In fact, Furillo was not the first Dodger with whom O'Malley sought a reconciliation. Jackie Robinson, who had not always gotten along well with Walter O'Malley during his career with the Dodgers, was miffed when he was traded to the Giants in December, 1956. "He was offended by that and retired," Peter O'Malley said. But afterwards, "My dad and he corresponded quite a bit in very friendly terms."

When the Dodgers decided to retire Robinson's number in 1972, O'Malley reached out to Robinson through Don Newcombe. "I met with Don Newcombe," he said. "I said, 'Don, do you think Jackie would come out?' and he said, 'I don't know.' I said, 'Why don't you see if he has any interest?' Don talked to Jackie, and Don told me Jackie said he would be happy to come out. That was a happy ending and I'm very happy that I did that."[14] On June 4, 1972, Robinson attended the ceremony where the Dodgers retired three numbers: his, Campanella's and Koufax's. Robinson died less than five months later, on Oct. 24.

In Erskine's view, "Peter O'Malley has been a jewel, for what he has done for the Dodger organization," not only for keeping up with the Brooklyn players and providing help and opportunity for many of them, but also for seeking to reconnect the Los Angeles Dodgers to their Brooklyn roots.

"He has made a second career of keeping in touch with guys, and sending articles, sending e-mails, if anything happens related to the Dodgers, even when he was selling the team (in 1998)," Erskine said. "Another thing Peter did, quietly, was to take care of players who needed it, particularly Campanella." After the famous catcher was paralyzed in a 1958 accident, the Dodgers made him a scout and a catcher's coach during spring training in Vero Beach. In 1978, he moved to Los Angeles to work as assistant to Newcombe, who was the Dodgers' director of community relations. Campy died in 1993.

The Dodgers, under both Walter and Peter O'Malley, "extended Roy's life—who knows how long?—by including him back in the organization," Erskine said. At one point, Tommy Lasorda, who became Dodgers manager in 1976, asked Campanella to coach. Added Erskine, "I recall Lasorda said to Roy, 'I want you to coach my players,' and Roy said, 'I can't coach.' So Lasorda said, 'Do you know anything about baseball? If you know anything about baseball, you can help my players.' Roy had a special place in Dodger Stadium, where he and Roxie (his wife) could come. Campy was the ultimate example but quietly, behind the scenes, without fanfare, Peter took care of guys who were struggling."

Moreover, O'Malley sought to reconnect the legacy of the Brooklyn Dodgers with the Los Angeles team. "When Peter became president, he began to reconnect," Erskine said. "The Brooklyn fans still hate the fact that the team left, but now the Los Angeles fans recognize that the history of the franchise was in Brooklyn and Los Angeles, and Peter's responsible for that. I don't think most teams that move keep the history alive. I think it's unique that, in this case, the history is kind of unbroken, from the city that gave up a team to the city that got the franchise."[15] Of course, the 1972 retirement of the three uniform numbers—two worn by players who epitomized the Brooklyn Dodgers, while Koufax was born in Brooklyn and played for both teams—was a turning point.

Other links between the Brooklyn Dodgers and the Los Angeles Dodgers include the continuity of Dodgertown in Vero Beach, the Dodgers' spring training home from 1948 through 2008 (the Dodgers moved their spring training home to Glendale, Arizona, in 2009), as well as the long careers of Lasorda, who joined the team in 1949, announcer Vin Scully, who joined in 1950, and executive Bill DeLury, who joined the team as an office boy in 1950. The fantasy camps, all held at Dodgertown, and Erskine himself also contribute to the bond. Erskine joined the team in 1948, when Dodgertown opened, and he worked at 46 fantasy camps, including the last one in 2008. (The camps ended when spring training was moved to Arizona for the 2009 season.) "It's amazing that my career was so extended," Erskine said. "I told Peter O'Malley one time, 'I've done so many fantasy camps that you've paid me more than your dad did.'"[16]

Peter O'Malley has also worked hard to restore the image of his father, particularly in connection with the Dodgers' move from Brooklyn. In recent years, a series of books has made a strong case that the move was not initially something that O'Malley sought or even envisioned. Rather, he was pushed toward that course by the imperious Robert Moses, who presided over New York's municipal construction programs for decades and who was unwilling to provide an acceptable site for a new ballpark for the Dodgers to replace aging Ebbets Field. Moses vehemently opposed Walter O'Malley's efforts to build one on the corner of Atlantic Avenue and Flatbush Avenue in Brooklyn. In general, Moses' urban vision was focused primarily on the enhancement of access and opportunities for the automobile, rather than for mass transit. It is a vision that has come to be discredited as time has passed, due to a variety of factors including the 1974 publication of *The Power Broker*, the Pulitzer Prize–winning biography of Robert Moses. Subsequently, Moses' role in forcing the departure of the Dodgers has been explored in the 2003 book *The Last Good Season* and the 2009 book *Forever Blue*, a biography of Walter O'Malley for which Peter O'Malley cooperated.

On Oct. 9, 2003, the 100th anniversary of the birth of Walter O'Malley, Peter O'Malley and his sister started a web site, walteromalley.com, to provide biographical information on Walter O'Malley and the history of the move from Brooklyn. "I think that when the move was made and the family arrives here (in Los Angeles), my dad's got a full plate," Peter O'Malley said. "He doesn't have a place to play temporarily, he's got to build a stadium and there are challenges before him on that. So he just didn't focus on what was happening back east, where he was getting banged. I think the beauty of the web site, which lays out thousands of documents, (is that it shows) his efforts over ten years to address the aging of Ebbets Field. That was really lost. That was really never understood.

"In 1946, which is 12 years before the move, he writes a letter to (engineer Emil Praeger, who designed proposed new ballparks in Brooklyn), citing the aging of Ebbets Field. Then he becomes president of the ballclub and he was focused on Ebbets Field. Ebbets Field isn't going to last a whole lot longer, and we've got to deal with the future. So it's this longtime effort and they (wanted) to keep the team in Brooklyn. He had no idea of trying to move somewhere, to leave New York, particularly as interested as he was in television and media. So that piece has been lost over the years, but I think it's finally been realized, this guy not only wanted to stay here and build a stadium, he wanted to do it privately, and not ask the taxpayers. That's been totally lost until recently."

Asked whether he sought to repair a misunderstanding of his father, Peter O'Malley, who was 71 at the time, offered a rationale that has guided him. "It's not a question of misunderstanding or repair. It's a question of, as we all get older, I think if fences have been broken for whatever reason over the years, it's a good idea to try to mend them while you can."[17]

The Furillo family has appreciated O'Malley's fence-mending efforts, although a resentment over the team's action lingers. "My family has the deepest respect for Peter O'Malley," said Carl Furillo, Jr. "My father had a lot of respect for him, my mother speaks very highly of him, and my brother and I both think highly of him. As far as bringing my dad back into baseball, I thank him for doing that, but it was a little late. I wish it could have been sooner, because my father loved the game. But I know Peter was trying to make peace. I know he wanted to do what he thought was right, and he acted as soon as he was in a position to do something. What he did was very satisfying to my father and my mother. It was very important to them."[18]

So Furillo was largely at peace with the Dodgers by December 1988, when he and several family members went to Benton, Pennsylvania, for a long weekend of hunting. He shot a buck. "I was off to the far right, and I went over there," recalled Carl Jr. "Dad had dragged the deer a short distance to a spot, where I found him sitting on a stump looking like somebody had poured a five-gallon bucket of water on him—that's how bad he was sweating. I said, 'Sit here.' I got the deer and started dragging the deer down the hill and he came with me.

"We got to the bottom, a friend of mine took the deer, and I gave Dad back his gun and he says, 'Let's walk out across the field.' Dad liked to talk, we talked a lot, and as we're walking out I said, 'How do you feel?' and he said, 'I feel good, I must have a touch of the flu.' Then I had to go to work, and I said to my brother, 'Keep an eye on Dad.' And Dad came home two days later, with two deer on the back of his Suburban.

"I came out—I was next door—and again, it looked like somebody had poured a five-gallon bottle of water on him. He says, 'I'm all right' and I said, 'No you're not. You're going to the doctor.' Mom took him and when she came back, she was upset. She said, 'Your dad has fluid around his heart. He has congestive heart failure.' Dad was taking his medicine, but he had a tendency to push himself. He always wanted to get it all done.

"I had planned a fishing trip for his birthday on March 8. We were going to go to Pulaski, New York, and fish, my treat. But on January 21 (1989), around six in the morning, I got a call from my brother. He said, 'You'd better get down here, something is wrong with Dad.' I said, 'What's wrong?' And he said, 'Just get down here.' I got in the car and went down to the house and I saw the coroner, who I knew very well, and the ambulance. My mom looked at me and said, 'Your dad is dead.' He had died in his sleep of a massive heart attack. So I asked the coroner if I could spend some time with my dad. I sat down and talked to him. I said, 'Why now, why'd you do this now?' I left out the emotion. I just wanted to talk with him. Then I came downstairs, I went over to my Mom. I said, 'Do you want me to handle everything?' She said yes and I called the funeral home and they came down and got him."[19]

18. THE RIGHT WAY TO LEAVE

Furillo died on a Saturday. Shortly afterwards, Carl Erskine got a phone call from Peter O'Malley, who asked that he meet O'Malley and Sandy Koufax in Philadelphia, where they would get a cab to the funeral home in Reading on Wednesday, January 25. The funeral was delayed, in order to allow visitors to come from around the country. Among the guests were teammates Cal Abrams, Joe Black, Carl Erskine, Sandy Koufax, Clem Labine, Billy Loes and Johnny Podres, as well as O'Malley. Sal Maglie and Pee Wee Reese sent regrets, saying they were too ill to attend.

Several teammates who came had been close to Furillo. "Joe Black and my father were good friends; they called each other once a month," said Carl Jr. "Joe was married four or five times. My dad said, 'What are you doing?' And Joe Black said, 'I can't keep them but I love being married.'" Koufax too had been close to Furillo. "He was my dad's roommate, and my mom used to make him buttermilk cakes," said Carl Jr. "He was like a son to her."[20] Speaking to *The Reading Times*, Koufax recalled that when he joined the team, "Carl was my friend, and in a way he was a big brother to me. He helped me through the early years when I didn't know what I was doing. Both Carl and Fern were like fam-

An unidentified woman, Peter O'Malley, Johnny Podres and Joe Black (left to right) were among the Dodgers who attended Carl Furillo's funeral. After baseball, Joe Black and Furillo talked frequently on the phone (Reading Eagle Company).

ily. They took me into their home. I watched their boys grow up. Most of my memories of Carl are personal. We lived together for a good portion of the year for three or four years. The thing would stand out about Carl was he was my friend."[21] At one point during the funeral, Koufax, acting on Peter O'Malley's behalf, asked Fern Furillo if she would accept a blank check from O'Malley, but she declined.

Recalled Erskine, "We walked into the funeral home and Fern came right to the door along with his two sons and met us and greeted us. Then Fern says to Peter O'Malley, 'Would you say a few words in the service today?' Peter said, 'Well I think one of his teammates should do that, I think Carl here should do that.' It was five minutes later, so I didn't have time to get scared."[22] As he spoke, Erskine stood "white-haired and wearing a black tie, by the sprays of flowers near the open casket to give the eulogy," wrote Dave Anderson in *The New York Times*.[23]

According to Erskine, "One thing I said was, 'Carl was a worker, he came to work, he didn't come to play.' I said I saw him do something

Carl Erskine, Peter O'Malley and Sandy Koufax (left to right) attended Carl Furillo's funeral. Erskine delivered a moving eulogy. He called Furillo "a lunch bucket guy" who always did his job (Reading Eagle Company).

I never saw anybody else do at any level. I saw him, in Ebbets Field, throw runners out at all four bases: home, third base and second base, and twice I saw him throw runners out at first base. That was a unique thing about Carl, the Reading Rifle, his throwing arm was strong.

"Then I said Carl was a strong man, he was physically stout, he wasn't big and burly, but he was very strong. I saw him in two fights, he didn't start either one, but he won both of them. One was in spring training, a guy on the Dodgers, I wouldn't want to name him, but he did things inappropriately. Furillo was a lunch-bucket guy. He went to work, and he couldn't tolerate players who were half-hearted or flippant about their job, and he felt like this is too important to screw around with. The other fight was with (Leo) Durocher. I say Carl won the fight, no question he had the upper hand in that fight. He was a strong man, but he was not a belligerent person.

"Then I mentioned he had two sides, he was very strong-willed, almost on the stubborn side, but then he had a sensitive side. Our old manager, Charlie Dressen, when he wanted to compare things, he would say they were 'like dirt and ice cream.' Carl Furillo was like steel and velvet. You saw the tough side mostly, but he did have a very tender side."[24]

Furillo died relatively young, at 66. In many ways, despite his bitter battle with baseball, he died happy, because he was a man who was comfortable with himself. When he believed in something, he did not back down. Of course, it helped that Peter O'Malley reached out to him. But he found satisfaction not only in the exalted life of a Brooklyn Dodger in the 1950s, but also in more mundane things: his family, his hobbies, and his work, including his final job as a security guard, surrounded by friends. "Dago, stick to your guns,"[25] Fern had told him, and that is what he did.

Appendix: Furillo's Career Statistics

NAME: Carl Anthony Furillo
BORN: March 8, 1922, Stony Creek Mills, Pennsylvania
DIED: January 21, 1989, Stony Creek Mills, Pennsylvania
FIRST ML GAME: April 16, 1946
LAST ML GAME: May 7, 1960
BATTED: Right
THREW: Right

MINOR LEAGUE RECORD

		Games	AB	R	H	2b	3b	HR	RBI	SB	BA
1940	Pocomoke	71	235	36	75	15	3	9	39	4	319
1940	Reading	8	30	3	11	0	1	0	2	0	367
1941	Reading	125	482	87	151	23	16	10	76	8	313
1942	Montreal	129	445	55	125	21	6	3	51	13	281

Major League Record

		Games	AB	R	H	2b	3b	HR	RBI	SB	BB	SO	BA	OBP	SLUG
1946	Brooklyn	117	335	29	95	18	6	3	35	6	31	20	284	346	400
1947	Brooklyn	124	437	61	129	24	7	8	88	7	34	24	295	347	437
1948	Brooklyn	108	364	55	108	20	4	4	44	6	43	32	297	374	407
1949	Brooklyn	142	549	95	177	27	10	18	106	4	37	29	322	368	506
1950	Brooklyn	153	620	99	189	30	6	18	106	8	41	40	305	353	460
1951	Brooklyn	158	667	93	197	32	4	16	91	8	43	33	295	344	427
1952	Brooklyn	134	425	52	105	18	1	8	59	1	31	33	247	304	351
1953	Brooklyn	132	479	82	165	38	6	21	92	1	34	32	344	393	580
1954	Brooklyn	150	547	56	161	23	1	19	96	2	49	35	294	356	444
1955	Brooklyn	140	523	83	164	24	3	26	95	4	43	43	314	371	520
1956	Brooklyn	149	523	66	151	30	0	21	83	1	57	41	289	357	467
1957	Brooklyn	119	395	61	121	17	4	12	66	0	29	33	306	358	461
1958	Los Angeles	122	411	54	119	19	3	18	83	0	35	28	290	343	482
1959	Los Angeles	50	93	8	27	4	0	0	13	0	7	11	290	333	333
1960	Los Angeles	8	10	1	2	0	1	0	1	0	0	2	200	200	400
	Totals	1806	6378	895	1910	324	56	192	1058	48	514	436	299	355	458

World Series Record

		Games	AB	R	H	2b	3b	HR	RBI	SB	BB	SO	BA	OBP	SLUG
1947	Brooklyn	6	17	2	6	2	0	0	3	0	3	0	353	450	471
1949	Brooklyn	3	8	0	1	0	0	0	0	0	1	0	125	222	125
1952	Brooklyn	7	23	1	4	2	0	0	0	0	3	3	174	269	261
1953	Brooklyn	6	24	4	8	2	0	1	4	0	1	3	333	360	542
1955	Brooklyn	7	27	4	8	1	0	1	3	0	3	5	296	387	444
1956	Brooklyn	7	25	2	6	2	0	0	1	0	2	3	240	296	320
1959	Los Angeles	4	4	0	1	0	0	0	2	0	0	1	250	250	250
	Totals	40	128	13	34	9	0	2	13	0	13	15	266	338	383

Chapter Notes

Introduction

1. Carl Furillo interview, 1970, Flushing, NY.
2. Ibid.
3. Carl Furillo, Jr., interview, April 8, 2009.
4. Carl Erskine interview, Sept. 29, 2008.
5. Peter O'Malley quoted in *Reading Eagle*, January 26, 1989.
6. Carl Furillo, Jr., interview, April 8, 2009.
7. Carl Erskine interview, Sept. 29, 2008. The eulogy is quoted from memory as there is no written record.
8. Ibid.
9. Ibid.
10. Carl Furillo, Jr., interview, April 8, 2009.

Chapter 1

1. Carl Furillo interview, 1970, Flushing, NY.
2. Carl Furillo, Jr., interview, April 8, 2009.
3. Carl Furillo interview, 1970, Flushing, NY.
4. Carl Furillo, Jr., interview, April 8, 2009.
5. Carl Furillo interview, 1970, Flushing, NY.
6. Carl Furillo, Jr., interview, April 8, 2009.
7. Jerry Kobrin, "Fresco Thompson Sees Big League Prospect in Stony Creek Product," *Reading Eagle*, 1941, date not available.
8. Ibid.
9. Carl Furillo interview, 1970, Flushing, NY.
10. Kobrin, "Fresco Thompson Sees Big League Prospect in Stony Creek Product," *Reading Eagle*, 1941.
11. Gene Hermanski interview, Sept. 30, 2008.
12. Carl Furillo interview, 1970, Flushing, NY.
13. "Promoted to Peeps," *Reading Times*, 1940, date not available.
14. Gordon Williams, "In the Realm of Sports," *Reading Times*, Sept. 27, 1947.
15. Tom Oliver, quoted in "Tom Oliver Recalls Time When He Was Embarrassed by Furillo's Arm," by Bill Reedy, *Reading Eagle*, July 24, 1946.
16. Carl Furillo interview, 1970, Flushing, NY.
17. Fresco Thompson, quoted in "Fresco Thompson Sees Big League Prospect in Stony Creek Product," by Jerry Kobrin, *Reading Eagle*, 1941.
18. Carl Furillo interview, 1970, Flushing, NY.
19. Kobrin, "Fresco Thompson Sees Big League Prospects in Stony Creek Product," *Reading Eagle*, 1941,
20. Carl Furillo interview, 1970, Flushing, NY.
21. "Carl Cashes In on Popularity," unidentified Reading newspaper, Aug. 20, 1941.

22. Elmer Ferguson, "The Gist and Jest of It," *Montreal Herald*, 1942, date not available.
23. Carl Furillo interview, 1970, Flushing, NY.
24. Elmer Ferguson, "The Gist and Jest of It," *Montreal Herald*, 1942.
25. Ibid.
26. Lloyd McGowan, "Furillo Quite a Fellow, Royals Fandom Finds," *Montreal Star*, May 19, 1942.
27. Carl Furillo interview, 1970, Flushing, NY.
28. Bill Reedy, *Reading Eagle*, June 1, 1942.
29. Dink Carroll, "Furillo Draws Praise as Sure Major League Prospect from Manager and Several Scouts," *Montreal Gazette*, September, 1942.
30. "Montreal Keeps Furillo on Reserve List," *Reading Eagle*, Oct. 22, 1942.
31. "Furillo Inducted Into Army at Allentown," *Reading Eagle*, Nov. 5, 1942.
32. Carl Furillo, Jr., interview, March 10, 2010.
33. Carl Furillo interview, 1970, Flushing, NY.

Chapter 2

1. Carl Furillo interview, 1970, Flushing, NY.
2. Ibid.
3. Ibid.
4. Gordon Williams, "In the Realm of Sports," *Reading Times*, Feb. 22, 1952.
5. Mike Gaven, quoted by Williams, "In the Realm of Sports," *Reading Times*, Feb. 22, 1952.
6. Leo Durocher, quoted by Associated Press, "Carl Furillo to Get Full Opportunity," unidentified Reading newspaper, April 19, 1946.
7. Carl Furillo interview, 1970, Flushing, NY.
8. Ibid.
9. Ed Head's comments to Associated Press, quoted in "Head Lauds Furillo's Great Catch That Saved No-Hitter," unidentified Reading newspaper, April 24, 1946.
10. *New York Times*, quoted in "Head Lauds Furillo's Great Catch That Saved No-Hitter," unidentified Reading newspaper, April 24, 1946.
11. Jerry Kobrin, "Carl Furillo Gleams in Shibe Park," *Reading Eagle*, April 25, 1946.
12. Carl Furillo, quoted by Jerry Kobrin, "Carl Furillo Gleams in Shibe Park," *Reading Eagle*, April 25, 1946.
13. Jerry Kobrin, "Carl Furillo Gleams in Shibe Park," *Reading Eagle*, April 25, 1946.
14. Charlie Dressen, quoted by Jerry Kobrin, "Carl Furillo Gleams in Shibe Park," *Reading Eagle*, April 25, 1946.
15. Dixie Walker, quoted by Jerry Kobrin, "Carl Furillo Gleams in Shibe Park," *Reading Eagle*, April 25, 1946.
16. Carl Furillo, quoted by Jerry Kobrin, "Carl Furillo Gleams in Shibe Park," *Reading Eagle*, April 25, 1946.
17. Carl Furillo interview, 1970, Flushing, NY.
18. Ibid.
19. International News Service, "Furillo, Reese Lone Survivors of Lip's Early Season Dodgers," unidentified Reading newspaper, Oct. 3, 1946.
20. Carl Furillo interview, 1970, Flushing, NY.

Chapter 3

1. Happy Chandler with Vance Trimble. *Heroes, Plain Folks, and Skunks: The Life and Times of Happy Chandler*. Chicago: Bonus Books,1989.
2. Ibid, page 229.
3. Carl Furillo interview, 1970, Flushing, NY.
4. While Furillo says he was a rookie, he was about to start his second season with the Dodgers in the spring of 1947. Also, while he says he was in a Navy barracks in Panama, some accounts say it was an Army barracks.
5. Bobby Bragan interview, April 13, 2009.
6. Harold Parrott, *The Sporting News*, Feb. 3, 1973.
7. Carl Erskine, e-mail to author, Jan. 30, 2010.
8. Carl Furillo, Jr., interview, Jan. 30, 2010.
9. *The Jackie Robinson Story*, screenplay by Arthur Mann and Lawrence Taylor, release by Eagle-Lion, 1950.
10. Carl Furillo, Jr., interview, April 8, 2009.
11. Jackie Robinson, *I Never Had it Made*. New York: Harper Collins, 1972.
12. Arnold Rampersad, *Jackie Robinson: A Biography*. New York: The Ballantine Publishing Group, 1997.
13. Carl Erskine, e-mail to author, Oct. 19, 2009.
14. Bill Traugher, "Tommy Brown Recalls His Career," SABRgrafs, written in 2005 and published by the Society for American Baseball Research, Sept. 14, 2009.
15. Pee Wee Reese, quoted by Peter Golenbock in *Bums*. New York: G.P. Putnam's Sons, 1984.

16. Buzzie Bavasi, in an e-mail to Bill Ninfo, quoted in *Carl Furillo: The Forgotten Dodger*. Bloomington, IN: 1stBooks Library, 2002.
17. Kirby Higbe with Martin Quigley, *The High Hard One*. New York: Viking Press, 1967.
18. Bobby Bragan interview, April 13, 2009.
19. Gene Hermanski interview, Jan. 31, 2010.
20. Ralph Branca interview, April 27, 2009.
21. Lester Rodney interview, Nov. 14, 2009. Rodney died Dec. 20, 2009.
22. Carl Erskine, e-mail to author, Feb. 17, 2010.
23. Carl Furillo, Jr., interview, Feb. 16, 2010.
24. Bobby Bragan interview, April 13, 2009.
25. Jack Lang interview, 2006.
26. Carl Erskine interview, Sept. 29, 2008.
27. Roy Campanella, quoted by Larry Stewart, in "Carl Furillo, Dodger Outfielder for 15 Seasons, Is Dead at Age 66" in *Los Angeles Times*, Jan. 22, 1989.
28. Roger Kahn, "Views of Sport: Carl Furillo, 1922–1989," *New York Times*, Jan. 29, 1989.
29. Ibid.
30. Research by Lyle Spatz indicates the photograph was taken on May 12, 1947, the only day the Dodgers were home between May 9 and May 23. The picture includes Al Gionfriddo, who joined the team in a May 3 trade, but does not include Howie Schultz, who was sold on May 10.
31. Carl Furillo, Jr., interview, Jan. 15, 2010.

Chapter 4

1. Carl Furillo, quoted by Doc Silva in "Carl Furillo Joins Holdout Ranks," *Reading Times*, Feb. 6, 1947.
2. Ron Fairly interview, Nov. 6, 2009.
3. Roger Kahn, *The Boys of Summer*. New York: Harper & Row, 1972.
4. Roger Kahn, "Views of Sport: Carl Furillo, 1922–1989," *New York Times*, Jan. 29, 1989.
5. Carl Furillo, quoted by Doc Silva in "Carl Furillo Joins Holdout Ranks," *Reading Times*, Feb. 6, 1947.
6. *Reading Times*, Feb. 12, 1947.
7. Carl Furillo, quoted in "Carl Furillo Ends Brooklyn Holdout," *Reading Times*, Feb. 17, 1947.
8. Lester Bromberg, story in unidentified Reading newspaper, March 9, 1947.

9. Carl Furillo, quoted by Lester Bromberg, in Reading newspaper, March 9, 1947.
10. Bobby Bragan interview, April 13, 2009.
11. Jackie Robinson, quoted by Mike Gaven in *The Sporting News*, Jan. 16, 1957.
12. Leo Durocher, quoted in "The Furillo Case," *Reading Times*, April 8, 1947.
13. Mike Gaven, *New York Journal-American*, quoted in "The Furillo Case," *Reading Times*, April 8, 1947.
14. Carl Furillo interview, 1970, Flushing, NY.
15. Bill Reedy column, *Reading Eagle*, April 11, 1947.
16. Stan Baumgartner, "Phils Won't Hold Still as Shills—See Rickey Offer as Buildup," *The Sporting News*, April 16, 1947.
17. Bobby Bragan interview, April 13, 2009.
18. Carl Furillo interview, 1970, Flushing, NY.
19. Carl Furillo, quoted by Gordon Williams, "In the Realm of Sports," *Reading Times*, July 1, 1947.
20. Gene Hermanski interview, Jan. 31, 2010.
21. Carl Furillo, quoted by Gordon Williams, "In the Realm of Sports," *Reading Times*, July 1, 1947.
22. Gordon Williams, "In the Realm of Sports," *Reading Times*, July 1, 1947.
23. Carl Furillo, quoted by Gordon Williams, "In the Realm of Sports," *Reading Times*, July 1, 1947.
24. Gordon Williams, "In the Realm of Sports," *Reading Times*, July 1, 1947.
25. Carl Furillo interview, 1970, Flushing, NY.
26. Bill Reedy column, *Reading Eagle*, July 27, 1947.
27. "Furillo 'Burns Up' Cubs," *The Sporting News*, Sept. 17, 1949.
28. Carl Furillo interview, 1970, Flushing, NY.
29. Bobby Bragan interview, April 13, 2009.
30. Carl Furillo interview, 1970, Flushing, NY.

Chapter 5

1. Carl Furillo interview, 1970, Flushing, NY.
2. Joan Hodges interview, January 18, 2010.
3. Carl Furillo interview, 1970, Flushing, NY.
4. Les Biederman, "Rickeys Sr. and Jr. Tell of Contract Parleys; Furillo Always Late

Signer—But Never Balked," *The Sporting News*, March 2, 1955.
5. Carl Furillo, quoted in "Carl Furillo Joins Ranks of Holdouts," *Reading Times*, Feb. 6, 1948.
6. Carl Furillo, quoted by Gordon Williams, "Rickey Meets Salary Demands Via Telephone," in *Reading Times*, Feb. 24, 1948.
7. Carl Furillo, quoted in "Furillo Likes Dodgers," *Reading Times*, March 8, 1948.
8. "Birthday Cakes by the Box in March," *The Sporting News*, March 3, 1948.
9. Bobby Bragan interview, April 13, 2009.
10. Carl Furillo interview, 1970, Flushing, NY.
11. Ibid.
12. Bill Reedy column, *The Reading Eagle*, April 13, 1948.
13. Mike Gaven, *New York Journal-American*, quoted in "The Baseball Front," *Reading Times*, April 27, 1948.
14. Carl Furillo interview, 1970, Flushing, NY.
15. Bill Reedy column, *The Reading Eagle*, June 29, 1948.
16. Dick Young, *The Daily News*, quoted in *Reading Times*, May 4, 1948.
17. Les Biederman, "Pirates Foiled in Repeated Efforts to Get Furillo from the Dodgers," *The Sporting News*, May 26, 1948.
18. Carl Furillo, quoted in *Reading Times*, June 24, 1948.
19. "'The Arm' Obtains Marriage Permit," *Reading Times*, June 22, 1948.
20. Carl Furillo, quoted in *Reading Times*, June 24, 1948.
21. Fern Furillo, quoted in "'The Arm' Obtains Marriage Permit," *Reading Times*, June 22, 1948.
22. Bill Ninfo, *Carl Furillo: The Forgotten Dodger*. Bloomington, IN: 1stBooks Library, 2002.
23. Carl Furillo interview, 1970, Flushing, NY.
24. Ibid.
25. Carl Erskine interview, Sept. 29, 2008.
26. Carl Erskine, e-mail to author, Feb. 4, 2010.
27. Fern Furillo, quoted by Carl Furillo, Jr., in interview, March 24, 2010.
28. Carl Furillo, quoted by Gordon Williams, "The Baseball Front," *Reading Times*, Oct. 1, 1948.
29. Gordon Williams, "The Baseball Front," *Reading Times*, early October, 1948.
30. *The Sporting News*, December 8, 1948.
31. Whitey Kurowski, quoted in Bill Reedy column, *Reading Eagle*, Dec. 10, 1948.

Chapter 6

1. Carl Furillo interview, Flushing, NY, 1970.
2. Burt Shotton, quoted by Gordon Williams, *Reading Times*, March 18, 1949.
3. Gordon Williams, "In the Realm of Sports," *Reading Times*, April 15, 1949.
4. Burt Shotton, quoted in "Furillo's Arm Rates with Any in Business," unidentified Reading newspaper, April 28, 1949.
5. Carl Furillo interview, Flushing, NY, 1970.
6. Fay Vincent interview, April 17, 2009.
7. Carl Erskine interview, Sept. 29, 2008
8. Bob Cooke, *New York Herald Tribune*, quoted in Bill Reedy column, *Reading Eagle*, July 24, 1949.
9. Ralph Branca interview, April 27, 2009.
10. Clem Labine, quoted by Rich Ziemba in "Teammates Remember ex–Dodger," *Reading Times*, Jan. 26, 1989.
11. Carl Furillo interview, Flushing, NY, 1970.
12. Ibid.
13. Carl Furillo, quoted by Gordon Williams, "In the Realm of Sports," *Reading Eagle*, April 17, 1949.
14. Carl Furillo interview, Flushing, NY, 1970.
15. Bill Reedy column, *Reading Eagle*, July 24, 1949.
16. Burt Shotton, quoted by Chet Hagan in "Brooklyn Manager Credits Berks Slugger for Dodgers' Success," *Reading Eagle*, Sept. 24, 1949. Hagan later became an Emmy Award–winning NBC News producer.
17. "25 Years Ago," *The Sporting News*, Aug. 10, 1974.
18. Carl Furillo interview, Flushing, NY, 1970
19. Carl Furillo quoted in "Feud and Injury Helped Furillo to Batting Diadem," *The Sporting News*, Dec. 16, 1973.
20. Milton Gross, "The Sport Profile: Brooklyn's Good Right Arm," *Sport Magazine*, June, 1950.
21. Carl Furillo interview, Flushing, NY, 1970.
22. Bill Paddock, "Dodger Snapshots," *The Sporting News*, Oct. 12, 1949.
23. Carl Furillo interview, Flushing, NY, 1970.
24. Pee Wee Reese, quoted by Bill Roeder in "Hats Off" column, *The Sporting News*, Oct. 12, 1949.
25. Dick Young, "Flock Pins Series Hope on Recovery of Furillo," *Daily News*, Oct. 4, 1949.
26. Chet Hagan, "Dodger Hopes in Se-

ries Ride with Furillo, *Reading Eagle*, Oct. 4, 1949.
27. Jackie Robinson, ibid.
28. Burt Shotton, ibid.
29. Chet Hagan, "Shotton's Judgment in Playing Crippled Furillo Questioned," *Reading Eagle*, Oct. 6, 1949.
30. Carl Furillo, ibid.
31. Burt Shotton, ibid.
32. Carl Furillo, ibid.
33. Carl Furillo, quoted by Chet Hagan in "Dodger Hopes in Series Ride with Furillo," *Reading Eagle*, Oct. 4, 1949.
34. Carl Furillo interview, Flushing, NY, 1970.
35. Franklin Lewis, in "Bests and Worsts of Big Series," *The Sporting News*, Oct. 19, 1949.
36. Carl Furillo interview, Flushing, NY, 1970.

Chapter 7

1. Carl Furillo interview, Flushing, NY, 1970.
2. Carl Furillo, quoted by Gordon Williams, "In the Realm of Sports," *Reading Times*, Jan. 6, 1950.
3. Gordon Williams, "In the Real of Sports," *Reading Times*, Feb. 23, 1950.
4. Frank Eck, *Associated Press*, quoted in Bill Reedy column, *Reading Eagle*, April 2, 1950.
5. Harold Parrott, ibid.
6. Milton Gross, in "The Sport Profile: Brooklyn's Good Right Arm," *Sport Magazine*, June, 1950.
7. Carl Furillo interview, Flushing, NY, 1970.
8. Bill Reedy column, *Reading Eagle*, Aug. 8, 1950.
9. Carl Furillo interview, Flushing, NY, 1970.

Chapter 8

1. Carl Furillo interview, Flushing, NY, 1970.
2. Bill Reedy column, *Reading Eagle*, Feb. 11, 1951.
3. Gordon Williams, "In the Realm of Sports," *Reading Times*, Feb. 10, 1951.
4. Bill Reedy column, *Reading Eagle*, Jan. 7, 1951.
5. Jackie Robinson, quoted in unspecified article, quoted in ibid.
6. Carl Furillo, quoted in Camel advertisement, 1951.
7. Carl Furillo interview, Flushing, NY, 1970.
8. Oscar Ruhl, "The Ruhl Book," *The Sporting News*, July 11, 1951.

9. Carl Furillo interview, Flushing, NY, 1970.
10. Fern Furillo, quoted by Chet Hagan in "Carl Furillo Admits Being Very Tired," *Reading Eagle*, Oct. 2, 1951.
11. Carl Furillo interview, Flushing, NY, 1970.
12. Carl Furillo, quoted in "Dodgers Mum on Pennant, Pulling Together—Furillo," unidentified Reading newspaper, July 10, 1951.
13. Carl Furillo interview, Flushing, NY, 1970.
14. Charlie Dressen, quoted in Bill Reedy column, *Reading Eagle*, July 17, 1951.
15. Pat Robinson, in "Carl Furillo May Develop into Greatest Leadoff Man," INS story published in unidentified Reading newspaper, Aug. 10, 1951.
16. Fred Down, "Carl Furillo, Monte Irvin Most Under-Rated Stars," UPI article published in unidentified Reading newspaper, Sept. 13, 1951.
17. Carl Furillo, quoted by Milton Richman of UPI in Bill Reedy column, *Reading Eagle*, Sept. 7, 1951.
18. Bill Reedy, ibid.
19. Carl Furillo interview, Flushing, NY, 1970.
20. Ibid.
21. Chet Hagan, "Carl Furillo Admits Being Very Tired," *Reading Eagle*, Oct. 2, 1951.
22. Ralph Branca interview, April 27, 2009.
23. Carl Furillo interview, Flushing, NY, 1970.

Chapter 9

1. Carl Furillo interview, Flushing, NY, 1970.
2. Carl Furillo, quoted by Gordon Williams, "In the Realm of Sports," *Reading Times*, Feb. 18, 1952.
3. Gordon Williams, "Furillo Aims High," *Reading Times*, March 25, 1952.
4. Carl Furillo, ibid.
5. Carl Furillo, quoted by Gordon Williams, "In the Realm of Sports," *Reading Times*, May 26, 1952.
6. Carl Furillo interview, Flushing, NY, 1970.
7. Carl Furillo, quoted by Gordon Williams, "In the Realm of Sports," *Reading Times*, Oct. 29, 1952.
8. Carl Furillo interview, Flushing, NY, 1970.
9. Dick Young, "Carl Furillo Undergoes Surgery on Both Eyes," *Daily News*, Jan. 9, 1953.

10. Carl Furillo interview, Flushing, NY, 1970.

Chapter 10

1. Carl Furillo, quoted in "New Pact Gives Slight Increase Over '52 Salary," unidentified Reading paper, Jan. 14, 1953.
2. Carl Furillo, quoted in "Furillo Refuses to Blame Eyes for Bad Year," *United Press International*, published in unidentified Reading paper, March 10, 1953.
3. Carl Furillo, quoted by Fred Down, in "Furillo Figures He'll Hit Better Than .300 in '53," *United Press International*, published in unidentified Reading paper, April 29, 1953.
4. Carl Furillo interview, Flushing, NY, 1970.
5. Judith Testa, *Sal Maglie: Baseball's Demon Barber*. Dekalb: Northern Illinois University Press, 2007.
6. Carl Furillo, quoted in "Accidental Slips by Sal and Carl," *The Sporting News*, May 6, 1953.
7. Walter O'Malley, quoted in Judith Testa, *Sal Maglie: Baseball's Demon Barber*, Dekalb: Northern Illinois University Press, 2007.
8. Carl Furillo interview, Flushing, NY, 1970.
9. Carl Furillo, quoted by Peter Coutros in "Low, the Poor Skoonj!" *Daily News*, May 22, 1955.
10. Larry Goetz, quoted in "Furillo, Beaned by Rush, Raps Double on Next Trip," *The Sporting News*, July 29, 1953.
11. Babe Pinelli, quoted in "Pinelli has Perfect 1.000 Attendance Mark as Ump," *The Sporting News*, March 2, 1955.
12. Carl Furillo interview, Flushing, NY, 1970.
13. Dick Young, in "Furillo's Finger Broken in Row with Leo—'I'm Gonna Get Him,'" *Daily News*, Sept. 7, 1953.
14. Carl Furillo, ibid.
15. Leo Durocher, quoted in "Carl Furillo Breaks Bone in Left Hand," *Associated Press*, published in unidentified Reading paper, Sept. 6, 1953,
16. Carl Furillo, quoted by Gordon Williams, "In the Realm of Sports," *Reading Times*, Sept. 8, 1953.
17. Charlie Dressen, quoted by Roscoe McGowan in "Close Shaves Follow Homers as Campy Battles with Barber," *The Sporting News*, April 28, 1954.
18. Ernie Harwell, in "Biggest Thrills of the Season," *The Sporting News*, Jan. 6, 1954.
19. Carl Erskine, e-mail to author, May 30, 2009.
20. Carl Furillo interview, Flushing, NY, 1970.
21. Joan Hodges interview, Jan. 18, 2010.
22. Carl Furillo interview, Flushing, NY, 1970.
23. Charley DiGiovanna, "Furillo Home Run in Series DiGiovanna's No. 1 Thrill," *The Sporting News*, Sept. 28, 1955.
24. Carl Furillo, quoted by Gordon Williams, "In the Realm of Sports," *Reading Times*, Oct. 5, 1953.

Chapter 11

1. Carl Furillo interview, 1970, Flushing, NY.
2. Ibid.
3. Carl Furillo, quoted in *Reading Times*, Jan. 27, 1954.
4. Carl Furillo interview, 1970, Flushing, NY.
5. Ibid.
6. Carl Furillo, quoted by Harry Dilser in "Furillo Foursome Off Monday for Annual Jaunt to South," *Reading Times*, Jan. 21, 1955.
7. Carl Furillo, quoted in "Quickie Quotes," *The Sporting News*, May 25, 1955.
8. Roscoe McGowan, "Furillo Offers No Alibis—Could Have Nailed Dark," *The Sporting News*, May 4, 1955.
9. Roscoe McGowan, in "Hats Off," *The Sporting News*, May 11, 1955.
10. Peter Coutros, "Low, the Poor Skoonj!" *Daily News*, May 22, 1955.
11. Carl Furillo, ibid.
12. Carl Furillo, quoted by Dick Young, in "Furillo Wants No Part of Rest for Regulars," *Daily News*, Sept. 13, 1955.
13. Carl Furillo, quoted in "Furillo's Single Hits Sign, Dodger Wins A Suit of Clothing," unidentified Reading paper, Oct. 1, 1955.
14. Carl Furillo interview, 1970, Flushing, NY.
15. Carl Erskine, e-mail to author, May 30, 2009.
16. Carl Furillo interview, 1970, Flushing, NY.
17. Lester Rodney interview, Oct. 31, 2009.
18. Carl Furillo, quoted in *Reading Times*, Oct. 5, 1955.
19. Walter Alston, quoted by Dick Young, in "Dirty Play on Diamond Helps Breed Juvenile Delinquency, Asserts Furillo," *The Sporting News*, March 14, 1956.

Chapter 12

1. Carl Furillo interview, 1970, Flushing, NY.

2. Tom Villante, e-mail to author, Dec. 5, 2008.
3. Interview with Sal Maglie, April 11, 1969, Seattle, Wash. The interview was conducted at Sicks' Stadium, where the Seattle Pilots were playing their inaugural home game. Maglie was the pitching coach.
4. Judith Testa, *Sal Maglie: Baseball's Demon Barber*. DeKalb: Northern Illinois University Press, 2007.
5. Interview with Carl Furillo, Jr., Dec. 16, 2009.
6. Judith Testa, *Sal Maglie: Baseball's Demon Barber*. DeKalb: Northern Illinois University Press, 2007.
7. Interview with Carl Furillo, Jr., Dec. 16, 2009.
8. Judith Testa, *Sal Maglie: Baseball's Demon Barber*. DeKalb: Northern Illinois University Press, 2007.
9. Interview with Carl Furillo, Jr., Dec. 16, 2009.
10. Tom Villante, e-mail to author, Dec. 5, 2008.
11. Carl Furillo interview, 1970, Flushing, NY.
12. Carl Furillo, quoted by Doc Silva, in "Salute to Sports," *Reading Times*, Oct. 25, 1956.
13. Interview with Carl Furillo, Jr., Dec. 16, 2009.
14. Bill Reedy column, *Reading Eagle*, March 10, 1956.
15. Carl Furillo, quoted by Dick Young, "Clubhouse Confidential," *The Sporting News*, March 3, 1928.
16. Carl Furillo, quoted by Doc Silva in "Salute to Sports," *Reading Times*, April 13, 1956.
17. Interview with Carl Furillo, 1970, Flushing, NY.
18. Ibid.
19. Pete Hamill, *New York Post*, Sept. 11, 1969.
20. *Associated Press*, "Furillo's Homer In 10th Beats Reds 5–4," *Reading Times*, Sept. 17, 1956.
21. Doc Silva, "Salute to Sports," *Reading Times*, Sept. 21, 1956.
22. Carl Furillo, quoted by Dick Young, "Riled by 'Over the Hill Hints,' Furillo Says Only Illness Balked Bat Crown," *The Sporting News*, March 6, 1957.
23. Dick Young, ibid.
24. Furillo, ibid.
25. Carl Furillo, in "Carl Furillo to Sell Home at Stony Creek," *Reading Times*, Oct. 4, 1956.
26. Ibid.
27. Carl Furillo interview, 1970, Flushing, NY.
28. Ibid.
29. Carl Furillo, quoted in "Brooks Consider Invitation for Japanese Junket in Fall," *The Sporting News*, May 9, 1956.
30. Carl Furillo, quoted by Doc Silva, "Salute to Sports," *Reading Times*, Dec. 11, 1956.
31. Carl Furillo interview, 1970, Flushing, NY.
32. Ibid.
33. Letter from Roscoe McGowan, quoted by Doc Silva, "Salute to Sports," *Reading Times*, Dec. 11, 1956.

Chapter 13

1. Carl Furillo interview, 1970, Flushing, NY.
2. Quoted by Emanuel Perlmutter in "Dodgers Accept Los Angeles Bid to Move to Coast," *New York Times*, Oct. 9, 1957.
3. Doc Silva, "Carl Furillo Signs '57 Dodger Contract," *Reading Times*, Jan. 8, 1957.
4. Doc Silva, "Salute to Sports," *Reading Times*, Jan. 15, 1957.
5. "Furillo Climbs in Hit Parade," *The Sporting News*, May 29, 1957.
6. Carl Furillo, quoted in "Durocher, Furillo Bury Ax," *The Sporting News*, August 14, 1957.
7. Roscoe McGowan, in *The Sporting News*, Sept. 18, 1957.
8. Team-by-team summary of 1957 season, *The Sporting News*, Oct. 2, 1957.
9. Carl Furillo interview, 1970, Flushing, NY.
10. Ibid.
11. Dick Young, "Furillo .300 on the Nose for 12 Seasons," *The Sporting News*, Oct. 16, 1957.
12. Carl Furillo interview, 1970, Flushing, NY.
13. Dick Young, "Training Tidbits from Arizona to Florida," *The Sporting News*, March 5, 1958.
14. Carl Furillo interview, 1970, Flushing, NY.
15. Joe King, "Deterioration Rap Denied by Alston, Furillo," *The Sporting News*, May 21, 1958.
16. Carl Furillo interview, 1970, Flushing, NY.
17. Ibid.
18. Carl Erskine, e-mail to author, June 28, 2009.
19. Carl Furillo interview, 1970, Flushing, NY.

Chapter 14

1. Ron Fairly interview, Nov. 6, 2009.

2. Ibid.
3. Joe King, "Fairly Finds Pal in Furillo, Whose Job Ron Seeks," *The Sporting News*, April 1, 1959.
4. Ron Fairly interview, Nov. 6, 2009.
5. Carl Furillo interview, 1970, Flushing, NY.
6. Carl Erskine interview, Sept. 29, 2008.
7. Carl Furillo interview, 1970, Flushing, NY.
8. Ibid.
9. Bill Becker, "Bad Hop Good Break for Furillo," *New York Times*, Oct. 4, 1959.
10. Carl Furillo, ibid.
11. Walter Alston, ibid.
12. Carl Furillo interview, 1970, Flushing, NY.
13. Ron Fairly interview, Nov. 6, 2009.
14. Carl Furillo, Jr., interview, Dec. 30, 2009.

Chapter 15

1. Carl Furillo interview, 1970, Flushing, NY.
2. *The Sporting News*, March 9, 1960.
3. Frank Finch, "Furillo Fights to Keep Dodger Job," *Los Angeles Times*, Feb. 28, 1960.
4. Buzzie Bavasi, ibid.
5. Carl Furillo, ibid.
6. Buzzie Bavasi, letter to Roy Hamey, Feb. 24, 1960.
7. Roy Hamey, letter to Buzzie Bavasi, March 7, 1960.
8. Bucky Harris, letter to Buzzie Bavasi, March 11, 1960.
9. Bob Hunter, in *The Sporting News*, March 9, 1960.
10. Jimmy Cannon, "Furillo Forecast Fate to Cannon," *Los Angeles Herald-Express*, May 19, 1960.
11. Carl Furillo, Jr., interview on Oct. 4, 2009.
12. Bob Hunter in *The Sporting News*, April 6, 1960.
13. Carl Furillo interview, 1970, Flushing, NY.
14. Ibid.
15. Buzzie Bavasi, letter to Ford Frick, May 27, 1961.
16. Carl Furillo interview, 1970, Flushing, NY.
17. Ibid.
18. Carl Furillo, in transcript of hearing before Commissioner Ford Frick, June 16, 1961.
19. Ibid.
20. Carl Furillo interview, 1970, Flushing, NY.
21. Carl Furillo interview, 1970, Flushing, NY.
22. Gerald Eskenazi, "Furillo Waiting on Deck for Baseball's Call, but Phone Doesn't Ring," *New York Times*, Sept. 1, 1968.
23. Carl Furillo interview, 1970, Flushing, NY.
24. Buzzie Bavasi, letter to Ford Frick, May 27, 1961.
25. Arthur Cowan, quoted by Dan Hafner in "Furillo Considers Suing Club," *Los Angeles Examiner*, May 19, 1960.
26. Carl Furillo, ibid.
27. Fern Furillo, quoted by Jeanne Hoffman, in "Mrs. Furillo Prefers to Have Carl in Outfield, Not Home," *Los Angeles Times*, May 19, 1960.
28. Jimmy Cannon, "Furillo Forecast Fate to Cannon," *Los Angeles Herald-Express*, May 19, 1960.
29. Carl Furillo, ibid.
30. Buzzie Bavasi, letter to Carl Furillo, May 23, 1960.
31. Bob Hunter, "All's Well That Pays Carl Well," *Los Angeles Examiner*, July 1961, date not available.
32. Carl Erskine interview, Sept. 29, 2008.

Chapter 16

1. Ford Frick, in findings issued July 13, 1961, following June 16, 1961, hearing.
2. Ford Frick, in testimony at June 16, 1961, hearing.
3. Ibid.
4. Buzzie Bavasi, quoted in Bill Ninfo, *Carl Furillo: The Forgotten Dodger*. Bloomington, IN: 1stBooks Library, 2002.
5. Carl Furillo interview, 1970, Flushing, NY.
6. Carl Furillo interview, 1970, Flushing, NY.
7. Buzzie Bavasi, quoted in "The Furillo Case," *Baseball Monthly*, April, 1962.
8. Interview with Carl Furillo, Jr., Oct. 4, 2009.
9. Carl Furillo interview, 1970, Flushing, NY.
10. Ibid.
11. Ibid.
12. Ibid.
13. Carl Furillo, quoted by Dan Hafner, in "Furillo Fires Blacklist Charge," *Los Angeles Examiner*, March 29, 1961.
14. Gene Autry, quoted by United Press International, in "Furillo Tale Denied by Gene Autry," *Los Angeles Mirror*, March 3, 1961.
15. Jean Hoffman, in "Carl Furillo to Huddle with Frick," *Los Angeles Times*, June 3, 1961.

16. Carl Furillo interview, 1970, Flushing, NY.
17. Ibid.
18. Paul Caruso, in testimony at June 16, 1961, hearing.
19. Harry Walsh, in testimony at June 16, 1961, hearing.
20. Carl Furillo, in testimony at June 16, 1961, hearing.
21. Furillo and Walsh, ibid.
22. Harry Walsh, in note, May 23, 1961.
23. Ford Frick, in findings issued July 13, 1961.
24. Ibid.
25. Bob Hunter, "All's Well That Pays Carl Well," *Los Angeles Examiner*, July 1961, date not available.
26. Carl Furillo interview, 1970, Flushing, NY.
27. Carl Furillo, quoted in "The Furillo Case," *Baseball Monthly*, April, 1962.
28. Carl Furillo, quoted by Frank French, "Carl Furillo's Charges Ignored by Dodgers," *Los Angeles Times*, Jan. 9, 1962.
29. Irv Noren interview, Sept. 30, 2009.
30. Carl Furillo interview, 1970, Flushing, NY.
31. Ford Frick, quoted in "Frick Denies Blacklist," *New York Times*, Jan. 9, 1962.
32. Buzzie Bavasi, ibid.
33. Fay Vincent interview, April 17, 2009.

Chapter 17

1. Carl Furillo interview, 1970, Flushing, NY.
2. Ibid.
3. Ibid.
4. Ibid.
5. Ibid.
6. Ibid.
7. Ibid.
8. Carl Furillo, Jr., interview, March 12, 2010.
9. *The Sporting News*, Aug. 7, 1965.
10. Roger Kahn, *The Boys of Summer*. New York: Harper & Row, 1972.
11. Carl Furillo interview, 1970, Flushing, NY.
12. "Furillo Mellowing," *The Sporting News*, June 5, 1971.
13. Carl Furillo interview, 1970, Flushing, NY.
14. Carl Furillo, quoted by Jack Lang, *The Sporting News*, Sept. 13, 1980.
15. Robert Erb interview, Jan. 30, 2010.
16. Carl Furillo, Jr., interview, Oct. 4, 2009.
17. Carl Furillo, quoted by Gordon Edes, "At Last—Furillo, Dodgers Are Together Again," *Los Angeles Times*, Feb. 25, 1985.

18. Jack Ferenchick interview, Jan. 25, 2010.
19. Ibid.
20. Robert Erb interview, Jan. 20, 2010.
21. Jon Furillo interview, Feb. 2, 2010.
22. Robert Erb interview, Jan. 30, 2010.
23. Carl Furillo, quoted by Robert Erb, Jan. 30, 2010.
24. Robert Erb interview, Jan. 30, 2010.
25. Carl Furillo, Jr., interview, Feb. 5, 2010.
26. Ibid.
27. Bill Ninfo, *Carl Furillo: The Forgotten Dodger*. Bloomington, IN: 1stBooks Library, 2002.

Chapter 18

1. Peter O'Malley interview, Sept. 23, 2009.
2. Ibid.
3. Carl Furillo, quoted by Gordon Edes, in "At Last—Furillo, Dodgers Are Together Again," *Los Angeles Times*, Feb. 25, 1985.
4. Carl Erskine interview, Oct. 13, 2009.
5. Ibid.
6. Dick Young, *The Sporting News*, June 25, 1984.
7. Carl Furillo, quoted by Bill Madden, in "Something Special: Dodgers, Brooklyn," *The Sporting News*, June 25, 1984.
8. Bill Madden, ibid.
9. Carl Furillo, ibid.
10. Peter O' Malley interview, Sept. 23, 2009.
11. Carl Furillo, quoted by Gordon Edes, in "At Last—Furillo, Dodgers Are Together Again," *Los Angeles Times*, Feb. 25, 1985.
12. Buzzie Bavasi, ibid.
13. Carl Furillo, ibid.
14. Peter O'Malley interview, Sept. 23, 2009.
15. Carl Erskine interview, Sept. 29, 2008.
16. Ibid.
17. Peter O'Malley interview, Sept. 23, 2009.
18. Carl Furillo, Jr., interview, Oct. 4, 2009.
19. Carl Furillo, Jr., interview, April 8, 2009.
20. Ibid.
21. Sandy Koufax, quoted by Rich Ziemba in "Ex-teammates Bid Farewell to Furillo," *Reading Times*, Jan. 26, 1989.
22. Carl Erskine interview, Sept. 29, 2008.
23. Dave Anderson, in "Sports of the Times: Steel, Velvet and a Wall in Brooklyn," *New York Times*, Jan. 26, 1989.
24. Carl Erskine interview, Sept. 29, 2008.
25. Fern Furillo, quoted by Gordon Edes, in "At Last—Furillo, Dodgers Are Together Again," *Los Angeles Times*, Feb. 25, 1985.

Selected Bibliography

Books

Allen, Maury. *Brooklyn Remembered: The 1955 Days of the Dodgers.* Urbana, IL: Sports Publishing, 2007.
Chandler, Happy, with Vance Trimble. *Heroes, Plain Folks, and Skunks.* Chicago: Bonus Books, 1989.
D'Antonio, Michael. *Forever Blue.* New York: Riverhead Books, 2009.
Eig, Jonathan. *Opening Day: The Story of Jackie Robinson's First Season.* New York: Simon & Schuster, 2007.
Erskine, Carl, with Burton Rocks. *What I Learned from Jackie Robinson.* New York: McGraw-Hill, 2005.
Falkner, David. *Great Time Coming: The Life of Jackie Robinson, from Baseball to Birmingham.* New York: Simon & Schuster, 1995.
Golenbock, Peter. *Bums.* New York: G.P. Putnam's Sons, 1984.
Higbe, Kirby, with Martin Quigley, *The High Hard One.* Lincoln: University of Nebraska Press, 1967.
Kahn, Roger. *The Boys of Summer.* New York: Harper and Row, 1972.
Ninfo, Bill. *Carl Furillo: The Forgotten Dodger.* Bloomington, IN: First Books Library, 2002.
Prince, Carl E. *Brooklyn's Dodgers: The Bums, The Borough and the Best of Baseball.* New York: Oxford University Press, 1996.
Rampersad, Arnold. *Jackie Robinson.* New York: Alfred A. Knopf, 1997.
Robinson, Jackie. *I Never Had It Made.* New York: G.P. Putnam's Sons, 1972.
Shapiro, Michael. *The Last Good Season.* New York: Doubleday, 2003.
Stout, Glenn, and Richard A. Johnson. *The Dodgers: 120 Years of Dodger Baseball.* New York: Houghton Mifflin, 2004.
Testa, Judith. *Sal Maglie: Baseball's Demon Barber.* DeKalb: Northern Illinois University Press, 2007.
The Sporting News. Official World Series Records. St. Louis: Sporting News Publishing Co., 1976.

Interviews

Bobby Bragan, by telephone, April 13, 2009.
Ralph Branca, by telephone, April 27, 2009.
Robert Erb, by telephone, Jan. 30, 2010.
Carl Erskine, by telephone, Sept. 29, 2008; Oct. 13, 2009.
Ron Fairly, by telephone, Nov. 6, 2009.
Jack Ferenchick, by telephone, Jan. 25, 2010.
Carl Furillo, several interviews were conducted at his home in Flushing, NY, and at the site of the World Trade Center, winter and spring, 1970.
Carl Furillo Jr., by telephone, April 8, 2009; Oct. 4, 2009; Dec. 30, 2009; Jan. 15, 2010; Jan. 30, 2010; Feb. 5, 2010; Feb. 16, 2010; March 10, 2010; March 12, 2010; March 24, 2010.
Jon Furillo, by telephone, Feb. 2, 2010.
Gene Hermanski, by telephone, Sept. 30, 2008 and Jan. 31, 2010.
Joan Hodges, by telephone, Jan. 18, 2010.
Jack Lang, by telephone, 2006.
Sal Maglie, at Sicks' Stadium, Seattle, during Seattle Pilots opening day, April 11, 1969.
Irv Noren, by telephone, Sept. 30, 2009.
Peter O'Malley, in his office in Los Angeles, Sept. 23, 2009.
Lester Rodney, by telephone, Oct. 31, 2009 and Nov. 14, 2009.
Fay Vincent, by telephone, April 17, 2009.

Newspapers

Because I had access to a Carl Furillo scrapbook kept by a fan, and because local coverage of Carl's career was so intense, I relied heavily on stories in *The Reading Eagle* and *The Reading Times*. I also relied heavily on *The Sporting News*, which is available online. The scrapbook also had clips from *The Montreal Gazette*, *The Montreal Herald*, and *The Montreal Star*. I also used *The Daily News* and *The New York Times*. Stories from *The New York Herald-Tribune* and *The New York Journal American* are quoted in the columns of the Reading newspapers.

Web Sites

I repeatedly used *Baseball Almanac* for scores and dates.

Index

Aaron, Hank 102, 116
Abbott and Costello 42
Abrams, Cal 76, 179
Addis, Bob 85
Agee, Tommie 115
Alexander, Grover Cleveland 131
All-Star Game 56, 94
Alston, Walter 10, 103, 104, 105, 107, 108 116, 117, 131, 138, 139, 140, 146; praises Furillo 109, 134–135, 139
Amoros, Sandy 108, 142
Anderson, Dave 180
Antonelli, Johnny 102
Aparicio, Luis 134
Arkema 166
Ashburn, Richie 75, 76, 119, 121
Asheville Tourists 53–54
Associated Press 24, 71, 116, 161
Atlanta Crackers 138
Autry, Gene 153

Banta, Jack 65
Barney, Rex 56, 58, 62
Bauer, Hank 100
Bavasi, Buzzie 34, 35, 79, 80, 82, 88, 93, 102, 104, 112, 118, 126, 132–133, 136–140, 142–148, 150, 151, 153–161, 174, 175
Bay Ridge, Brooklyn 6, 7
Becker, Joe 143, 156
Berle, Milton 42
Bessent, Don 127
Bevans, Floyd 47
Big Apple supermarket 163
Black, Joe 89, 90, 96, 172; close to Furillo 179

Blackwell, Ewell 75, 113
Blades, Roy 58
Boggess, Dusty 102
Boston Braves 24, 45, 49, 52, 58, 67, 80, 82, 84, 85, 90
Boston Red Sox 113, 137, 155, 158
Bowman (baseball cards) 43, 91
The Boys of Summer 40, 165
Bragan, Bobby 30–36, 42, 48, 53, 133, 143, 156
Branca, Ralph 35, 45, 56, 62, 65, 82, 85, 89, 172, 173; criticizes Dressen for overusing pitchers 86
Bromberg, Lester 41
Brooklyn Dodgers: acquire Furillo 14; aged in 1957 122–123; great team assembled 24, 49–50; as historic team 47; last game 120; last hurrah 133; links to LA Dodgers 175–176; lose 1947 World Series 47–48; lose 1949 World Series 67–69; lose 1950 pennant 70, 75–77; lose 1951 pennant 78, 84–86; lose 1954 pennant 102, 103; paid lower salaries 91; reach 1946 playoffs 27; win 1952 pennant 89; win 1953 pennant 97; win 1955 pennant 105, 107; win 1955 World Series 107–109; win 1956 pennant 115–116
Brooklyn Eagle 25, 42
Brown, Tommy 34, 58
Bums 34
Burdette, Lew 133
Burgess, Smoky 104
Burr, Harold 25
Byerly, Bud 137

197

Campanella, Roxie 176
Campanella, Roy 4, 36–37, 49, 63, 65, 66, 85, 97, 101, 103, 107, 111, 112, 113, 114, 115, 118, 120, 122, 123, 130, 172, 173, 175, 176; accident 123; close to Furillo 36–37, 123; joins Dodgers 53
Campanis, Al 15, 16, 103
Cannon, Jimmy 138–139, 147
Caputo, Joe 161
Carl Furillo: The Forgotten Dodger 7
Carl Furillo's (restaurant) 118
Caruso, Paul 150, 151, 153, 154, 155, 156, 157, 159
Casey, Hugh 30, 33, 45
Cashman, Terry 63
Cashmore, John 104
Cerv, Bob 108
Chandler, A.B. 28, 32, 41–42
Chavez Ravine 121
Chicago Cubs 26, 47, 58, 82, 90, 95, 96, 102, 115, 165
Chicago White Sox 133
Chock Full o' Nuts 119
Cimoli, Gino 119, 131
Cincinnati Reds 65, 75, 116, 139
Clemente, Roberto 21, 62
Coleman, Jerry 68
Collier's 62
Collins, Jack 84
Comeback Player of the Year (1953) 94, 97
Conley, Gene 105
Connie Mack Stadium 107, 127
Corriden, John 48
Coutros, Peter 105
Cowan, Arthur 144, 145, 149, 150
Cox, Billy 48, 49, 90, 95, 100, 103, 104
Craig, Roger 114, 132
Crockett, Davy 105

The Daily News 54, 59, 67, 90, 92, 96, 105, 166
Dallessandro, Dominic 15
Dark, Alvin 102, 105
Dascoli, Frank 85
Davis, Tommy 138, 140
Day, Laraine 42, 81–82
Daytona Beach, Fla. 16, 20, 22–23, 88
DeLury, Bill 176
Demeter, Don 132
Depression 9, 10; impact on Furillo 11, 170
DiGiovanna, Charley 100, 111
DiMaggio, Joe 12, 47, 48, 55
Donovan, Dick 135
Down, Fred 84
Dressen, Charlie 27, 73, 79, 82, 86, 88, 89, 90, 92, 97, 139, 145, 147, 153, 155, 156, 181
Drysdale, Ann Meyers 122
Drysdale, Don 4, 113, 117, 125, 129, 131, 132, 173; biggest thrill 122
Duren, Ryne 130

Durocher, Leo 7, 21, 22–23, 26, 27, 34, 41, 42, 43, 52, 53, 54, 55, 56, 58, 64, 73, 74, 75, 81, 99, 115, 165, 181; fights with Furillo 93–97, 181; mends fence with Furillo 121
Durslag, Mel 143, 156

Eastern Shore League 12
Ebbets Field 3, 10, 26, 48, 62, 75, 84, 85, 95, 110, 114, 129, 173, 177; Furillo's first visit 24; Hit Sign, Win Suit 107
Eck, Frank 71
Eddington, Robert 12, 14
Edward, Bruce 41, 53
Ehlers, Arthur 13
Eisenhower, Dwight 118
Engelberg, Morris 42
Ennis, Del 26, 44, 54, 75, 80, 104, 121
Erb, Robert 166, 168, 169
Erskine, Carl 6, 7, 65, 73, 86, 89, 90, 97, 103, 105, 106, 107, 114, 123, 125, 127, 135, 148, 150, 151, 165, 172, 173, 175, 176, 179; delivers eulogy 62, 180–181; on Furillo and Robinson 32–34, 36, 49; joins Dodgers 56, 57, 58; retires 132–133; watches 1955 game 108
Essegian, Chuck 146

Fairly, Ron 39, 127–129, 132, 135
Ferenchick, Jack 167, 169
Ferguson, Elmer 16, 17, 18
Finch, Frank 137
Flushing, N.Y. 5, 163
Ford, Whitey 118
Forever Blue 177
Fox, Howard 88
Franks, Herman 74, 96
Frick, Ford 140, 145, 149–150, 153, 154, 156, 158, 159, 161
Furillo, Carl: asks to be benched 60, 65–66, 69; best season 93–98; charges blacklisting 149, 153, 160–161; on contract talks with Rickey 50–51, 71; early relationship with Bavasi 79–80, 102; early relationship with Dressen 79, 82, 83, 92, 101; early relationship with Durocher 21–22, 26, 43 73–75; early view of Hodges 82; expects trade to Braves 139; faces eye problems 87–88, 91–92; feelings for Brooklyn 9, 26, 123, 124; fights Tommy Brown 58; first son 60, 64; friendly with Robinson 29, 36, 38, 45, 55, 80–81, 109; greets Maglie 111; Hall of Fame 63, 84; kisses Robinson 36, 108, 109, 119; last game 140–141; last hunting trip 178; as leadoff hitter 83, 88; liked reporters 40; love for hunting 5, 50, 164; marriage 55–56; mentors Fairly 127–129; mother's death 12; moves to right field 61, 63, 64; as pitcher 14, 41; platooned 26, 44, 45, 54–55; re-

buts Robinson 124–125; refuses to fly 107; rejects Purple Heart 19; relations with umpires 95; throwing arm 61–63, 65–69, 83; wins 1959 playoff game 130, 134, wins 1959 Series game 130, 134–135, 137
Furillo, Carl, Jr. 5, 7, 10, 11, 19, 33, 36, 38, 58, 64, 72, 99, 112, 113, 135, 139, 151, 164, 167, 169, 170, 171, 178
Furillo, Fern (Reichart) 6, 7, 36, 50, 55–56, 58, 64, 72, 73, 81–82, 102, 122, 146, 170, 172, 173, 174, 178, 179, 180, 181
Furillo, Jon 5, 81, 99, 168, 178
Furillo, Michael 9, 10, 12, 52, 60, 61, 65, 66, 67; death 69, 81
Furillo, Nick 12
Furillo, Tony 13
Furillo and Totto's deli 163

Galan, Augie 23
Gang Busters (radio show) 18
Gaven, Mike 23, 42, 43, 54
Gilliam, Jim 37, 90, 97, 104, 107, 108, 115, 125, 132
Gionfriddo, Al 47, 52
Goetz, Larry 94, 95
Golenbock, Peter 34
Gomez, Ruben 95, 97, 102
Gregg, Hal 48
Griffin, John 135
Gross, Milton 66, 73

Haddix, Harvey 119
Hall of Fame 4, 63, 84, 113, 121
Hamey, Roy 137–138
Hamill, Pete 115
Hamner, Grady 90
Haney, Fred 153
Haring, Josh 11, 12, 14
Harris, Bucky 47, 54, 138
Harwell, Ernie 97
Hatten, Joe 45, 56, 65, 82
Havana, Cuba 29, 41
Hawaii Islanders 160
Head, Ed 24
Hearn, Jim 85, 96
Heinrich, Tommy 68
Hemond, Roland 153
Hermanski, Gene 12, 23, 35, 43, 44, 53, 82
Higbe, Kirby 30, 34
High Noon 111
Hodges, Gil 4, 5, 49, 50, 58, 63, 65, 76, 82, 90, 94, 101, 103, 104, 108, 113, 115, 122, 123, 124, 125, 127, 130, 132, 138, 173; famous slump 97–99; Mets manager 136, 165; moves to first base 53
Hodges, Joan 50, 99
Hodges, Russ 86
Holmes, Tommy 24, 54
Hopper, Clay 21–22

Hotel Bossert 108
Howard, Elston 108
Howard, Frank 138
Howell, Dixie 44, 114
Hughes, Jim 173
Hunter, Bob 138, 139, 142, 148, 156, 159

Idlewild Airport 119
International News Service 27, 83
Irvin, Monte 84, 89
Italians, discrimination against 10, 31–33

Jackie Robinson: A Biography 33
The Jackie Robinson Story (movie) 4, 31, 33
Jackson, Joe 62
Jackson, Randy 114
Jansen, Larry 89
Jensen, Jackie 138
Jones, Puddinhead 75, 86
Jones, Sheldon 74

Kahn, Roger 37, 40, 165
Kansas City A's 107
Kefauver, Estes 154, 160
Kerlan, Robert 140, 154
Kiner, Ralph 54
King, Clyde 86
King, Joe 128
Kittle, Hub 160
Klippstein, Johnny 102
Kluszewski, Ted 95
Kobrin, Jerry 11, 15, 25–26
Konstanty, Jim 75
Koslo, Dave 74
Koufax, Sandy 4, 6, 73, 102, 117, 119, 122, 129, 131, 135, 165, 167, 173, 175, 176, 180; close to Furillo 179
Kurowski, Whitey 59

Labine, Clem 63, 85, 86, 97, 107, 125, 127, 179
LaGuardia, Fiorello 18
Lang, Jack 36, 66
Larker, Norm 132, 140
Larsen, Don 118
Lasorda, Tommy 176
The Last Good Season 177
Lavagetto, Cookie 24, 27, 47, 96
Lawrence, Brooks 105
Lazzeri, Tony 131
Lewis, Franklin 69
Life 90
Littlefield, Dick 119
Litwhiler, Danny 81
Loes, Billy 89, 90, 97, 107, 179
Lombardi, Vic 45, 48
Long Island Press 36
Look 119
Lopata, Stan 76
Lopez, Al 134

Los Angeles 6, 118, 119, 121, 124
Los Angeles Angels 153
Los Angeles Coliseum 124, 131–132, 134, 143, 151
Los Angeles Dodgers 123, 124; connect to roots 175, 176; finish seventh in 1957, 125; win 1959 pennant 131, 133–134; win 1959 Series 134–135
Los Angeles Examiner 153
Los Angeles Herald Examiner 142, 145
Los Angeles Herald-Express 147
Los Angeles Rams 150
Los Angeles Red Devils 160
Los Angeles Times 36, 137, 143, 146, 147, 153, 160, 173

Mack, Ray 47
MacPhail, Larry 14, 16, 42
MacPhail, Lee 16
Maglie, Sal 85, 94, 95, 107, 114, 118, 119, 120, 122, 165, 179; joins Dodgers 110–113
Mann, Arthur 31, 50
Mantilla, Felix 134
Mantle, Mickey 63
Marciano, Rocky 97
Martin, Billy 108
Martyn, Bob 138
Masi, Phil 25
Mauch, Gene 48
Mays, Willie 42, 63, 89, 102
McCormick, Mike 143
McDevitt, Danny 132
McDougald, Gil 108
McGowan, Roscoe 105, 119, 122
Medwick, Joe 27, 61
Meyer, Russ 97
Miksis, Eddie 53
Milwaukee Braves 97, 102, 105, 107, 116, 120, 122, 123, 130, 131, 133, 135, 139, 156
Mize, Johnny 54, 89, 90
Montreal 15, 16, 17, 142
Montreal Canadiens 17
"Montreal Embargo" 21
Montreal Expos 17
Montreal Gazette 18
Montreal Herald 16, 17
Montreal Royals 16, 19–24, 28–29, 42, 43, 65
Montreal Star 18
Moon, Wally 129, 132, 140
Morenz, Howie 17
Morgan, Bobby 90
Moses, Robert 110, 176, 177
Mueller, Don 102
Mullin, Willard 102
Mulvey, Dearie 78
Mulvey, James 78
Munger, Red 67
Musial, Stan 54, 67, 90, 95, 104, 121, 137

Naples 9
National Football League 9
National League playoffs 27, 47, 81, 84, 130, 133–134, 135, 139
Neal, Charlie 119, 125, 132
New York Giants 7, 74, 75, 78, 82, 84, 89, 94, 96, 102, 103, 105, 116, 119, 175
New York Herald Tribune 62, 94, 119
New York Journal-American 23, 42, 54, 138
New York Mets 82, 109, 115, 136, 160–161, 164, 166
New York Post 115
New York Times 24, 88, 134, 145, 180
New York World-Telegram 41
New York Yankees 24, 47, 48, 60, 67, 70, 89, 100, 107, 116, 120, 137–138, 148, 155, 158, 166, 169
Newcombe, Don 65, 67, 76, 85, 86, 88, 89, 107, 113, 114, 118, 122, 127, 173, 175, 176
Ninfo, Bill 34, 150, 170
Noren, Irv 160

Oliver, Tom 14, 25
O'Malley, Peter 6, 152, 165, 171, 172, 173, 174, 175, 176, 177, 178, 179, 180, 181
O'Malley, Walter 56, 78, 79, 84, 91, 101, 102, 107, 110, 119, 120, 124, 125, 144, 171, 172, 175, 176, 177
Otis Elevator Co. 163
Ott, Mel 56

Pafko, Andy 47, 54, 82, 83, 84, 88, 89
Page, Joe 47, 48, 54
Palica, Erv 96
Panama City, Panama 29–30, 33, 37
Paper, Lew 34
Parrot, Harold 30, 31–33, 71
Patterson, Red 142
Pennside Junior High School 10
Perfect: Don Larsen's Miraculous World Series Game 34
Philadelphia A's 61, 75
Philadelphia Phillies 25, 44, 47, 58, 77, 80, 84, 85, 86, 88, 90, 104, 107, 110, 119, 140, 141, 161, 169; Whiz Kids 75–76
Philley, Dave 137
Pignatano, Joe 134
Pinelli, Babe 95
Pitler, Jake 95, 107
Pittsburgh Pirates 21, 49, 55, 59, 67, 79, 116, 120
Pocomoke City, Md. 12, 14, 19
Podres, Johnny 107, 108, 117, 121, 122, 125, 131, 132, 179
Pollett, Howie 67
Polo Grounds 85, 96, 121
Porter, Paul 153, 156, 157
Post, Wally 127
The Power Broker 177

Index

Praeger, Emil 177
Purple Heart 19

Queen, Mel 55

Rackley, Marvin 53
Rampersad, Arnold 33
Randolph, Willie 169
Reading Brooks 14, 22, 61
Reading Chicks 12, 14
Reading Eagle 11, 15, 18, 19, 25, 43, 54, 65, 67, 68, 81, 85
Reading Times 11, 14, 22, 39, 40, 44, 52, 71, 88, 90, 109, 116, 118, 179
Reedy, Bill 43, 45, 54, 65, 71, 75, 80, 84, 113
Reese, Pee Wee 4, 6, 24, 27, 31–32, 34, 41, 45, 49, 54, 56, 63, 76, 80, 85, 86, 104, 108, 109, 111, 120, 122, 131, 132, 134, 152, 165, 179: praises Furillo 67
Reiser, Pete 23, 34, 41, 43, 44, 45, 47, 48
Repulski, Rip 142
Reynolds, Allie 100, 107
Rice, Grantland 54
Richman, Milton 84
Rickey, Branch 4, 16, 21–28, 31, 35, 39, 40, 42, 43, 44, 52, 56, 58, 59, 60, 71, 78, 79, 83, 124; best trade 48–49; negotiating style with Furillo 50–51
Rickey, Branch, Jr. 21, 22, 40, 50, 51, 52, 61, 71, 147
Rilsan plant 167
Rizzuto, Phil 107
Roberts, Robin 75, 76, 77
Robinson, Jackie 3, 4, 16, 17, 23, 28–38, 42, 43, 45, 46, 49, 53, 58, 60, 63, 65, 66, 67, 73, 77, 79, 80, 81, 85, 90, 101, 103, 104, 105, 108, 109, 115, 118, 120, 122; attacks Dodgers and apologizes 124–125; leaves Dodgers 110, 111, 119, 120; number retired 175; plays pro basketball 160; praises Branca 86; praises Furillo 68
Robinson, Pat 83
Robinson, Rachel 109
Rodney, Lester 35, 109
Roe, Preacher 6, 48, 49, 56, 65, 67, 86, 89, 97, 104
Roebuck, Ed 151
Roosevelt Stadium 110
Roseboro, Johnny 125, 132, 134
Rush, Bob 95, 134
Ruth, Babe 82

St. Catherine's Church 56
St. Louis Cardinals 21, 23, 26, 27, 47, 58, 66, 67, 70, 90, 102, 105, 123, 148
Sal Maglie: Baseball's Demon Barber 94, 112
San Francisco Giants 121, 131, 133, 139, 143, 146, 165

Sauer, Hank 54, 139
Schoendienst, Red 121
Scott, Lee 143
Scully, Vin 176
Shea Stadium 5, 163, 165
Sherry, Larry 127, 129
Shibe Park 25, 85
Shotton, Burt 42, 44, 45, 46, 48, 56, 58, 60, 61, 62, 64, 65, 66, 67, 69, 70, 71, 73, 79, 147
Shuba, George 53, 93
Silva, Doc 39, 40, 116, 121
Simmons, Curt 75, 104
Sisler, Dick 76, 77
Sisler, George 27
Skowron, Moose 109
Slaughter, Enos 54, 67, 121, 148
Smith, John 56, 78
Snider, Duke 4, 48, 49, 53–54, 61, 62, 63, 65, 66, 71, 76, 82, 84, 90, 96, 97, 103, 107, 113, 114, 122, 123, 124, 125, 127, 130, 131, 165, 167, 172, 173
Sorensen, Ted 115
Spahn, Warren 90, 134
Spatz, Lyle 38
Spooner, Karl 114
Sport Magazine 66, 71, 73
Sporting News 26, 31, 44, 45, 47, 55, 58, 67, 69, 97, 121, 122, 128, 138, 139, 165, 173
Staley, Gerry 90, 134
Stanky, Eddie 24, 27, 31, 41, 49, 52, 58
Stengel, Casey 138
Stevens, Ed 41
Stoneham, Horace 56, 119
Stony Creek Mills 9, 10, 12, 16, 18, 51, 52, 69, 96, 113, 118, 126, 153, 162, 164
Sukeforth, Clyde 16–17, 18, 19
Summers, Bill 107
Swoboda, Ron 164

Talkin' Baseball (song) 63
Taylor, Harry 45, 61
Testa, Judith 94, 112
Thompson, Fresco 15, 16, 22–23, 25, 79, 80
Thompson, Hank 105
Thomson, Bobby 47, 85, 86, 165
Toots Shor's 112
Topps (baseball cards) 43, 91, 130
Torgenson, Earl 90
Toronto Maple Leafs (baseball) 17
Traughber, Bill 34

United Press International 84, 153
University of Southern California 127
Urban League 125

Valo, Elmer 61
Vaughan, Arky 41
Vernon, Mickey 121

Vero Beach 6, 103, 104, 109, 113, 123, 124, 128, 137, 138, 151, 152, 171, 173, 175, 176; Peter O'Malley remembers 172
Villante, Tom 111, 112
Vincent, Fay 62, 161

Wade, Ben 89
Wade, Jake 24
Wagner, Charley 15
Walker, Dixie 23, 25, 27, 30, 31, 33–35, 37, 41, 43, 44, 45, 49, 53, 62, 64, 83; traded to Pirates 48
Walker, Rube 6, 82, 117
Walsh, Harry 144, 145, 153, 155, 156, 157
Walteromalley.com 177
Ward, Preston 55
Warneke, Lon 105
Warwick, Carl 138, 140
Westrum, Wes 102, 164
Whalen, Polk 12, 13
White, Bill 169
Whitman, Dick 23, 41, 43

Wilks, Ted 70
Williams, Dick 89
Williams, Gordon 14, 22, 44, 45, 58, 61, 71, 80, 88
Williams, Stan 125
Williams, Ted 121
Wills, Maury 132
World Series: (1919) 134; (1946) 27; (1947) 47–48; (1949) 60, 67–69; (1950) 76; (1952) 87, 8–90; (1953) 100; (1955) 3, 36, 47, 104, 107–109; (1956) 47, 110, 116–118; (1957) 123; (1959) 130, 133–135, 146; (1960) 21; (1969) 5, 136, 165
World Trade Center 5, 163, 166
Wrigley Field (Los Angeles) 120

Yankee Stadium 108
Young, Dick 54–55, 59, 67, 92, 96, 105, 116, 123, 124, 173
Yvars, Sal 94

Zimmer, Don 108, 125, 132

www.ingramcontent.com/pod-product-compliance
Ingram Content Group UK Ltd.
Pitfield, Milton Keynes, MK11 3LW, UK
UKHW042005140426
5217IPUK00015B/991